DO YOU BELIEVE IN ANCIENT ASTRONAUTS?

Atlantis? Extraterrestrial Temples on Earth? Monuments on the Moon? The Country of the Blue Men? The Devils from Space? Tombs for Eternity? Saturn in America? Doors to Infinity?

Some of archeology's most baffling mysteries are re-examined in light of new scientific evidence that extra-terrestrial beings once existed on Earth . . .

※

NOT OF THIS WORLD
may make a believer of you!

not of this world

Peter Kolosimo

Translated by A. D. Hills

BANTAM BOOKS
TORONTO · NEW YORK · LONDON

A NATIONAL GENERAL COMPANY

*This low-priced Bantam Book
has been completely reset in a type face
designed for easy reading, and was printed
from new plates. It contains the complete
text of the original hard-cover edition.*
NOT ONE WORD HAS BEEN OMITTED.

RLI: | VLM 9 (VLR 8–10)
IL 9–adult

NOT OF THIS WORLD
*A Bantam Book / published by arrangement with
University Books, Inc.*

PRINTING HISTORY
*University Books edition published April 1971
Bantam edition published November 1973*

Published simultaneously in the United States and Canada

Bantam Books are published by Bantam Books, Inc., a National
General company. Its trade-mark, consisting of the words "Bantam
Books" and the portrayal of a bantam, is registered in the United
States Patent Office and in other countries. Marca Registrada.
Bantam Books, Inc., 666 Fifth Avenue, New York, N.Y. 10019.

PRINTED IN THE UNITED STATES OF AMERICA

Contents

Stone within stone
Where was man?
Air within air
Where was man?
Time within time
Where was man?

from CANTO GENERALE by
Pablo Neruda

PART ONE

SHIPWRECKS
FROM THE STARS

CHAPTER ONE

WHO SHOT THE DINOSAURS?

There was once a man called Mr. Zebra, but known as Horace Reid, who was earning his living in Chicago in 1965 and constantly on the look-out for special news items in his daily reading of newspapers and listening to the radio. He was a strange type of investigator, this Mr. Zebra. He was not interested in the apoplectic headlines about the Vietnam War or the violent state of affairs along the Indo-China frontiers; and neither could the very different bit of news about the engagement of Princess Beatrix of the Netherlands give him any kind of thrill: the agonized questions in the papers about this had no effect on him. On the other hand our friend would be most perturbed to read an article of the following sort:

"Near a small town in Illinois, Professor Forrestor of State Normal University has found, with the aid of his archeological students, a new Indian tumulus about 400 years old. Various skeletons have been brought to light, together with buried weapons, necklaces and an assortment of objects. This is a remarkable discovery, if not sensational. As a result there has been a unique find: that of the body of a Red Indian, one-armed, and holding a broken vase full of coins bearing the stamp of an Indian head.

"Professor Forrestor thought at first that he had been the victim of a joke on the part of his students, who however emphatically denied it. In fact an examination, very carefully carried out, has confirmed that both the mutilated Indian and the vase with the coins were buried at the same time. Experts from Illinois University and the authority there are now on their way to the site of the excavations."

Now it so happens that the coins with the Indian head were minted in the United States not long ago. It was precisely this which caused Mr. Zebra to turn, in his confusion, to the skies above—but literally. That is to say he was calling up a distant planet by means of a special machine, and as a result a beautiful blonde descended from the planet and landed near Chicago, her mission being to help him solve the riddle. But it was a riddle only for earthly inhabitants, not for Mr. Zebra and his colleague; because these two, being secret agents of a huge space-organization, knew only too well how the 1965 "pennies" had come to be in the possession of a man living in or around 1565. The perpetrators of this and other practical jokes were the offspring of a highly developed extraterrestrial race who had escaped from the eye of their master and had seized a ship capable of travelling across space and time.

The blonde and her friend set about studying every possible method of doing away with this anachronism which would have caused an uproar among human scientists. They thought of replacing the coins with others and of doing something which would have supported the hypothesis that the whole business was a students' joke; they even thought of digging a tunnel under the site to give people the idea that the money had been buried recently. But nothing of this materialized and the business might well have taken a nasty turn if the brilliant Mr. Zebra had not come to make everything topsy-turvy.

"Souvenirs" from another World

This of course is just fiction, being one of the more far-fetched passages taken from Wilson Tucker's *Able to Zebra*.[1] But it cannot be said that it is entirely a matter of pure imagination on the part of the American writer. Space agents and money aside, he is dealing with sheer fantasy only in one point: that the discovery of modern coins in an ancient tomb might have brought about a state of pandemonium among the archeologists.

If he had wanted to be a little more realistic, Tucker would certainly not have made his Mr. Zebra and girl-friend confused: we can assure him that nothing at all would have really happened: the scholars would simply have glanced absent-mindedly at the heap of coins and then shrugged their shoulders and gone away muttering something like "utterly impossible", "stupid" or "a childish prank".

Readers will object that this is all Utopian, but it is not so; it concerns the would-be keepers of universal knowledge, those holy scientists surrounded by their own aura of infallibility.

"Assuming that the Bible can never err and that the account of past events represents a guarantee for the accurate prediction of the future," wrote St. Augustine of Hippo (354–430), "it is absurd to say that man has been able to cross the vast ocean and reach the other side for the purpose of establishing the human race." Well, from his time to ours, methods have not changed: everything is pulled down if it can be demolished at all, with a wave of the banners of orthodoxy and a screen of sophism—even stubbornly denying or simply ignoring all the evidence and proofs.

Is it necessary to recall that in 1790 the Paris Academy of Sciences let loose a torrent of abuse against the physicist Chladni because he upheld the view that meteorites were of cosmic origin, declaring "that it is absurd to believe that stones could ever have fallen

[1] Published in Italy under the title *Z for Zebra*, translated by Mario Galli ("Urania", Mondadori, Milan, 1.1.1967).

from space on to Earth"? Or would it be sufficient to
go back to the first half of the past century, when the
sea depths were decreed to be officially unsuitable for
any form of life because of lack of oxygen beyond a
depth of two hundred metres and they were therefore
covered with a sheet of permanent ice? Probably nothing could ever dislodge the sceptics from positions clung
to for their very life. "The mistakes of the past," they
would reply, "do not permit us to push science into the
realms of fantasy." A reasonable and logical argument,
provided that those frontier areas are not considered
as being unchangeable and that one is not inclined to
remove them from regions belonging until very recently
to science fiction, or to reject such new ideas arising
as products of an arbitrary speculation.

This is not to say that we are here trying to claim
some scientific recognition for Wilson Tucker and his
coins. We can, however, begin with another coinage:
that of the bronze money discovered by chance in
1871 during excavations near Chillicote, Illinois, over
forty-two and a half metres in depth.

Forty-two and a half metres is nothing if measured
horizontally; but make a hole of this depth and it will
soon seem to have gone a good half of the way towards
the centre of the Earth. Of course, we would not have
scratched the surface of the world any more than if
we had tried marking a ball of glass with a pin, but we
would have pushed back into time an amazing distance,
reaching a layer which was in the open air at a time
when on our planet—as far as human history is known
—there was not only no money but nobody to make
it or spend it!

Unfortunately the coins, having been reduced to flat
discs of irregular shape, could tell us nothing about
their origin. However, the idea that they could have
been left there in times relatively close to ours as a result of earthquake or from other causes, can be excluded at the start; they could really only have been
lost or left where they had been discovered, countless
thousands of years ago.

This, it is clear, is not mere fantasy. It is one simple ring of a long chain of bewildering mysteries that crop up all over the world today and have done so during the past century.

In 1851, at Illinois again, two copper rings were found, or rather their remains, at a depth of about thirty-six and a half metres. And in June of the same year, an explosion revealed at Dorchester (Massachusetts) a bell-shaped jar made of an unknown metal and decorated with floral patterns in silver; and the vase came out of a solid mass of rock which had been formed in the remotest antiquity.

For many years there has been going around the story of a doctor who in California found a fine piece of quartz containing gold, which he took home as a souvenir. The rock broke by accident and a small metal trifle of some sort emerged, the shape of which reminded one of a bucket handle. We have not succeeded in discovering the doctor's name or in finding out what became of it. Still, this does not warrant our thinking of it as a mere fable because it has been discussed in serious scientific journals and a similar object has been discovered since then. The second "bucket handle" was unearthed at a considerable distance from the first, in a cave at Kingoodie, in northern England. It was contained in a block of stone 23 centimetres long and undoubtedly formed during the Pleistocene era (from 8,500 to 700 thousand years ago); scholars give it an age of at least 10 to 12 thousand years but the possibility that it is much, much older is not excluded.

The most amazing discoveries, compared with which Tucker's imagination seems pale, took place in 1869 and 1885. In this latter year an Austrian mine produced the strangest metal cube which is now kept in Salisbury Museum. The coal beds in which it was found are undoubtedly of the Tertiary period (from 70 to 12 million years ago) and the object when analysed was found to consist of iron and carbon, with a small amount of nickel. "A meteorite," say some experts, basing their opinions on these dates. A cubic meteorite, with one of the two opposite faces perfectly rounded? Certainly we could admit that it is an object from space but then we would feel obliged to accept one of these two hypotheses: either it has come somehow from another world or it has been extracted here on Earth from a mass from outer space.

The first idea is unacceptable; even if it had had the luck to be kept unaltered from the start, the object would have been reduced to a shapeless crumb as a result of atmospheric attrition. But then the second idea is as fantastic as thinking that it might have been made by someone on Earth: in fact to make a meteorite like this is well-nigh impossible, unless one has at one's disposal all the resources offered by modern technology.

In November 1869 a tiny object upset the scientific world: an object which itself did not even exist any longer but which had left an irrefutable trace: a screw 5.08 centimetres long which had remained for countless thousands of years wasting away inside a rock from the so-called "Abbey Gallery" in Treasure City, Nevada. When the rock actually came to be split at that point the screw (which one imagines was of iron) no longer existed. But the marks of the thread were still clearly visible and perfectly showed the spiral formation. "The stratum in which it was found is extremely old," say the experts of the San Francisco Academy of Sciences. "This discovery could antedate human history by millions of years." At the time there was a great deal of fuss made about it but the arguments died down: silence fell upon the "screw of Treasure City" as on many other astounding events.

Something equally sensational which made the scientists start talking and then go dumb was found in a carboniferous vein in Cow Canyon, again in Nevada, 25 miles east of Lovelock: it was the imprint of a human foot stamped in the very middle of the Tertiary Period; a graceful footprint, the impression from a well-balanced and agile human being living at a time which traditional archaeologists say, was still extremely far from our monkey-like ancestors!

Siberian mysteries

Who attacked the bison hundreds of thousands of years before our clumsy and growling ancestors started to use stones as weapons? It seems right to ask the question seriously, after looking at the skull of a bison, a prehistoric one, exhibited at the Museum of Paleontology at Moscow. The fossil was found to the west of the River Lena in the autonomous Republic of Yakutsk and something at once arrested the attention of the scientists. This was a round hole in the forehead which could never have been produced by a spear. It is thought that the hole could have been made only by a bullet from a gun, but this could not possibly have been carried out in recent times because the edges of the aperture had become calcified—which proves that the animal must have survived its nasty adventure.

These are the opinions of the curator of the Moscow museum, Professor Constantin Flerov. If he is asked who could have gone hunting bison with a prehistoric Siberian rifle, Flerov shrugs his shoulders and smiles. His colleagues are less careful than he is and do not hesitate to say: "Only one explanation is possible—the one linking it with the landing on Earth, at various times, of explorers from space very long ago."

It is a hypothesis which in these areas does not fail to have a deep effect. We are among the people of Yakutsk, that strange race which came up here from Turkey after having lived at the foot of the Altai Mountains. "Sleep," the people of Yakutsk sing to their dead, whose coffins they put among the branches of trees so as to favour their removal by divine powers. "Sleep until the spirits come down from the stars on their shining chariots." Which spirits? Those of which the Shahmanists speak, the Mongolian and Siberian priest-wizards who describe to us the mysterious beings who come to call the dead on their "flying shells" and throw off their "cloaks of darkness" when they wish to reveal their true features, similar to ours? It certainly does not need great imaginative powers to see in the "shells" some space vehicle or other (is it not at least odd that we have coined the terms Teller, Saucers, Soucoupes, i.e. flying saucers?) and a space suit in the term "detachable skin".

If we go further to the west we shall meet the "baba", those strange funeral monuments that are dotted around the "kurgani", the oldest cemeteries in Siberia which are an insoluble riddle to the archaeologists. Let us look at one of them closely. It is made from a mass of stone and its top part has been sculptured in the form of a human being. An enigmatic Mongolian face is smiling, eyes half-closed, at the two objects which his hands are clasping—a dagger and a sphere. "The dagger cuts through the darkness, the sun of life," we would be told, if we borrow once more from Shahmanistic wisdom. Let us imagine, however, space ships cutting through cosmic darkness towards a globe remembered in the traditions of a vanished people as a symbol of life beyond the dark chasms: coming down southward we shall arrive in the Siberian Tunguses, where in 1908 the meteorite fell, which according to Kasanzev was not a meteorite but an interplanetary cruiser with nuclear propulsion: it had gone out of control and burnt up a few kilometres from the ground. "Siberia," says the Russian scholar and writer, "and many other regions of the world are perhaps huge museums containing evidence of cosmic encounters." And of collisions too, we would add, not only suggesting the bison episode but also an unfortunate Neanderthal man whose skull came to light near Rhodesia's Broken Hill.

The skull of the hominid seems to demonstrate clearly the hole made by a bullet and on the other side the aperture where the bullet went out again. It is impossible that this can be a case of the famous cranial trepaning of prehistoric times: in the Siberian example no one would have risked operating on a bison (and that without anaesthetic) while in the African one, the double hole forces one to abandon the theory. One could say, then, that the so-called Neanderthal men had never practised any surgical intervention of such a nature—the only holes (the majority anyway) which these anthropomorphic cannibals made in the heads of others were meant for the extraction of brains which were used as food.

Another sensational idea is also attributed to some Soviet scientists: that certain bones belonging to gigantic saurians were smashed by explosives. The idea has clearly come from the fact that some discoveries bear fractures which do not seem to admit of any other explanation, because of the way in which they were lying and of the positions of the skeletons in relation to the surrounding ground. In effect, if it is admitted that the Earth might have had visits from space long ago, we cannot expect the astronauts to have renounced the use of weapons against those mountains of flesh and blind fury.

A Prehistoric Zoo

Nice, May 1964. Ten minutes away from the packed "Promenades des Anglais," full of its usual stupid gossip and sophistication, an elderly man and a young blonde girl are walking carefully into one of the "Lazzaretto Grottoes", completely prehistorical. Down there we find no echoes of the latest receptions and films and races; down there we have the traces of horses which, like other animals' bones left, ran for their lives. Down there the two scholars—François Octobon and Uoëlle Chochon—move among the oldest possible groups dancing around camp fires, thus bringing to mind some film scene which only a "time machine" could have produced.

The witnesses of an unthinkably distant past still sleep, unsuspected, near us underneath the skyscrapers, or a couple of yards from the proud monuments of our civilization or from fashionable beaches; just as in the "Lazzaretto Grottoes", the chief of which experienced the gaping holes made by dynamite at the start of the century, when it was intended to build a place for accommodating people next to a bathing pool. In those surroundings, three thousand year old remains turned up; nothing exceptional, nothing to hold up the destructive work. Yet the explosives brought to light bones of elephant which had disappeared from the Mediterranean shores at least a thousand centuries ago, together with some stone implements cut in very rudimentary fashion. This accidental discovery interested scholars but not for long. Science got tired of the Nice grottoes but in 1950 a retired marine official—François Octobon himself—took up the excavations again; at first by himself and then later supported by a number of young and enthusiasitc paleontologists and speleologists. With the patience of a Carthusian monk, Octobon revealed layer after layer. And in May 1964 his assistant saw a strange white spot emerging; it was the brow of a creature which existed 150,000 years ago, as the examinations of it showed.

An ape of some sort? No. The thickness of the bone excluded such a possibility, likewise the traces of the cerebral vessels which indicated a mental activity far from insignificant. The instruments found nearby also support this: it is a fact that no ape can light a fire or make stone axes, knives, rasps and graving tools. "Classical texts," Marc Ambroise-Rendu wrote in connection with this, "point to the appearance of graving-tools 40,000 years before Christian times." Well, the "Lazzaretto Man" compels us to have another look at these and other notions. Already he knew how to make awls, daggers and extraordinary clubs, the weight of which would seem to have been calculated scientifically. But the most amazing piece is a small handle made of deer bone. This was very skilfully split and scapula bones inserted: they are prehistoric razors! And Jean Piveteau, the brilliant French paleontologist, said: "It was a genuine man, living in the same epoch as that which saw the appearance of pithecanthropus on the other Mediterranean coast in North Africa."

Who could this man be who showed the need for having such instruments, and who felt compelled to shave himself? Those who support the idea of the prehistoric cosmonauts point to fascinating theories and speak of spatial explorers left on Earth, compelled to use all their technical skill in a savage and hostile world; or they talk about primitive-men being approached by space travellers and thus they began to build the rudiments of civilization.

However that may be there is, for our supporters of the spaceship idea, a still tastier morsel; and it is likely enough that others may turn up on the Côte d'Azur, since the devoted work of Commander Octobon has shown the way forward to a series of promising researches.

"At a distance of 20 kilometres from the 'Lazzaretto Grotto' a young member of the French central organization for scientific research is after a man who lived a million years ago, at the time of australopithecus, an ape-man whose remains were discovered in the Far East and in South Africa," Marc Ambroise-Rendu tells us again. "Henry de Lumley has brought to light in the Vallonet cave at Roquebrune-Cap-Martin, some traces of human life at the beginning of the Quarternary. The grotto is thus a real cemetery for exotic animals; and it is obvious that elephant, lions, the rhinoceros, the hyenas and macaco monkeys did not go by themselves to die in this 25 square metre cave. Whale bones have also been found there. Somebody had dragged their booty into the Vallonet from who knows where . . ."

This is an undertaking that can be attributed to human beings only with some difficulty. But let us suppose that we in order to establish ourselves, land on a planet rich in various forms of life. Among the first things in the programme would be the study of local fauna: and here our vehicles would dash off in every direction in search of animals to capture and exhibit small temporary zoos, entrusting them to the hardly merciful hands of the experts. But would it be only the study of animals? In the French cave some discoveries make one think that the inhabitants too had taken part in some way or other in organizing the harvest. But as collectors—or the ones collected? . . .

CHAPTER TWO

THE DEVILS FROM SPACE

"To believe nothing or everything," Pierre Bayle, the French forerunner of Voltaire said, "are extremes of no value." And it is precisely on these two positions that we find those who retard or hinder the solution of the big scientific mysteries: on the one hand the reactionaries from all discipline protecting themselves by their scepticism and on the other, the visionaries, the madmen and swindlers, the sellers of humbug. The latter are encouraged by a certain section of the Press for the sole purpose of increasing circulation and thus exploiting the public's insatiable thirst for magic.

There is the history of the flying saucers. Pure illusion the hard sceptics declare, laughing at official reports and unimpeachable evidence based on sound documents. "Space-ships sent by a highly developed civilization to guard against nuclear suicide," the initiated reply. Or "as safe as the sun: we have ourselves spoken to those from Venus, Mars and Centaurus".

We would willingly abstain from questioning George Adamski if he had not left our hopeless world and

14

bequeathed to his creditors something which unluckily was to be exploited for a long time in every way by the victims of space travel absurdities. It is hardly conceivable how such people could have fallen for Adamski's revelations. Some of his imaginings are so childish that one might call the worst science fiction cartoons and fancies inventive masterpieces by comparison. The effect of our dead friend's doings turned out to be so crude that it might be enough to make our less sophisticated readers shake their heads.

Let us look at Adamski leaving his snack-bar at the foot of Mount Palomar on his way to take photos of flying saucers. He photographs them in the sky and, when the amazed public are about to burst with curiosity at this, he tells them that someone has come from Venus and agreed to supply him as local sausage-maker with a new kind of hors d'œuvre.

Flying Saucers have Landed was Adamski's first book. Some just go away convinced that scepticism here is better than faith but a few others fall down before him in adoration, asking only that they too should have final illumination from one who is intimate with the spacemen. And Adamski is ready to accept them: he leaps on to a saucer and is off to the moon to have a look at the peaceful lakes and healthy forests there —and then return to write another book, this time *Inside a Spaceship*. And then? The ideal would be to give to the world some small proof of interplanetary fraternization by exhibiting a lunar chronometer or at least producing a photo of a martian skyscraper. But since lunar chronometers and martian skyscrapers are rather difficult to falsify then our celebrated astronomer comes along with material evidence in his third book *Goodbye, Flying Saucers!* to give us the only authoritative statement sanctified by sacred texts from Venus . . .

The Fantasy Bible

"As a student of philosophy and science for many years," this same master condescends to tell us in his rough English, "I have taught that the other planets were inhabited; and this some time before I had seen flying saucers or had had the pleasure of meeting their occupants personally . . . Accurate researches based on the Bible are bringing to light various relationships with space visitors. A priest told me in fact that he had found about 350 reports and relationships of this nature . . ."

Let us collect a few other pearls from the Adamski science:

"In St. John (14, 2) we read: 'In my Father's house are many mansions. If it were not so I would have told you. I go to prepare a place for you.' This house or mansion clearly demonstrates that if we evolve enough we can go to other worlds and live as He was preparing to do. This is clear from the following: (14, 3) 'And if I go and prepare a place for you I will come again and receive you unto myself, that where I am there ye may be also.'

"Christ has given us plenty of evidence about his arrival from another world. In St. John (8, 23) we find: 'And he said unto them: you are from beneath; I am from above; ye are of this world; I am not of this world.' This shows that we are of this world and were born in it; that Jesus was in this world but not born of it—He came from another one. This is one of the best references to a being from another planet presented to us willingly as coming precisely for that purpose of guiding and helping those who are still climbing the evolutionary ladder.

"The Bible teaches us that we can become like Christ and do even greater things. It teaches us that He begot many brothers and that many of us will one day be able to reach the same state as Christ (Romans 8, 29). This agrees entirely with the declarations made by space visitors when it was said that the Earth was like the lowest class in a school. As we progress we shall travel to the planets like one going from the first to the second class, thence to the third; from class to class and planet to planet. From time to time someone wishes to return to Earth to help those who are beginning to climb: this is very much like our sending of missionaries to foreign lands. Some choose to be born here like Jesus, others to come into this world and live like one of us: several hundreds are doing so today. The Bible offers us direct evidence that other worlds are inhabited. The Book of Genesis (6, 2 and 6, 4) describes the sons of God who 'came in unto the daughters of men and they bare children to them, the same became mighty men which were of old, men of renown'. These sons of God were evidently sufficiently similar to human beings to enable them to give women children. They were made of flesh and blood like us. They are confident that nobody will state that spirits or angels will descend here on Earth and have relationships with these women; they must be human like you or me. This is definite proof that other planets are inhabited and have been for a long time.

"It has been mentioned many times that the flying-saucers leave their parents ships to explore Earth and then return to the same ships. How often? A perfect description of this form of activity can be found in Isaiah (60, 8) 'Who are these that fly as a cloud and as the doves to their windows?' "

And even now it is not finished: the sausage-maker is not in fact happy to keep to his theories and claims, by means of his pamphlets, to have shared a seat on an interplanetary organization with Christ himself!

"As most of you know," he says in the course of his rhetoric, "I had the privilege in March 1962 of taking part in a conference on the planet Saturn. Nine hours after leaving Earth the cosmic ship landed there. I admit this sounds incredible because of the amazing distance but I will try to explain how it is possible. There is no speed limit for conscious thought. Well, the ship which took us to Saturn was built on the same principles as the laws of the conscious mind. Scarcely had we left Earth when we began to function on the same principles as those on which the human mind is built . . .

"In the first part of this report I described the procedure following the landing and the buildings in which the conference took place. I described those who were sitting at my table but I said nothing about there being twelve other tables. At these tables there were seated twelve Great Souls, one at each table and with them sat the governor of each of the planets. These Great Souls were once known as 'Messiah' on Earth. Now you will ask here: Who was the Great Soul sitting at our table? It was the representative of the other twelve, the conscious conscience personified in one being. On Earth we would classify him as the conscience of the creator that we call Christ. This however does not mean Jesus because Jesus is a personality and Christ is conscious conscience or cosmic conscience. Jesus as an individual taught himself to allow conscience to be expressed in him and he was thus able to say, 'I, as a part of this Earth, am one with my creator, so I can state that I and my Father are one!' All the 'Messiahs' present had been on Earth once and each of them had come down in order to show the true way to live. Earth had not been the only planet visited by them: the same service was accorded to Mars so I was told . . ."

We think that is about enough of these blasphemous idiocies; but we may just once more refer to the "crusade for the truth concerning the people of other worlds", which is "obvious" Adamski asserts and he ends by asking: "Many of you are saying to yourselves 'What can we do about it?' Here I am giving you an idea of how you can help the cause. We need money to cover the cost of sending our literature to every country so let us hear something of you whether you wish to help or not in this crusade. Even cents will do because with these we can publish information on the subject . . ."

Thus do these Adamski psalms finish in triumph: and to think that there are people amongst us who are prepared to swear on the revelations of this charlatan if not actually to believe in his reincarnation! If there are still some who hesitate to accept Adamski's most liberal interpretation of the Old and New Testaments, who object that . . . well, no matter, it may well have happened some other way. Never fear. Here is something to support the sausage-maker's explanatory notes, taken straight from the Book of Enoch and is more "realistic" even than the Bible.

"The Book of Enoch, which was brought from Abyssinia in three copies by the great Scottish scholar James Bruce round about 1772," the Frenchman Robert Charroux tells us, "was copied from a Hebrew original which was also written in Chaldean and Aramaic— originals which many textual scholars consider as being the oldest manuscript in the world on this subject. Some Catholic scribes made a number of interpolations, being very pious, and claimed there were chapters announcing the coming of the Son of Man or the Messiah. But these passages can easily be disclosed. Enoch is a mysterious character who was taken over into Israeli traditions. But his existence is much older than that of the Hebrew civilization."

Quoting the Book of Enoch ("When the sons of men multiplied in those days daughters were born of them, elegant and beautiful. And when the angels, the sons of heaven had seen them they fell in love with them and said to each other: 'Let us choose women of the race of men and have sons by them'") Charroux comments thus: "Here already we have an atmosphere different from that of the Bible. The women had existed only a short while on Earth, otherwise they would have been seen by the sons of heaven before now. Are they angels? Yes, in the sense meant by the Incas when they saw the Spaniards landing or by those tribes who went into the jungles when the first airmen came. Orejona, the woman from Venus who landed near Lake Titicaca according to tradition in the Andes was defied later, is it not so?"

Let us begin by saying that the information supplied by Charroux (apocryphal and edited not in ancient times but in the Christian era) is quite fantastic and we see that the Frenchman accepts as an indisputable fact the complex Orejona story (the woman with the long ears, who having come from Venus was supposed to have copulated with a tapir and thus generated the human species), which was given with some reserve in his previous book. It is not entirely a question of Andes traditions, but of a legend which a Spaniard named Bertran Garcia claims to have discovered in a secret manuscript (which nobody had ever seen) belonging to the historian Garcilaso de la Vega. A nice piece of evidence indeed!

It is depressing to see how Charroux, a writer who is certainly not rigidly scientific but at least appreciated by some for his brilliant deductions, has sunk down to the histrionic level of Adamski. And it is still more melancholy to note that this is the end of many an investigator who, having seriously approached unusual problems, falls for the charms of crude theories, queer associations of ideas and interpretations. Thus they compromise themselves as they are unable to withdraw from the positions they take up and end by having to resort to distortions and falsehoods.

Apart from discrediting themselves, they obviously increase the destructive and slanderous effect which the champions of orthodox scientific conservatism have on the genuine students who are engaged in revolutionary research.

Professor Lucifer

In America the sects who predict the imminent end of the world are now losing ground and are encouraging reports of the following sort in their bulletins: "Leo V. Bartsch, of Coos Bay, Oregon, Fourth Street, 744 South, has published several letters about his conversion to Christianity because of the flying saucers. He declares that they are sent by angels." (*The Christian Sion Advocate Humanitarian,* Nean Bay, Washington, July-August, 1966.) To compensate for this the supporters of the Adamski Foundation are advancing in full sail and forming groups full of the esoteric and fantastic, of chauvinism and madness, altogether making a strident uproar like the organization of the Sons of Jared, the hostile societies of Watchers who long ago sent ruthless, living robots to subjugate Earth.

"More than 8,000 years ago," we are assured by

these hunters of space witches, "the first Watchers were created like the androids of Hub. Hub is an enormous planet at the centre of the universe, the home of beings which are the best developed in the cosmos and they belong to the Antique Race. To Make the Watchers there was an El called Lucifer who was not only the head of the ruling council but also a skilful biologist. Lucifer tried to create a perfect race, but the creatures escaped from his hands before they had souls; thus they were androids, simply robots of flesh and bone. Lucifer continued with their production against the advice of other members of the council so he was removed from office and summoned to court. But under his guidance the Watchers, supported by the ignorant inhabitants of other planets rebelled against the leadership of Hub. The battle, which took place near these heavenly bodies, was terrible but short, just as it is pictured in the Apocalypse (12, 7): 'And there was war in the heavens: Michael and his angels fought against the dragon but he did not prevail and his abode was no longer to be found in the heavens. And the great dragon, the ancient serpent that is called Devil and Satan, the deceiver of the whole world, was cast down onto Earth and his angels were cast down with him . . . Woe to the Earth and to the Sea, since the Devil has come unto you with much colour, knowing that time is short.'

"The Watchers are the fallen angels of the Bible. Michael, elected head of the council in place of Lucifer, commanded the Hub fleet. As a result of their attitude regarding capital punishment the people of Hub decided to send the Watchers to the primitive planets to warn the inhabitants of these about civilization. Hundreds of celestial bodies were chosen, among them the Earth. Lucifer, with two hundred Watchers, was left on Mount Hermon in present-day Lebanon; as those people know who are familiar with the works of Richard Shaver and George Hunt Williamson, the Antique Race had a colony on Earth at the same time. T. Lobsang Rampa, in his *Third Eye* tells of having seen the mummies of three members of this race in a Tibetan cave; and the famous statues on Easter Island are a primitive representation of El.

"In the regions of Hermon there were the tribes of Adam, led by Jared who lived on the mountain and of Cain who frequented the valley underneath. The watchers contacted the latter and members of Adam's tribe attached themselves to it despite the appeals of Jared. The beings from space taught men of Cain's tribe astronomy, astrology, the workings of metals and fibres, farming and various other practical activities; but they did it for their own ends, because they were not of the best and neither did they have any intention of improving themselves. They convinced them that gold was a precious metal, instituted the first banking system and introduced the use of money. Soon the members of the Cain tribe began to carry out raids and the Watchers taught them how to make weapons of metal: swords, lances, knives and breastplates; and since spirits were essential to the Watchers they started up their production here. They also brought in cock-fighting and dog-fights, horse-racing and gladiator contests. With this came gambling and the result was brawls, corruption and sexual depravity. Gabriel, Michael, Uriel and Raphael, now called archangels, commanded the ships sent to control the Watchers. They saw that these had not kept their word and took steps to arrest them. Some escaped but others were sent to the planetary prison on Mercury where life was only possible in an area bounded by extremes of temperature.[1] The archangels led Enoch, the son of Jared, to Mercury and his description of that planet became one of the sources of the Christian idea of Hell. In effect, there is no written or logical proof of anything from which it is possible to say how God may have formulated the slightest threat of eternal punishment for his creatures; where this does seem possible the Scriptures have been altered by the Watchers or badly inter-

---

[1]This senseless account was written when it was still not known that Mercury rotates and people thought Mercury was exposed to enormous solar heat on one side and the cold cosmos on the other.

preted. When for instance Jesus says: "Get thee hence, accursed ones, into the eternal fire prepared for the devil and his angels", he is speaking of the Watchers' end and of Mercury . . .

"The Watchers established themselves like divine kings in Lebanon and controlled Nineveh, Tyre and Babylonia. The city of Ur was one of their headquarters. They eventually dominated Egypt and replaced the Pharaoh's son with one of their own, killing Solomon and putting in his place a boy who resembled him . . . The Caesars and the Roman generals who persecuted the Christians, were Watchers; and when they saw that they could not eradicate the religion by massacres they decided to stop. During the following centuries the church was almost completely controlled by Watchers who made themselves popes, cardinals and bishops . . . In our day a Watcher, who gave up all claim to decency, was Al Capone . . . Russia is governed by Watchers . . . and they are also in our government and assemblies, in the cloak of respectability, of course, but actually as savage as those we have mentioned. The Watchers are white and are accepted as members of the white races; which is just why the populations of Africa, India and the East have been dominated by foreign masters like the colonial powers and the communist bosses in the Kremlin . . ."

If we want to know something further about the Watchers, it is enough to glance at the publications of their deadly foe *The Jaredite Advocate*. Thus we shall learn that the low-born androids from Hub organized massacres of innocents: Socrates, Archimedes, Alexander, Hannibal and Julius Caesar today give vent to their sadistic instincts by crippling taxes put on the innocent citizens of the United States. And this is not all: Professor Lucifer's henchmen are claiming high office in every country, aiming of course at making slaves of the whole of humanity. The heroic *The Jaredite Advocate* does not hesitate in giving names: the fierce invaders from space include Leonid Brezhnev, Charles de Gaulle, Joseph Saragat and Gamal A. Nasser. The paper also supplies the overwhelming proof of their origin. In fact we can read under two photos appearing in June 1965: "To the left, Russia's Marshals Zukov and Krylov; on the right, King Olaf of Norway and the Jugoslav President Tito . . . have a good look at all four of them—they seem to be brothers: and they are, because all of them belong to the race of flesh and blood robots created by Lucifer . . ."

Fortunately the Sons of Jared are on the alert and ready to save ignorant humanity by selling the oldest masterpeices at a dollar a copy. (*The Lamentations of Jared* dictated by Jared to his son Enoch, a book written around 5800 B.C. . . , *The Prophecy of Nathan* as written by Nathan, saint and advisor of King David of Israel . . . the future of Israel and of the new Israel, or the United States . . . predicts television and the assassination of J. F. Kennedy . . .) In the newspaper clips of the time, their political editor achieves quite a propaganda venture into the past and future, visting Mars, the Alpha system of Centaur and a no better identified "Olympus Planet" and at the same time defending Earth before the Council of Five Thousand Masters. Unfortunately he finds only one brave Watcher who condemns him to a long stay in the best-equipped psychiatric hospital on Saturn.

Being provided with these highly edifying examples, we do not want to conclude that the Bible is ignored by everybody as a source of information. It undoubtedly contains references to events which are not simply religious and which deeply influence human history. We have already spoken about it[2] and outlined some hypotheses by genuine scholars, a number of whose theories are bold but not haphazard. But between this and the interpretation of Scripture in spatial terms there is however a gulf—filled solely with a sea of pious absurdities.

It can be said that the future will give us things which will shed light on many passages in the Old Testament; but until we have such it will be best to proceed very carefully. It is, of course, clear that fol-

[2] *Terra senza Tempo (The Timeless Earth)* by the same author: Sugar Publishing House, Milan.

lowing the systems cherished by the deceased Adamski and his Sons of Jared, we could weave all sorts of fantasies around cosmic eras—for that matter we could do the same with the Snow-White fairy-tale or with a railway timetable.

Imagine the whole world upset by some cataclysm and that books written by us reach our descendants and suppose that the books deal with astronauts or a science fiction concerning intelligent worms on the planet Desdemona: what sort of conclusions might they feel justified in reaching? That men, having managed to project themselves into space, had discovered a planet called Desdemona and had contacted the intelligent creatures on it? Or that before the catastrophe the Earth was inhabited by flying creatures gifted with fearful powers, by invisible women and highly civilized animals? Or would our descendants try to obtain confirmation of what they had read instead of drawing such arbitrary conclusions, and devote themselves to the study of old texts and archaeological remains? Unless extremely primitive, they would undoubtedly take the second course of action. Therefore it will be better for us too to proceed in this way, confining ourselves to the study of less vague references as supported by eloquent traditions, historical allusions and discoveries. A sensational enough picture will emerge without even having to disturb fallen angels and Watchers or intellectual devils.

CHAPTER THREE

WANDERING PROPHETS

If there is one figure in the Old Testament who seems, like Noah, to have gone all round the world it is that of Elijah. The biblical story is well-known: Ahaziah, King of the Israelites, fell from a railing somehow and injured himself badly. His faith in the local medicine must have been far from steady if he thought it advisable to send his men abroad to consult the priests of a mysterious god called Beelzebub. But on the way there the men met the prophet Elijah who, seated on a mountain-top seemed to show little understanding of Ahaziah's ideas, accusing him of something akin to blasphemy and predicting certain death for him. ("And is it perhaps because there is no god in Israel that you come to consult Baalzebub, god of Ekron?")

Ahaziah furiously sent an official and fifty men to arrest Elijah but the latter, before anybody could lay hands on him, had disintegrated them at one stroke. ("Let fire come down from heaven and consume thee and thy fifty", the hill-top solitary ordered. "And there came down fire from heaven and consumed him and his fifty", says the Bible.) A second group met the same fate and a third miraculously saved itself by piously begging for mercy. After the king Ahaziah had duly died Elijah went up into the sky in a whirl of fire. "And they travelled on talking together", the Old Testament says again, referring to the prophet and to his disciple Elisha, "behold, there appeared a chariot of fire, and horses of fire and parted them both asunder and Elijah went up by a whirlwind into heaven."

There are interesting things about this account: the destroying flame which was at his command (this occurs in tradition all over the world and seems to allude to cosmic vehicles and their propulsion) and the fact that Elijah does not go away suddenly as a result of one of those mythological ecstasies or rather abductions which are so good for explaining something which otherwise would be inexplicable but announces his departure beforehand almost as though he were expecting someone to come and fetch him. And these things seem all the more impressive when it is remembered that they occur in populations often very far from each other. An Amazonian source tells us quite clearly about a certain Elipas who, settling down on a hill in the company of a snake goes off to cure the natives and "use strange magic of fire and water". The matter continued until the local gods were annoyed by the competition and tried to welcome him with feasting and then let loose the "wicked men of the forests". It was a huge fiasco: the snake spurted flame and burnt up the forests, charring the land and making the rivers boil, after which Elipas lectured the survivors, telling them that from then on they would have to do without his miracles; he then went up into the air, riding on the serpent in a whirl of fire.

It is not possible to know if Amazonian traditions are older or later than the Christian era. "But it seems inadmissible to me", wrote the anthropologist R. Lodge, "that such primitive natives, even if already in contact with missionaries, could have acquired such a detailed knowledge of the Old Testament; and also because there are no traces amongst them of other such memories, if we exclude the myths concerning the deluge, the biblical origin of which is highly unlikely."

So it is pertinent to consider how the imagined celestial vehicles, often described as chariots of fire in the Mediterranean areas, become "birds of flame" or "fiery serpents": we find them in this form in the whole of central and southern America and another legend obtained by Marcel F. Homet, again in the Amazon area, supplies us with a further version of the story of Elijah: where our friend does not go off riding on a serpent but is swallowed by it!

The biblical prophet is not unknown even in Asia: referring to it indirectly, the British scholar, Raymond W. Drake, calls our attention to the Indian heroes who "leap into the skies on flying chariots to engage in aerial combat, destroying their enemies with 'explosive arrows', and annihilating whole armies with instruments which remind one of our atomic bombs . . . The tellers of these stories lived in a simple world and compared aerial machines to birds or animals—just as centuries later the American Indians were to see the train as a horse of iron." Here, then, are the "fiery steeds of the Bible!"

Serpents among the clouds

The Divine Archer, Tsu-yu, who could be a kind of Chinese Elijah, used to hit his enemies with fiery darts and then return into the sky. And in Siberia we have one still more like his biblical colleague: a warrior with "dazzling arrows" who, in the Shahman legend, offers his prophecies seated on a mountain, blows up anybody who dares to laugh at him and in the end, disgusted by human incredulity, flies away in a shell of gold.

Having perhaps a claim to the goodwill of this mythical hero, several Russian research workers have gathered all the versions of this legend and they conclude that the chief points agree. *The Northern Neighbours*, a Canadian journal, stresses this and adds: "The Elijah legend is spread in various parts of the world and

Elijah himself is often called 'The Thunderer'. Some tribes link the story with the fiery serpent myth, telling us also how the people swallowed by this reptile return to the world with new and marvellous ideas. Not much imagination is needed to think of this as a space ship. But there is an odd reference in several old texts to men who watched in a forbidden box and who were 'punished with the loss of all their hair'; the 'box' might have been some nuclear apparatus, since radioactivity causes precisely that loss of hair (among other things)." Do these things sound like fables? Wait: many primitive religions have rites during which the faithful go into caves and later emerge with increased awareness.

Ceremonies of this sort take place in Central America, Asia, Oceania and Africa. Other magical rites which resemble them closely have prevailed since time immemorial in those regions of the "black continent" where, among the objects of the cult, we find several extremely ancient trifles made of glass occupying an important position: they are of unknown origin and the natives call them stone ear-rings.

"When white people ask for more detailed information in connection with these," the French scholar Serge Hutin wrote, "they are told that the ear-rings were brought by white men who had come down from the sky." And among the tribes around the Gulf of Guinea curious traditions exist which confirm these apparently fantastic beliefs. Georges Barbarin tells us that a British major one day saw the members of a tribe, with their chief and wizards leading it, going towards the seashore where a canoe was approaching them. Two white-painted natives got out of it and, after having received signs of submission from the assembled company, went into their boat again. When asked what this meant, the negroes replied that it was a custom handed down from the very earliest times and was meant to perpetuate the tradition that white men had come once from the sky and from an island now no longer in existence. They reached the mainland in order to impose laws and administer justice. These far-sighted advisors appear in the lore of almost all the countries in the world. For instance, Raymond W. Drake writes: "The very oldest documents declare that China in ages now lost was ruled for 18,000 years by a race of divine kings: it can also be read in the so-called Tchi manuscript, which establishes fascinating parallels with Indian, Japanese, Egyptian and Greek legends; in the 'Ramayana' and the 'Kojichi' traces of it can be found, likewise in the 'History' of Manetho and in in Hesiod's 'Theogony'.

"The Chinese text 'Huai-nan-tzu' (chap. 8) describes to us an idyllic era in which men and animals lived in a sort of Eden, united in their cosmic awareness. The climate was mild and there were no natural disasters —the planets did not deviate from their orbits—crimes were unknown and the world's population prospered. 'Spirits' often came down to Earth to teach the divine wisdom, but our generation then became greedy and perverted. The 17th book of the 'Shan-hai Ching' refers to a troubled race called Miao which collided with its 'high lord' and then 'lost the ability to fly and was exiled'.

"In another work, the "Shoo-ikng' (4th Part, Chap. 27) it is said that: 'When the Mao-tse (the perverted antediluvian race who withdrew into caves and whose descendants might have been discovered in our day near Canton) brought trouble to the whole earth (according to ancient documents) and were helped in this by Tchi-yoo, the world was full of robbers . . . Chang-ty (a king of the 'divine dynasty') saw that his people had lost all virtue and ordered Tchang and Lhy (two 'Dhyan Chohans'—semigods) to cut all communication between sky and earth. From then on there was no longer ascent or descent."[1]

Let us return to Elijah: we shall see that before going away on his fantastic chariot of fire he gave his cloak to Elisha, thus conferring on him a part of his extraordinary powers. The Bible says here (2nd Kings 2,

---

[1] The explanatory comments here are those of R. W. Drake. The sections given are taken from his volume *Spacemen in the Ancient East*.

14):"And he took the mantle of Elijah and smote the waters and said, Where is the Lord God of Elijah? And when he also had smitten the waters, they parted hither and thither: and Elijah went over . . . Now the inhabitants of the city said to Elijah: Behold, the situation of this city is pleasant, as my lord seeth: but the water is naught and the ground barren. And he said: Bring me a new cruse and put salt therein; and they brought it to him. And he went forth unto the spring of the waters, and cast the salt in there and said: Thus saith the Lord, I have healed these waters. There shall not be from thence any more death or barren land. Thus the waters were healed unto this day."

Thus the spatial hypotheses appear to be anything but heavy and clumsy: it does not take a wild imagination to think of some interplanetary explorer landing on our globe and forced to use arms against a gang of crude, superstitious people and then to withdraw so as not to aggravate the situation. As for Elisha, imagine finding ourselves in a hostile country (like Elijah) and gaining the friendship of a native more open-minded than his fellows, then letting him stay in our camp and using him as a guide and source of information. When we left would it not seem natural perhaps to give him something with which he could possibly defend himself against his kinsmen—something which would ultimately benefit his own society? Let us consider for a moment Elijah's magic cloak: we cannot help thinking of the feather-cloaks worn across the shoulders by ancient central and southern American kings. The "serpent of fire" is also the "plumed serpent"; the plumes undoubtedly symbolizing flight. We find these among the Olmecxs, the Toltecs, Aztecs and the Maya. Quetzalcoatl (the son of the sky-god, Mixcoalt, whose name means "serpent of the clouds"), the legendary white king who "taught all the sciences to mankind", wears a feather-cloak to symbolize his origin in a celestial ship; just like Kukumatz, his opposite number in Guatemala. And the other figures of the "solar races" wear their war-cloaks to reflect their hereditary and divine powers. The same meaning we can see at-

tached later to Montezuma's feathered crown, the final
emperor of ancient Mexico; and to the feather headgear
of all American Indians.

The Furore and the Stars

"Spread along the flank of the mountain
the great serpent sleeps
thirty awns long and eight wide.[2]
His belly is decorated with flints and resplendent
   glass.
Now I know the name of the serpent of the mountain.
Here it it: 'He who lives in fire'.
After having navigated in silence,
behold how Ra casts a glance at the serpent.

Suddenly his ship stops,
as for the one who is concealed in his boat
he holds himself in ambush . . ."

We are no longer in America but in the land of
pyramids and this passage is taken from the *Book of
the Dead,* a number of sacred texts attributed to the
god Thoth and his priests, perhaps sometime before
3500 B.C. Here the cosmic serpent reappears, this time
on the shores of the Mediterranean and "space" factors
emerge which can certainly surprise us with their details. The *Book of the Dead* refers to the struggle between Horus and Seth, among the "sons of light" and
the "sons of the dark". Perhaps we would be guilty of
levity if we let ourselves be tempted into finding parallels between these concepts and those which appear to
be the corresponding ones in pre-columbian mythology; but how can we forget the references to the
"white sons of light" so closely tied to the "serpents of
the clouds" and escape the fascination of that other
term ("sea of darkness", "heart of darkness" and
"spear in the dark") which seems to suggest not the
night but the eternal gloom of interstellar chasms?

[2]About 54 by 15 metres.

And the *Book of the Dead* does not encourage permanent stay on strictly mythological ground, with its threatening and shining serpent, motionless along the mountain-side, ready to unleash a flood of fire, and with the maddened Horus shouting into space: "I shall annihilate the devils; those who travel through the sky, those who live on Earth, and also those who reach the stars". Likewise the description—impressive in its realism—of the cosmic voids: "I approached the accursed zone into which they had fallen, sped towards the gulf, the stars . . . in truth they could not retrace their orbits of old because their path is destroyed . . ."

Had our world, perhaps ages ago, been shaken by the echoes of some frightful interplanetary conflict? What if it had been directly involved in an orgy of destruction? The idea may seem far fetched, but it is just as absurd to think that certain descriptions which have a bloodcurdling realism for us moderns have simply arisen from the fantasies of primitive peoples; or that the astonishing identity of myths all over the world can be simply accidental.

Shining shells which can fly are to be found in Mongolian Chinese, Japanese and Indian legends; golden discs hover in mid-air in America; winged plates stud the remote Egyptian past; from Persia we have "false stars" shining everywhere, harbingers of extermination and ruin—among the figures on the royal tomb of Nacch i rustem, near Persepolis, Darius The First is turning to Ahura Mazda, "the god of light", sculptured on a disc, not the sun which is pictured separately and higher up.

"The furore sparked off among the stars," says a Mongolian tradition, based unfortunately on unknown references, "lit up Suns of death . . ." And Raymond W. Drake tells us from China: "Some texts of the Chou dynasty about 2346 B.C. point to the appearance of ten suns in the sky, an item which reminds one of like visitations in ancient Rome, as recorded by Julian the Obsequious; or the "celestial prodigies" of medieval times cited by Matthew of Paris and similar phenomena oddly like the flying saucers today.

The manuscripts Chuang-tsu (chap. 2), Liu-shi-ch'unch'iu (12th Part, Chap. 5) and Hua-non-tsu (chap. 8) have a lively account of how the Earth was struck during the reign of the emperor Yao by a terrible calamity: an intense heat lit up the earth, the harvests were destroyed, frightful hurricanes lashed the cities and the countryside, the seas rose and boiled, submerging the fields, huge monsters were everywhere causing massacres and men feared the Apocalypse . . . The emperor Yao consulted his priests and sages who (as usual when there is dire need) were not much help. Desperate, he then asked the divine archer Tsu-yu, who was capable of flying and who ate nothing but flowers (thus showing a strange affinity to the modern spacemen for whom algae cultures are grown). The hero beat down the false suns, letting the true light shine on the follies of mankind; he exterminated the monsters entirely and saved Earth for ungrateful posterity, afterwards flying off to the moon."

Let us once more go through the accurate and unexceptionable collection of manuscripts gathered by the British scholar: "Some legends written in the Feng-shen-yen-i tell us of the strangest events that might have happened in a distant 'age of miracles', among which are aerial battles like those of the Mahabharata—the monumental ancient Indian poem. Rival factions fought for control of China, helped by celestial creatures who took part to assist the various groups, using spectacular weapons to do so. No-cha used his 'sky-earth bracelet' to defeat Feng-lin, who vainly shelters behind a smoke-producing curtain. Later the hero beat Chang Kuoi-fung (using his chariot of fire and wind) calling to his aid the bands of 'flying dragons of silver'. Weng-chang lashed Ch'ih with a 'magic whip' but is routed by an irresistible 'Yin-yang mirror' which sends out a lethal power. The wars were conducted with the techniques of genuine space-men. The combatants fired blinding rays and poisonous gases, 'dragons of fire' and spheres of flame, 'shining darts' and 'lightning'; they practised biological warfare and dropped capsules of 'celestial umbrellas', at the same time protecting themselves with 'cloaks of invisibility'; they must have had, if we go by the descriptions, radar or similar instruments, by means of which they could see and hear objects a hundred miles away; and here too we find a technology almost identical with that of the Sanskrit Mahabharata.

"More than any other peoples, the Chinese made the dragon the symbol of their civilization: they thought in fact that the 'celestial dragon' might be the father of the first dynasty of 'divine emperors'. As is known, the emblem of the dragon is prepared for Chinese art in a most fascinating way. The ancient texts show us fantastic monsters: the bodies covered in scales like armour, eyes flaming and jaws on fire, the beasts roar among the sky-winds and plunge into ocean depths, reducing whole cities to ashes with their burning breath . . .

"Could an illiterate Chinese of olden times imagine a dragon or have sufficient awareness of this idea to inspire him in art and religion? It is hard to credit it if we admit that 'flying things' of that sort have never existed. In fact to our eyes these pictures of dragons appear in an oddly familiar light: if we go through ancient texts we see the images of spaceships flashing by into space . . ."

Dragons of fire, thundering birds, winged and feathered serpents: though we might try to limit our fantasies we shall be compelled to admit that it is a question here of the mythological transfer of the same idea. Of an idea expressed very lucidly by (Professor Tchi Pen-lao declares) "those cylindrical flying machines symbolized on a pyramid arisen from Lake Kun-Ming as the result of an earthquake. The scholar thinks he can establish that "these regions saw the existence 45,000 years ago of an unknown, highly developed race . . ."

The City of Crystal

India is a country which has kept its traditions of flights and battles in the distant past most clearly: here it is not dragons, serpents or huge birds flashing through the skies but machines; not magic lanterns and false suns but with weapons the description of which is hardly hidden by mythological elements. James Churchward, the enigmatic English scholar whose researches are anything but negligible when he does not digress into theosophical speculations, tells us about a manuscript dealing with aerial navies around 15 to 20 thousand years ago. "Their fuel" he says in a work written decades before people spoke about artificial satellites and space ships, "is drawn from the air in a very simple and cheap way. The motor is something like a modern turbine: it works from one chamber to another and does not stop or stall unless switched off. If nothing happens it continues to function. The ship in which it is built could revolve as long as it liked around Earth, only falling when the parts of which it is made were burnt up." Fantasies? Let us hear what the Mysore International Academy of Sanskrit Studies has to say: "The manuscripts we present in translation from Sanskrit describe various types of automatic ships adapted for travel on land, sea or in air and from planet to planet. It seems that they could stop still in the sky and even become invisible; and that they might have instruments capable of detecting hostile aircraft even at a distance."[3]

We have plenty of confirmation from innumerable texts: the Samaranganasu-tradhara relates the history of fantastic flights on Earth and to the Sun and stars, a document from the pre-Christian era tells us in detail about the heavenly chariot of Rama.[4] ". . . the chariot was automatic, big and well-painted; it had two floors and many rooms and windows . . ." and Valmiki, the Indian Herodotus, sings in verse: "The sky-chariot which has a wonderful power and wings for speed, is gilded and lustrous throughout . . . it leaps above the

---

[3]The report has been published in India by the scholar Maharshi Bharadaja under the title "Aircraft of the Prehistoric Past".

[4]Son of Dasaratha, King of Adjudhia, seventh incarnation of Vishnu. Ravana, King of Lanka (Ceylon) stole his wife Sita whom Rama regained after a tremendous conflict.

hill and the wooded valley, winged like lightning or like Indra's javelin, lethal as the lamp of heaven, covered in smoke and flaming lamps, speedy and round of prow . . .

Hundreds and hundreds of similar stories await us in Indian folklore: behold the divine Maya aloft in "a circular chariot of gold, measuring 12,000 cubits in circumference and able to reach the stars" here too the "metal horse of the sky" belonging to King Satrugit, and the "sky-coach" of King Pururavas. Even in the fourth century A.D. we find a flying hero, the Buddhist monk Gunarvarman, who travels from Ceylon to Java on a machine like those of antiquity, discovered who knows where!

It is not thought that those of the prehistoric Indians were merely pleasure-trips. Like us they seem to have used aerial means both for recreation and for warlike operations, and the latter must have been terrible if we go by reports still reaching us. Ravana, the Demon King of Ceylon and mortal foe of Rama, "flew at his enemies (as a manuscript of 500 B.C says) dropping devices which caused huge destruction. Afterwards he was captured and killed, his machine being taken by the Hindu captain, Ram Chandra, who flew on it to the capital Adjudhia . . ."

And these are not just trifles. "The Bhisma Parva"— says Drake—"mentions weapons like the 'Rod of Brahma' and the 'thunderbolt of Indra' the effects of which were like nuclear explosions; the Drona Parva tells us about 'Mr. Mahadeva' and his frightening 'flying spears' (missles?) capable of ruining whole cities full of forts . . . and describes the fabulous weapons of Agni which annihilated whole armies, devastating Earth like hydrogen bombs".

Is it possible that no vestiges remain of these awful conflicts? There are countless witnesses—the researchers tell us—if we take the trouble to go and look for them. It is no simple undertaking of course, since jungle has claimed the ruins for thousands of years; but if we succeed in localizing all the dead cities of the subcontinent we should dot the map of India with as many points as can be found on an atlas of present-day sites.

From time to time, descriptions arise which leave us bewildered. The explorer De Camp, for instance, mentions having seen in the areas, between the Ganges and the mountains of Rajmahal, the charred ruins of something which could not be due to a simple fire, however violent: several huge masses seemed to be fused together and hollowed at various points "like lumps of tin struck by a stream of molten steel." The British official, J. Campbell, came across similar ruins more to the south and was struck by a very odd, half-vitrified floor which must have been an internal courtyard and appeared to have been formed by an unknown human power. Other travellers describe discoveries of ruined buildings, never seen before, in the heart of Indian forests. The walls were "like thick slabs of crystal" and these too were holed, split and corroded by agents unknown. The explorer and hunter, H. J. Hamilton, had the biggest surprise of his life when he went into a building of this sort containing a low dome.

"Suddenly," he says, "the ground gave way under my feet with a curious noise. I got into a safe place and then widened the hole, which had appeared, with my rifle-butt and lowered myself into it. I was in a long and narrow corridor which got its light from the space where the dome had split. At the bottom I saw a kind of table and chair, made of the same "crystal" as the walls. An odd shape was crouching on the seat, with vaguely human features. Looking at it from close by, I thought it might be a statue damaged in the course of time but then I glanced at something which filled me with horror: under the "glass" which covered that "statue" a skeleton could clearly be seen!" Walls, furniture, vitrified human beings . . . what huge secrets are lurking between the boundaries of the Mahabharata and the Drona Parva?

CHAPTER FOUR

THE SONS OF THE PLEIADES

Mr. John Spencer was not the type of man one would call the flower of gallantry: if he had been, he would have stayed peacefully in Manchuria and not set off in a frenzy of haste to face mad marches and cross nightmarish regions to turn up in 1920 in Mongolia, practically brought to death's door by fatigue and fever. It is said that he was dealing in arms and drugs; it was also said, in the newspapers of the day, that he even coined his own money. At any rate nothing more would have been heard of him had he not fainted, fortunately, on a path made by Buddhist monks who picked him up and took him into the famous lamasery at Tuerin, where they refreshed him. It was necessary in those days that he should be a guest of theirs. A white man of quite different standing, the American traveller William Thompson, an honest business man, fascinated by the lama world, had been for months a pleasant guest of the monastery. Thompson must have depicted the marvels and treasures of Tuerin with a somewhat excessive haste and enthusiasm if Spencer, without waiting for a

39

return to complete health, started to ramble around inside, suddenly full of interest for the wonders described by his fellow-countryman. One morning the adventurer discovered near the monastery a stone staircase with worn-out steps. Having pushed open a narrow door, without any trouble, he found himself in a polygon-shaped room, though it is not known if it had twelve, thirteen or more sides. On the various walls, Spencer looked at some incomprehensible patterns of a strange sort; but after having examined them thoroughly the design of one of them seemed to make sense. It was the representation of the constellation of Taurus, with which he was familiar for the simplest of reasons, having been born under that sign and carrying with him on his watch-chain an amulet from China with the same sign on it.

He followed the design with his finger, though without any special purpose—in fact almost playfully. Then as he prodded right at the end of the line, where an incision marked out the Pleiades[1] he was amazed to see the wall silently opening. The space in front was dark. Spencer hesitated a moment till curiosity got the better of him. He groped his way forward into the dark and was about to give up the exploration, when he saw a green light in the distance. Then his practical sense compelled him to go back and return with a big stone from outside, which he then used to prop the wall open so that it could not close and trap him.

He did not manage to discover the source of the green light, which seemed to him to come from the sharp corners of the ceiling. He considered it unnecessary to bother further with it and was satisfied that he was going along a narrow and solid gallery where there was no danger of collapse. The tunnel had several branches and Spencer decided to take the right one, although one was much the same as another and he did not want to run the risk of losing his way. Naturally he did not know that this was just the direction indicated by the Pleiades which was high on the right side of the

[1] Spencer did not even know that the Pleiades existed: a point which was later made clear by W. Thompson.

wall open wide in front of him! Finally he reached the
end, in a room where the green light was stronger and
harsher. Along one wall a number of rectangular boxes
were lined up (from 25 to 30 he said himself at the
time) which *seemed to be suspended about half a
metre from the floor*. Spencer ignored this, thinking it
might have supports he could not see, and instead gave
his attention to the boxes. He saw at once that they were
biers but instead of their impressing him he felt inclined
to congratulate himself, thinking that there must be
treasure buried with the remains. He found with pleasure that the lids could easily be lifted up, and started
his inspection. In the first three he discovered the bodies
of monks, clothed like those in the monastery, and in
the fourth, lay the body of a woman dressed in man's
clothing which must have been cut at least fifty years
ago. In the fifth there was an Indian wearing a cloak of
red silk and the sixth contained a man in a costume he
reckoned was made in 1700. He then began to consider
two other points: that the corpses were in a perfect
state of preservation and that they were not all of the
same epoch, becoming older the further he went towards the walls at the end of the room.

In the propenultimate box lay a man "wrapped in
white bedclothes" and in the last but one a woman
whose origin he could not establish. Of the longed-for
necklaces, etc., there was not the slightest trace. Spencer
was annoyed and when he lifted the last lid he was
rooted to the spot with amazement: the body of a man
was inside, dressed in a sort of silver mail and who in
place of a head had a ball of pure silver, with round
holes where the eyes should be and an oval thing full
of small holes in lieu of a nose—and there was no
mouth!

Spencer, recovering from his surprise, was about to
touch the object when he changed his mind suddenly as
the big round eyes of the dead man were wide open
and emitting a horrifying green gleam. So he quickly
dropped the lid and ran back shouting to the place he
had come from. After about ten yards he had the good
sense to stop and think, otherwise he would never have

been able to find the exit again. He returned to the exit after a long walk but when he came out he had another shock: darkness had fallen in the valley. "I must have walked for two or three hours all told" he said afterwards. "It is impossible that I could have lost all sense of time to such an extent in there!"

A much perturbed John Spencer returned to the monastery and told Thompson, who did not seem very surprised, but told him off instead and said that he would have to tell the whole story to the priests. Next morning Spencer was called by one of the monks who welcomed him smiling, treating him with a kindness which Spencer hardly dared to believe. "My poor friend" the monk said, "your fever has played a dirty trick on you! Why didn't you expect to be cured by visiting our holy places?" This friendliness encouraged Spencer to ask for explanations about the vaults and the "corpse without a mouth". But the lama shook his head: "There are neither corpses nor vaults down there: come with me if you feel strong enough." They went down to the odd room together and the priest touched a wall with his finger. It opened on to a gallery and the two men walked for not more than ten minutes when they reached a small room containing a table like an altar. On this ledge there was a row of some small biers, with a length of not more than 12-13 centimeters. The priest carefully uncovered them one after the other—they contained perfect statuettes, copies of the creatures discovered by Spencer.

"This is what you really saw," said the monk, smiling. "They are images of people who have enriched the world with their wisdom and so we honour them. It was your fever, my poor friend, which made you think you were standing in front of real sarcophagi. And as you can see, there is no green light but only the yellow one from our humble lamps." Spencer did not dare to reply (in certain circumstances he could be the epitome of caution) but he was unable to stop himself asking the priest who the person with the round head might be, the first one in the row. "A high lord who came from the stars" replied the monk, pointing to some lines on the wall behind the altar: once again it turned out to be the Constellation of Taurus and once more Spencer's glance was directed to the Pleiades!

Pocket-sized Biers

When Spencer saw Thompson again he said he had not the slightest doubt about the truth of his adventure. "It might easily be that I still had some fever" he said, "but I absolutely reject the idea that I dreamt it all or was the victim of delirium. I lost the heel of one of my shoes down in the labyrinth and scratched my hands at least a dozen times when I was feeling the stones for any possible snags. I touched the clothes on that corpse and noticed the veins and wrinkles . . . the piece of wall which opened was on the left of the entrance whereas the opening the lama stood in front of was almost right in front, slightly to the right . . . the monk has tried to convince me by showing me a miniature copy of what I actually saw."

Spencer left the monastery a week later and nothing more was heard of him. William Thompson however, returned to the United States and told others about the whole episode (reported at that time in a review called *Adventure*) persuasively saying that Spencer's assertions were true. "I have on some occasions myself seen corpses in Mongolian monasteries, preserved intact for centuries, perhaps for thousands of years, and have heard people talk several times about silver men who had come from the stars".

There are too many legends surrounding the Tuerin monastery for Thompson's account to be snapped up like pure gold; still, it does contain many elements which blaze the trail to certain wild speculations which are not lacking in odd allusions. Spencer's lost hours between entering the cave in the morning and emerging at night could be explained by a long faint which was obliterated from his memory by the pressure of strong emotions. The gleam from the round eyes could be based on a light reflection on to what was probably not eyes but crystal discs. But there are plenty of tales about green lights in that maze of galleries which would stretch under the whole of central Asia; and huge crowds of pilgrims were able to worship in the Tibetan monastery of Khaldan, till the end of the fourteenth century, the corpse of the reformer Tsong Kaba which hung about twenty centimeters above the ground.

As for the tiny biers shown by the monk to Spencer, let us go to Scotland and listen to that restless collector of oddities called Charles Fort, who tells us the following things about a piece of news which appeared in *The Times* in London on July 20th 1836: "At the beginning of July some boys were after hares around the rock outcrop called King Arthur's Seat at Edinburgh when they came across a vein of slate in the rocks. When they removed the slate they discovered a small grotto containing 17 little coffins about 3 to 4 inches long which enclosed wooden figures of varying materials and styles. The coffins were arranged in two rows of eight each while the seventeenth seemed to mark the beginning of a new row. The discovery has been made more mysterious by the fact that they had been put separately in the grotto with a distance of several years between each. The coffins of the first row all seem to be damaged but the effects of time are not so evident in the second; thus the last coffin must have been put there in quite recent times."

This is not a question of humbug: there is a detailed report about the discovery, attached to copies of three of the coffins and the figures, in the archives of the "Society of Antiquarians of Scotland". And it is odd to notice how Fort, talking about a race of dwarfs from space accustomed to bury effigies of the departed, adds that the mystery could be cleared up by researches conducted in the Gobi Desert. What figures like those of Tuerin might not be found in other lamaseries, in the galleries and in the cities which, according to the legends, lie buried for countless thousands of years in central Asia, having been founded by creatures from space? If it is true we would have to come to the conclusion that Fort was wrong only in thinking a population of dwarfs was involved.

These ideas are certainly sensational but the accounts by Spencer and Thompson contain two items sufficiently important for the enquiry we intend to carry out: the reference to the Pleiades and the bizarre form of the "head" of the enigmatic being inside the first coffin. A "head" which was not in fact like a head but a space helmet supplied with eyepieces and projections in which we would be able to see a filter or, rather, a breathing system. Let us remember that the silver head *had no mouth*, just like the figures which a number of scholars think of as being written or carved to commemorate the coming of cosmic explorers to Earth ages ago in the mists of time: from the famous Great God of Mars found in 1956 by Henri Lothe a Sefar, in the Saharan plateau of n'Ajjer, to the white woman of Hoggar, likewise in the Sahara. "The style of their clothes is similar" says a famous Russian pilot "to our pressurized outfits and the helmet is the same as those we use today. The two oval shapes are perhaps inlets for eye-pieces, the eyes themselves probably looking through the transparent cover. The lines around the neck indicate the articulated parts facilitating head movements with the helmet on. Some designs have direct evidence of connections with the space-suit and antennae in the form of a grating."

In Australian caverns and on the rocks there we find innumerable designs of this nature, only a few of which have been accurately examined and photographed under the auspices of the National Museum but they are enough to show the extraordinary affinity with those of the Sahara. Heads without mouths, and clothes seeming able to suggest only overalls or suits: how can we interpret these extremely ancient rock pictures, considering that the aborigines lived and still live quite naked—"human symbols, as one anthropologist has put it, of a most remote prehistoric period"?

The most important figures are those of the Woomera area. One of them has on his chest certain marks which at once suggest the small orifices on some space-suits, while in another one there are two objects sketched which appear to be headphones. But the most curious drawing is the one on a rounded rock which can only be seen in its entirety from one point. "We are almost tempted to think that the artist must have wanted to show both a space-ship and the scene going on at the foot of the vehicle" a journalist says. A real space-ship? According to *Panorama* (published by Kilburn) there is no doubt. Records of the event, handed down from generation to generation, are still with us. "An old aborigine of a nearby tribe", we read, "says that the clear figure in the middle shows 'the great white man from the sky' and that the circle high up on the left is a space-ship. The semicircular marks lower down portray people instructed by the mysterious newcomers and the circles are the elders of the chief clans."

"These designs" Professor Alexei Kasanzev says, "allude to unknown beings who must have visited Earth several thousand years ago. We must continue to study and discuss them. We can talk it over with every conceivable argument but there is no justification for ignoring them." The resulting discoveries and details emerging from careful examinations confirm the validity of this statement. Let us read once more what the famous Russian scholar has to say: "There is for instance the cliff design discovered in an Alpine valley by the French archaeologist Emmanuel Anati (it is the Camonica Valley, above Lake Iseo) where you can see strange headgear (worn by anthropomorphic beings) detachable from the shoulders; they could be stylized representations of the "foreigners" hermetically sealed helmets. The external appendages of the "headgear" are also unusual. The figures are holding objects which seem to be a right-angled triangle and an isosceles triangle: one must conclude that they are geometrical symbols if the theory is rejected that they are bows and arrows (in which case the distortion would be excessive). Anati thinks that the culture discovered by him might be different from that of neighboring tribes—one of the higher level and with knowledge of metals and how to work them. It is difficult to say at what stage these people might have learnt about geometry but we would not be far wrong if we see in these triangles a symbolic expression of such knowledge.

"Recently G. V. Sciatskij, a worker from the central institute of crystalography, has found rock graffiti near the village of Okhna, 40 kilometers south of Fergana, on the river Sciahimardan. This graffiti is extraordinarily like the one found in the Alps: you can see the same stylized helmet separate from the shoulders and it shows similar external trappings.

"But the rock carving discovered in 1961 by the teacher, B. S. Scialatonin, in the mountain region of Sarmys near the Uzbeg city of Navoi is very interesting. It is at least three thousand years old and one woud say immediately that the central figure is a missile . . . the men shown inside are wearing a nasal object which could be a respirator".

Another rocket could be clearly pictured—again according to Kasanzev—on an Etruscan dish now kept in a Leningrad museum. He says "anthropoidal creatures of some sort can be seen wearing headgear which might well be space helmets: they are shown on board a ship which appears to move by rocket propulsion." At Meroe, the ancient Nubian capital, there is a "missile" near the base of a building which seems to have been an astronomical observatory! People say, nonetheless, that the pictures of cosmic ships are too rare (if not non-existent) to support the theory that prehistoric interplanetary ships once landed on Earth. Scholars reply to this by reviewing the stelae and monuments which closely suggest space-ships and point out that these are transformed into winged creatures and serpents or into mythological dragons of the kind we have mentioned; finally suggesting that it would be absurd to imagine interplanetary cruisers all being standardized on the same lines.

We already know now that space-ships with propulsion by nuclear or ionizing means are planned for the future with totally different aspects from the present-day ones. To give a practical example we might remember that within half a century, space would have to be crossed—according to the elaborate designs of Soviet

and American technicians—by ferries with the shape of
true ships, by vehicles meant for the Moon-Earth
stretch with equipment like shafts, discs, water-skis and
triangles; and by interplanetary ships consisting of a
complex of large spheres or cabins connected to each
other by means of very long booms (to avoid the danger of nuclear contamination) to cylindrical or spherical reservoirs. If, then, the ships supposed to land on
Earth came from various worlds with different forms of
life and technological levels the differences between the
space vehicles would obviously be enormous. And this
could give us an idea of the bewildering variety of unidentified flying objects appearing in our skies.

We can say that there are very old representations of
space-ships, things that we are not able to understand,
or at least not yet. If for instance we had no very clear
idea of the sort of structure a nuclear-propelled space-
ship might have, then the Indian bas-reliefs portraying
those odd spherical ships, which some Soviet scientists
believe are intended for space travel, then they would
appear to us to be completely incomprehensible. The
ones most remarkable are those patterns of the Gate of
the Sun at Tiahuanaco, in which we can see, according
to Kasanov, Zirov and others, automatic space-craft using solar energy. But the clearest and most puzzling one
is at Palenque; here we are up against a picture which
defies every interpretation except one—the spatial concept.

An Astronaut at Palenque

The pyramid of Palenque rises up from a huge field of
Maya ruins, eight kilometers from the Mexican town-
ship from which it takes its name. It was discovered
about 1950 and for years the expedition led by the
archaeologist Alberto Ruz Lhuillier was engaged upon
it. Months and months of extensive work were needed
to clear away the packed rubble inside the monument,
which had been there for centuries for reasons unknown. In the end the workers found themselves faced
with other revelations and mysteries. Palenque demol-

ished the idea held so tenaciously by traditional archaeologists that the American pyramids were clearly different from the Egyptian ones by never having been used as tombs: because in a large sarcophagus of red stone a skeleton came to light of a man one metre and 73 centimetres tall, whose face was covered with a mask of jade. To whom did these remains belong? To the "white god" Kulkan, according to some experts; to a senior Maya chief say other and more cautious scholars: but we know nothing about him; we know neither his name nor the time in which he lived. But everybody was struck by an odd fact: in order to uncover the tomb it was necessary to use complicated modern techniques like those employed for the tomb of Tutankh-Amon; but if the site was too narrow to facilitate the lifting of the slabs how had they been brought there and put in place?

Palenque may give us a final corroboration of what we have said about indecipherable designs to do with cosmic vehicles. The tombstone engravings were known to have the queerest and most varied interpretations, but when scholars not ignorant of astronautical matters began to consider them, the theory favoured was at the same time the simplest, most logical and fantastic.

The October 1966 number of the Turin review *Clypeus*, edited by a serious group of keen space biologists, appeared with a very odd photograph on its cover. One would have thought at first it was a science-fiction allegory, but it was the famous sarcophagous slab at Palenque!

The French contributors to this journal, G. Tarade and A. Millou, wrote: "When a race wishes to leave an indestructible message capable of resisting the effects of time they write it on stone, the only material which can defy eternity. This is what the Maya have done here. The clear, harmonious sculpture is one of the most beautiful and perfect known. The chief motif is surrounded by 24 symbols that remind one of the Sun Gate at Tiahuanaco, and are arranged as follows: 9 high up (i.e. the sky) 9 low down (Earth) 3 to the left (west) and 3 to the right (east). These hieroglyphics are certainly to do with the navigation of the ship. The man portrayed is wearing a helmet and looking in the direction of the ship's prow; his hands are busy and appear to be working levers, while his head is resting on a support and he has an inhaler in his nose. The bird on the prow is a parrot which for the Maya was a Sun-God symbol. Also on the bows we find three 'receivers' for accumulating energy, and elsewhere inside the ship there are others, in groups of three. The motor is in four parts and the system propelling it is behind the pilot . . . in the back a jet of flame is clearly visible".

When our science has progressed more the Palenque pictures and those of Tiahuanaco, and many other archæological sites, will be able to supply us with excellent ideas about the authors of astronautical progress if "interpreted technically", according to Kasanzev, Zirov and Agrest; and that it is not a matter of science fiction is borne out by a highly significant precedent if we turn to a document sent by NASA to the scientist Zeissig:

"Our people think that the theory concerning the uniform portrayed in the manuscripts sent by you is very interesting. A similar one has been prepared (under the auspices of the Los Angeles 'Litten Industry') which having been sent to the headquarters of the astronautical centre of NASA is now virtually complete. We also note that the communication devices and special parts for the eyepieces, the round hinges and joints together with the ideas for pressure maintenance listed by you and indicated in the photo have been included in the radical alteration made." What had Zeissig sent to the American society? The photo and the designs of some strange Japanese statuettes examined by him with his colleague Matsumura; figures with deformed heads, the limbs and trunk twisted unnaturally and covered in odd drawings.

In Japan the production of these had begun in the late Jomon period, and the statuettes were rough and elementary, obtained by simply shaping clay, after which clearly identifiable eyes, nose, mouth, hands, arms and legs were formed. Then suddenly they appeared in deformed state, and were known as dogu which one supposes were first modelled in earthenware and then copied in stone. Scholars were not a little puzzled by these figures: the places for the eyes on some of the dogu were taken up by oval protuberances with a horizontal slit in the centre, while in others it was a rectangular opening. In 1894 Doctor Shogoro Tsuboi said that these oval shapes put him in mind of the spectacles worn by some Eskimos against snow-glare but he was ignored by his colleagues who declared that they represented ancient armour. "Ancient armour"—on the plan of which the U.S.A. experts have based, as we saw, perfect space-suits!

"Matsumura and Zeissig," wrote Kasanzev, "were in fact certain that the Jomon costume faithfully copied a type of suit worn by visitors from other planets. The cosmonauts had to wear them in flight, not on Earth, adding gloves and boots to the same suits. In support of this theory, the two experts recall a figure of the god of wisdom, Hitokotonusi, who, according to an old Japanese fable, would have arrived on Earth to teach men wisdom and make them hand over all the weapons they owned. It is worth noting that this figure, with 'European' features in its anthropomorphic face, to whom is ascribed the oldest disarmament in the world, wears a Jomon suit with all the details except the helmet."

The contacts made by the creators of the dogu with men from space (how to describe them in any other way after the NASA experiment?) could have been neither sporadic nor brief. The statuettes existed in fact in considerable numbers in the prefecture of Kamegaoka, Aomori and Miyagi, among the ruins of the Tohoku and Kanto areas; and who knows in how many other districts. The sculptors certainly had the leisure for studying their models meticulously: not only did they reproduce different types of helmets (some with rectangular openings, others with eye-pieces) but also collected the details of suits which were not entirely alike even though made on the same principles. This is how the Japanese expert, Isao Washio, speaks about the suits: "The gloves are fixed to the forearms with a rounded attachment while the eye-pieces can be opened or closed. There are levers at their sides perhaps meant for manipulating these, while the 'crown' on the helmet is probably an antenna . . . the designs on the suits are not ornamental but correspond to devices suitable for regulation of pressure automatically!

"Those shown in the Jomon statuette" the American J. Ehernandez says, "are not the only citizens of other worlds to land on Japanese islands: before them and before the legendary Kaopas[2] the lands of the rising sun knew of other 'strangers' . . . the remains of their monuments can still be seen in the sea, perhaps becoming visible in certain hours of the day and in certain days of the year, and after showing their true features they then disappear rock by rock . . . here as in one of the most enigmatic corners of the world, at Marcahuasi." . . .

. . . and they carve the sky

Marcahuasi is not merely a high desert, burnt by the sun, parched with drought and beaten by the winds. It is also an amazing Moon crater 3,800 metres up in Peru to the west of the Cordigliera of the Andes. Three square kilometres of burnt-out horror which can be reached only by mule. What is to be looked for up there, apart from fever and madness?

Nevertheless Daniel Ruzo, a very famous Peruvian explorer, went up there, guided by vague trails, by unconnected and fantastic passages from ancient texts and legends. And he discovered, surrounded by prehistoric animal drawings dating at least back to the Secondary Era (from 185 to 130 million years ago) strange sculptures which seemed to mean nothing but became visible and revealed human faces at the summer solstice. And that was not the end of the wonders: Ruzo noticed a hill with the calm face of an old man on it. He photographed it and examined the negative—which then showed the features of a young man! What mystery did

[2]Which deals with other mysterious beings that Professor Komatsu Kitamura thinks are of extraterrestrial origin—see "Terra senza Tempo".

the enigmatic face of Marcahuasi conceal? Nothing we know of apart from a roll of film can make the change visible; and to carve such a work would certainly be difficult, even for an artist able to employ all modern techniques!

But the representatives of the "Masma culture" (from the name of a city and valley in central Peru) could certainly not have been short of resources if they were able to convert into a miniature paradise a place that not even we could make habitable with all the means at our disposal. The unknown pioneers built, among other things, a complete irrigation system thanks to which it was possible to get an enormous quantity of rainwater, which they conducted into the areas nearby during the drought. They also built a good dozen or so artificial lakes, two of which are still used today by the Indians. And they were not satisfied with practical results but erected on the banks of those lakes other masterpieces of their art which appear as strange to us as those of another world: human and animal figures reflected in the water, giving the impression, surely, of movement, ballet-dancing and fantastic metamorphoses.

The Spanish chroniclers of the Conquest tell us that the Inca, Tupac Yupanqui, was very familiar with the sculptures, together with others existing just as certainly in the less accessible parts of Peru: "The white men from the stars created them . . . created them in their likeness, in the likeness of the strangers living in the four quarters of the world . . ." a very earthly hint, this is; and indeed we see it expressed in stone images at Marcahuasi where there are symbolic white, yellow and black men and a fourth race which weathering has made unidentifiable.

"The white men from the stars": they had to arrive efficiently from the sky and shoot over all the continents, these beings whom the earthly races knew and marvelled at in the hey-day of prehistoric times! Would we perhaps have found near Nazca one of their astroports, on the plateau where enigmatic lines suggest traces of martian canals alternating with huge pictures of animals, known and unknown (among them the fabled "firebird") in a series of designs visible solely from above? Let us consider the statements of Professor John A. Mason of Pennsylvania University: though a rigid traditionalist he had to admit the extreme difficulty involved in carrying out a similar work without the aid of aircraft and felt obliged to recollect the myths of pre-inca origin in which there are frequent allusions to the descent of a divinity from the Pleiades.

Once again this constellation appears, as in Asia and Europe. On the island of Yeu in Vandea there are dome-shaped rocks which represent the Pleiades as they were seen in various epochs from the 10th to the 7th millennium B.C. It is odd that the Greeks baptized them with the name of the seven daughters of Atlas, the Titan condemned to hold up the sky on his shoulders; but the name comes from the word "pleo" (meaning "I navigate"). The Hellenes began navigation in May, when the Pleiades rose, and finished sailing when they set) and in Peruvian legends these stars are recorded as "celestial gates"!

It seems that what is equally worth considering is the likeness in the names given to the constellations by the various civilizations. Professor Jean Servier, a teacher of ethnology and sociology at Montpellier, says: "They are thought to be girls by the Indians of South America; virgins of the sun in the Inca empire; virgins of ice in Central Africa; and women present at the first circumcision by the Arunta Australians. To the Tuaregs they are the daughters of night and, in Greek mythology, the daughters of Atlas and Pleione, changed into stars by the gods. In the same way, Orion is consecrated to virility and to the chase by very different cultures, often far apart and for no apparent reason."

But let us turn to Yeu island: "They came from the void and formed Earth and sky" which we are tempted to explain by going back to the cyclopean works which are scattered all over the world. The French scholar, Serge Hutin, says that in Somerset there existed an extensive, drained swamp in very remote times which, by its canals and demarcation lines, took the form of an astronomical map. Also in Somerset, in ancient times, entire islands had been clearly reshaped by means we could not even imagine. And everywhere in Great Britain there are remains of mysterious labyrinths which make us think of other astronomical maps: the most important being the Mig-Maze near Leigh in Dorset, but most of it has vanished. Though during the last century its pattern could quite easily be seen. Here too there seemed to be a reflection of the Pleiades!

It is a strange fact that Somerset traditions link these odd configurations to the famous Caer Ariamhod (sky-temple in Gaelic) "the oldest British monument, built well before the Celts arrived"; and the "giant of Cerne Abbas" also undoubtedly has a pre-Celtic origin—perhaps of an age like that of the so-called Gog and Magog giants discovered on hills near Cambridge. All these figures can be seen solely from above and one has to be high up; their construction, too, must logically have been controlled from the air. Might we perhaps look for the answer in the Druid legends about the "magical machines capable of travelling on land, sea and air"? At the beginning of the Christian era the Irish Druid Ruith would have been able to handle one of these machines, the famous Roth Fail. And other instruments, once in the hands of the would-be wise men capable of controlling them would have plunged into the sea around the mountains and lakes of Ireland. There are some who swear they have seen a huge, flattened dome of silver rising from the bottom of Lake Neagh. And it is not only since then that they talk about flying saucers.

CHAPTER FIVE

THE RETURN OF THE GODS

We shall confine ourselves here to a discussion of the most important traditions re-examined by students of our unknown past and to their worthwhile ideas insofar as they are supported by archaeological evidence. If however we want to list the references to "prehistoric astronauts", not obscured or distorted by mythology, then a whole book would not be sufficient to contain them.

Let us therefore be content with a rapid survey. We can begin with the *'Popol Vuh'* (The book of the nations) from the Maya of Guatemala, which is clear enough in this connection. "They knew everything," we read there, "and they examined the four corners, the four points of the sky, *and the round face of Earth.*" Who were these men whose records lived on amongst nearly all the pre-Columbian cultures of America? "White men who came from the stars and from the sea" the *Popol Vuh* replies, hinting at a landing zone in the East, which could perhaps be identifiable with the legendary Atlantis; and the "Chilam Balam"[1] is still more specific: "Creatures arriving from the sky on flying ships . . . white gods who fly above the spheres and reach the stars."

"Once men could fly" we hear repeated again today in the legends collected by Harold T. Wilins (from the book *Mysteries of Ancient South America*). "Everything was sufficiently light and big stones were lifted . . ." The whole "red" America is full of such stories: the Haida Indians in the Queen Charlotte Islands (British Columbia, Canada) retain the tradition of "great sages descended from the stars on discs of fire", while the Najavos tell of "creatures who came from the sky and stayed a long time on Earth but finally returned to their world" carrying with them some forerunners of the Ogibway race who had wanted to follow them.[2] Even in the Brazilian jungles we hear fables having as their champions "flying stranger" and "wizards in flying boats".

Are they the same as those in Oceanic legend? Are the Papalaugi of the Maoris the "great wizards from the skies" who after staying here briefly "flew away on their coloured ships", promising to return? The hopeful natives are still waiting for them today, carrying out propitiatory rites in their honour.

But the Algonkin Redskins of Canada show less patience: a god called Glooskap came to them who taught them very interesting building techniques and how to hunt and grow food, killed off their enemies and worked various miracles of healing; after which he was probably a nervous wreck and went away promising he would return soon, but he took good care not to keep his promise. The Indians honoured him for some time in their rites but then, convinced it was no use cherishing further illusions, simply turned their backs on him, leaving him a place in history as "the lying god".

[1] This is the name given to a collection of Maya documents from Yucatan; the literal translation reads: "The far-seeing priest Jaguar": "Chilam" is the title of the greatest Maya priest.

[2] From the collections made by the ethnographers J. R. Swanton and W. Matthews.

The Tupi of the Amazon likewise gave up all hope that their solar hero would come back again, but they call to him sadly: "Why did you not return, son of the sky and of the wind?" Yes, why do the astronauts, who seem to have chosen Earth in the past no longer return? "Because, knowing what we are like, they do not want to run any risks" we are told with a mixture of gravity and flippancy by the writer P. H. Davis. Another Amercan, L. Scott thinks that the conditions no longer exist today which once upon a time induced them to pay us a visit; an argument which explains nothing. Besides which it would be absurd to make an investigation based on such assumptions; a worthwhile reply could only be supplied by the champions of cosmic cruisers. We must not think, however, that possible landings have followed regularly; it is true that the conjectured witnesses are very many but they refer to varying epochs, in all probability far removed from each other. And maybe it is not even correct to claim that the spacemen have not returned and do not do so: perhaps we should merely remark that for a long time we have had no direct contact with them. If so, our position could be likened to that of the inhabitants of a small centre who often see things dashing about high in the sky but for countless generations have not had the chance to see one come down and make friends with its occupants. Let us think about the mysterious and time-honoured romance of the flying objects": if we do we shall be led to believe that such things as flying saucers are more than just attractive hypotheses.

Three Suns and Three Moons

The expression unknown flying objects or unidentified (UFOs is the term in common use) covers all the phenomena seen in the sky which have no immediate explanation. Reports about such things often show after careful examination that their origin is in fact not at all msyterious. Often, certainly, but not always: "after 18 years of UFO study" says a Washington report, officially published in March 1965 "the U.S.A. has to admit it has no explanation for at least 663 sightings clearly made in detail and by people in full possession of their faculties. What is certain is that these things were not test balloons lost in the sky; neither were they light-refraction phenomena, or stars, aircraft, missiles or flying objects of man-made or known physical origin." (See *Shadows over the Stars*). Even if pilot Ken Arnold's encounter with nine huge "wheels of fire" drew the attention of the whole world to UFOs in June 1947 it still does not mean we are compelled to accept as fact an appearance, or re-appearance, of these flying mysteries. From time immemorial they have never stopped ploughing across our skies and some people have collected very trustworthy evidence.

One of the most accurate reports comes from Gianni Settimo, a young student of the problem and one of the founders of the Turin group, Clypeus, which attracted devotees of space phenomena. Settimo took up a career hardly made easy by all the speculators, madmen and credulous people involved: the aim being to strip the UFO problem of all its esoteric junk and puerile inanities about extraterrestrial aviation and space travel which these know-alls created. And it is just for this reason that we propose to use him for a quick but fluent review.

"But let us omit the fascinating though unverifiable ancient tales," he writes "and the suggestions which could lend themselves to fantastic interpretations. Let us keep to the clearest passages, to the chronicles. We could start with Cicero who tells us 'of the time in which two suns were seen . . . and when the sun of the night was seen, when noises were heard in the sky and the sky seemed to split and strange spheres appeared in it' (*De Divinitate*); and then make full use of the great Latin writers.

"The 'nocturnal sun' to which Pliny the Elder alludes in the second book of his *Naturalist Historia* (chap. 33) '. . . that is a light emanating from the sky at night during the consulate of S. Cecilio and G. Papirio and on many other occasions, such that the night be lit up as if it were day' could well be the polar

aurora. So science has always given us the explanation
of mysterious rains, similar to those the great historian
and naturalist tells us about in chapter 57: 'Rain of
milk and blood in the consulate of M. Acilio and G.
Porcio and on many other occasions; shower of flesh
during the consulate of P. Volumno and S. Sulpizio;
a rain of iron in Lucania; the objects which fell from
the sky had the look of iron sponges ... rain of wool
in the consulate of L. Paolo and C. Marcello, in the
district of Conza, where Tito Annio Milone must have
been killed the following year; after his death there was
also a shower of baked bricks, referred to in the
archives of that year'. But the sponges of iron could
certainly resemble those strange objects discovered in
recent times after the UFOs had gone through the
European and American skies (especially in Pennsylvania in June 1947 and in Liguria in April 1963) and
the woolshower which fell on Sesto Florentino, Florence
and Siena during a host of unknown flying objects in
October 1954.

"And here is Pliny the Elder referring to still more
sensational events: 'Brilliant beams appeared suddenly,
like those after the naval defeat which cost the Lacae-
demonians the Greek Empire' (chap. 26); 'Three
moons appeared together in the consulate of G.
Domizio and G. Fannio' (chap. 32); 'A spark from a
star grew bigger as it neared the Earth and after it had
reached the size of the moon shed a light like a cloudy
day, and then went back into the sky like a torch ...
mentioned by tradition as occurring only under the consulate of G. Ottavio and C. Scribonio, testified by
Proconsul Silanio and his retinue' (chap. 35); 'stars
have also been seen going everywhere without causing
violent winds ... during the consulate of L. Valerio and
G. Mario a burning shield crossed the sky at sunset,
from the west to the east, leaving a trail of sparks'
(chap. 36).

"Concerning the reference in Chapter 26 of Pliny
the Elder's book, Seneca had already written in his
Quaestionum Naturalium Libri 'The question is
whether we must consider these thundering beams and

meteorites as belonging to the same species, whose
appearance is very rare . . . and those fires which
sometimes exceed the size of the sun and that fiery
sky, of which history so often makes mention, and that
other light often confused with the star-light and which
is sometimes so low and near on the horizon as to make
us think it could be mistaken for a distant fire'. These
latter phenomena again suggest quite clearly the polar
aurora; as for the beams and the thundering meteorites
we could discuss them for a long time and quite uselessly even today.

"In the rarest book by Julian the Obsequious, the
historian living probably in the third or fourth century
A.D. one meets on almost every page these curious
celestial phenomena. What is remarkable above everything else is his description of the three moons, visible
first in the sky at Rimini, then in various parts of the
peninsula in 222 B.C.: the phenomenon, in fact, is
referred to by a number of other authors among whom
is Dione Cassio Cocceiano. And here some passages of
Julian's are just as odd: 'Three suns shone at the same
time that night and several stars glided across the sky
at Lanuvio' (175 B.C.) 'At Capua the sun shines at
night and two suns shone by day at Formia . . . On
the island at Kephalonia it seemed that a trumpet
sounded in the sky and a shower of earth fell. Something like a sun shone in the night at Pesaro' (163
B.C.); 'In Gaul they saw three suns and three moons'
(122 B.C.); 'Near Spoleto a ball of golden fire rolled
on the ground, seemed to become bigger and then
move across the ground towards the East—it was so
big it hid the sun' (91 B.C.)

"However, several of the facts recorded by Julian
had already been noted by Tito Livio (59 B.C.–A.D. 17)
from whose monumental work the writer just cited
might have taken his *Book of Prodigies*. The chief
Latin historians, then, describe things to us which are
still more disconcerting. Not only the spinning at great
height of objects like round shields and the bizarre apparition (217 B.C.) at Falerii Veteres (today called
Civita Castellana, in the province of Viterbo) during

which 'the sky seemed to crack like a great wound and across the opening shone a strong light', but also hints directly at the appearance of beings having little connection with Earth. 'There, in the calmness of the night' he writes, referring to an event of 235 B.C. 'both the consuls were visited, it is said, by the same apparition: a man of superhuman size and dignity who explained that he was the leader of one of the groups while the other groups fleet had to be offered to the Mani and to Mother Earth'. And it is certainly a vision which could perhaps be connected with that of Tito Livio (214 B.C.): 'At Hadria an altar was seen in the sky and near it human shapes in white clothes were being escorted' ".

Settimo carefully refrained from trying to explain the mysterious beings and neither can we do any more about it, except think of religious influences and of the miracles done by it in all times and places. We can, at the most, note the legendary characters of Inca tradition "balancing in the air on plates of gold"; likewise the Japanese "Kappas" which the ancient chronicles seem to portray to us as their next-of-kin, the "spirits" of the Shahman legends some of whom abandon their ships at a respectable height and come down from them quietly on to Earth as if down a moving and invisible ladder.

"Gods or space-men?" Raymond Drake asks.[3] We, being more cautious, say: many legends are based on fact: but it is hard enough and often impossible to decide whether it is a question of what seems most reasonable or whether it is something lying deep in time, for ever buried under a mass of buildings and mythological elements.

Still, before leaving ancient Rome, we must at least dwell a little on an interesting piece of evidence offered to us by another young student of the Clypeus group, Renato Gatto, who writes: "From time immemorial men have perceived mysterious objects cutting through the skies and they are impressed enough by

[3]It is the title of his book ('God or Space-men?' Ed. Ray Palmer, Amherst, Wisconsin, U.S.A.).

them to hand them down through tradition; this is why we find cliff drawings, bas-reliefs and perhaps monuments which make us think of such appearances.

"As an indication of the importance attached to these observations, there is among other things the fact that the Emperor Pertinace, during the three months of his brief reign, had some coins minted not with the imprint of some star or other (a common motif when it was a question of immortalizing events considered to be supernatural) but with a real sphere complete with strange antennae like those of our own artificial satellites. Many experts, after careful examination of the money, agreed that the object represented neither the sun, the moon nor any of the heavenly bodies. This certainty stems from the fact that the sphere's rays were arranged in a manner quite different from that usually used for the stars. Besides, the term 'Providentia deorum' leaves no doubt, since the faces of the coins clearly express an exaltation of the gods' providence. And probably the emblem of a woman is due to the simple fact that the word is of feminine gender. In short it would be a case of a minor deity whose powers were to be represented by this strange phenomenon. Is it too hazardous to think that it might represent an unknown flying object, one of those mysterious vehicles we call UFOs? If we look carefully at the coins we inevitably feel that the work was done very meticulously. The unknown artisan knew perfectly well what it was he had to, and wanted to, express; and the likeness of the object (including its antennae as we saw) to the satellites we have put in orbit round the Earth is, to say the least, amazing.

"These coins are exceedingly rare; but if some enthusiasts should wish to admire them in order to share our opinion, or produce their own, then they could visit the historical-archaeological museum at Alba, the Piedmontese city in the province of Cuneo, the fatherland of that very emperor Elvio Pertinace."

Then there is Roberto Pinotti, likewise of the Clypeus group, who says: "The theory according to which many strange phenomena cited by numerous classical writers tallied with unidentified flying objects seems to be confirmed by still other new facts arising. After history, archaeology and mythology it is the turn of numismatics to bring us to the same bold conclusions as those of eminent students like Kasanzev and Drake. There is an ancient Roman coinage with a mysterious emblem dating from around A.D. 193 and thus made in the time of Publio Elvio Pertinace. This money, discovered in Syria, concerns without any doubt one of the inexplicable events of which we have written testimony. During the rule of Commodo a particularly bright object crossed the sky; the historian Elio Lampridio hints at it: he is one of the 'scriptores historiae augustae' and it is in his *Life of Commodo*. Herodian, too, in his *History of the Empire after Marcus Aurelius* supports this with: 'There were many marvels in those days . . . *stars* were seen in mid-air and in broad daylight' (Book 1).

"Herodian, a Greek historian of possibly Syrian origin (born most likely at Antioch around A.D. 170) was at Rome in A.D. 203 though there is reason to believe he might have been there also in A.D. 192 when Commodo was emperor. We know that he was an objective writer, a lover of truth who turned to the immediate sources of the events and their protagonists so it is certain that the things he talks about are not fantasy but truth. Of course it is not easy to establish the precise chronology of the phenomena but Commodo took care to record them on several of his coins, with the impression of a 'star' on the reverse side; and there are some in which we can see a good seven 'stars'! Herodian's phenomena thus date from A.D. 189 to 190. One after the other the strange 'stars' appeared on large numbers of Syrian coins.

"The presence of such stars is always related to events considered supernatural. For example, Plutarch wrote that after the murder of Caesar 'many men of fire were seen fighting amongst them' and in the same section (*Life of Caesar*, chap. 68) he mentioned the appearance of extraordinary 'celestial fires'; Suetonius, too, confirmed that after the death of Caesar and during the days set aside for honouring him, 'a comet . . . shone for seven days—the Romans considered it to be Caesar's soul which went into the sky with the gods' (*Life of Caesar,* chap. 88) This is the origin of the 'stars' on Caesar's statues and on the coins bearing his image.

"But certainly the most sensational evidence is Pertinace's coinage (successor to Commodo) on which we see a flying globe, not a star. The same money shows us a woman who is lifting her hands towards a peculiar object which some experts say is not a representation of the sun, moon, star or comet since the position of the four 'rays' is not symmetrical with respect to this same sphere as is the case with drawings of the heavenly bodies. The enlargement of the photo is still more convincing: it can indeed be said that a light-effect has never before made things so clear in this way. All in all, we would be inclined to think that the globe could only be an unidentified flying object."

The scholar again notes how the feminine figure on the coins may symbolize a minor deity ("Providentia deorum" the text specifies: "The providence of the gods") and how it may be worth while to consider the question concerning the real essence of the myths.

Pinotti concludes thus: "Let us once again have a look at our flying globe. The question is whether its likeness to our modern satellites is completely accidental. Doctor Remo Cappelli, a famous coin expert and the author of important books on the subject, is an owner of some of the rarest coins and he supports the idea that this mysterious sphere may be, in effect, an extraterrestrial vehicle. He faced this burning problem with a courageous article in December 1960. Opinions can differ but it is undeniable that this astonishing coinage offers ample material for the liveliest discussions."

Charlemagne and the Airmen

The Middle Ages overwhelm us with showers of endless celestial wonders: but here we are on still more untrustworthy ground; because if on the one hand we have chronicles which are sufficiently detailed and abundant, on the other we must bear in mind all the angels and demons, the witches and magicians, used to persuade the masses to tour every conceivable corner of the known world. Gianni Settimo therefore does well to withdraw from the charm of the sorcerer's domain (although some things are enough to tempt every student of the subject) and to confine his documentation to the facts given as pure, inexplicable phenomena averse to doubtful allusions.

"Saint Bede, the Benedictine of Wearmouth known as the father of English history, lived from 672 (or 673) to 735," he says, "and reported in his *Historia Ecclesiastica Gentis Anglorum* (seventh chapter) a most peculiar thing which took place in 664. One night as some monks were praying at the cemetery tombs in the Barking monastery near the Thames, a huge light came down from the sky, and after covering them and settling a while on the other side of the abbey, finally disappeared into the depths of space. 'This light' Bede adds, 'was such as to make full sunlight seem pale in comparison. The following morning some of the chapel boys declared that its rays penetrated doors and windows with a dazzling brightness'.

"The historian refers to another four appearances of flying objects; these have been noted in the most numerous works. Let us quote Saint Gregory of Tours, *Historia Francorum:* 'A very bright sphere flew over French lands in 583'; and the *Annales Laurissenses:* 'In the year 776 flying shields appeared to guide the Saxons while they were besieging the horsemen of Charlemagne at Sigisburg'; the *Anglo-Saxon Chronicles:* 'In 793 in Northumbria the inhabitants were scared by powers appearing over them . . . there were dazzling gleams like lamps and red dragons were seen flying in the air' also the *Flores Historiarum* by the Benedictine Roger of Wendover: 'In 796 small globes were seen flying around the sun by people in various parts of England'.

"Alciun, the secretary and biographer of Charlemagne, and author of the *Vita Karoli*, states in the 32nd chapter of his work that in 810 when he was on his way from Aachen he saw a large sphere descend like lightning from the sky. It travelled from east to west and was so bright it made the monarch's horse rear up so that Charlemagne fell and injured himself severely. The mysterious spheres returned in force during the Spanish expedition of Pipin, son of Louis the Pious; and in the course of a bloody encounter in 827 we can actually read in the manuscript *Ludovici Pii Vita:* '. . . verily, this slaughter was preceded by terrible visions of things in the air; during the night they burnt like fires or shone like red blood'."

At this point we arrive in front of a host of reports which are as amazing as they are uncheckable, to take direct part in an invasion of devils and flying witches, against which both Charlemagne and his son, Louis the Pious, decree heavy penalties. Up to this point we have been on historical ground but we have not been able to accept the veracity of reports which French and British writers included in the famous *Capitolari,* a collection of decrees and allusions to them attributed, probably wrongly, to Alcuin.

But for curiosity's sake here is a strange story taken in part from the Abbot Montfaucon de Villars who wrote *Le Comte de Gabalis:* "Noticing the alarm and hositility in the population the aerial beings from space were upset when landing with their huge vehicle; they took some men and women, chosen from the best ones, in order to teach them and dispel popular evil . . . but when those women returned to Earth they were looked on as devils from space who had come to spread poison on the crops, then captured and executed after horrible tortures those people who practised diabolical arts . . . others had to submit to the same fate: the number of the wretches who met their death by fire and water was enormous. It was at last muttered everywhere amongst the people that they had been sent by Grimaldo, Duke of Benevento and master of magic, in order to destroy the rule of the Franks; in vain did these innocents protest that they were of the same race and had been carried off for a short while by extra-ordinary beings who had revealed marvellous things to them."

The most obvious objection is not unlike that used against the present-day champions of Mars and Venus: if the space creatures raiding through our skies had minded their own business they would have had no need to furnish the inhabitants of Earth with explanations of any kind. Can we imagine one of our astronauts who, being upset by people thinking of him as a sort of flying Satan, lands on the planet in order to give the primitive natives explanations? If, then, the airmen of the Carolingian period had really wanted to make excuses for causing trouble and to offer suitable ex-planations, would it not have occurred to them that the most reasonable thing to do would have been to land as a body, and ask audience of Charlemagne so as to organize a public meeting with the wise men of that time? They could not have lacked the means for defending themselves considering the cultural and sci-entific level attributed to them . . . and neither the necessary intelligence to understand the small powers of comprehension which the occupants of the flying machines would have encountered amongst the natives.

"In the Middle Ages," Settimo writes again, "we often witness phenomena with a religious significance attributed to them; thus, for instance, the 'celestial light' seen above the burial chamber of Jesus on May 13th 1120, with the object hanging for three days over Jeru-salem in 1200, after which it descended where the Saviour was crucified. There were many other phe-nomena besides these. Nevertheless, information is very scarce and thus perfectly reliable. Matthew of Paris, the English Benedictine monk of the monastery of Saint Albans who continued the work of Roger of Wendover, tells us for instance of an apparition in 1100, of a 'comet with an unusual type of movement . . . which, rushing from the east, went into the sky instead of coming down'; and also in England in Byland Abbey, York-shire, we have that 'great portent' falling on October 20th 1290 when 'a silver object like a ring was seen slowly flying.' The 'shining beams' of the ancient Romans, then, reappeared in various chronicles and even in Benvenuto Cellini's autobiography 'It was already night when we came to a certain rise in the ground, and as we were looking in the direction of Florence we both called out in a voice full of wonder: "Oh Almighty God, what marvellous thing do we behold above Florence? It was like a big beam of fire sparkling with a huge light . . ." '

"A fire-ball seemed to explode above Thuringia in 1548, dropping a substance like congealed blood; and in 1557 at Vienna the city was flown over by strange machines shedding light, while in the same year objects called 'green suns', 'red suns', 'flying dragons' and 'burning discs' appear in Poland and at Nuremburg. In 1558 there seemed to take place nothing short of a fight between two round shapes which hovered across present-day Austria and at Zürich three suns went by or 'three rings of light' said some others. In this Swiss city some stamps have actually been kept, those of the engraver Wieck, who recorded the appearance of very many 'flying discs' between 1547 and 1558.

"Collisions and fires amongst strange machines seem to have been witnessed on April 14th at Nuremberg, the chronicles talk about 'black, red, white and blue discs' and of two axle-driven machines; and on August 7th in 1566 Basilea was at the scene when a crowd of round black forms appeared in front of the sun, at an incredible speed; and in 1697 there were direct references to a 'round machine with a sphere at the centre and extremely luminous' which slowly crossed the sky at Hamburg and over other North German cities.

"Between 1760 and 1800 (we quote only the fewest possible references from many trustworthy sources) all Europe became aware of countless trifles which mysteriously flew in the air. Florence seems to have been one of the places preferred by these unknown 'scouts': they flew over several times and thus made a spectacular procession on December 19th 1781. Piedmont is the scene from 1808; and in this year the phenomena reappeared with astonishing speed. And not only this, but after these visions, sudden and violent fires broke out. Perosa Argentina was visited on April 2nd together with other regions of the Pinerolese, by luminous bodies discharging arrows at a low height; in the night between the 11th and the 12th an object shone on La Morra, while on the morning of the 12th a horseman was unsaddled at Carmagnola, just as Charlemagne was struck by a luminous object. On the 15th of the same month a 'shaft' flew over Torre Pellice and disappeared behind the Picco Vandalino; and on April 18th Mr. Simondi, the secretary to the Justice of the Peace at the same place—Torre Pellice—was woken up by a loud humming which did not stop. On going to the window he saw a luminous disc in the meadow opposite him, which then rose into the sky at a fantastic speed. Meanwhile on Mount Musiné, the lonely rocky cone which rises near Rivoli (13 kilometres from Turin) the 'Chariot of Herod' was flying, according to an ancient popular tradition, and strange shapes of light hovered with surprising force . . ."

Rivoli, the small town of the Turin "belt" preferred by the terrible Herod was not the only one "visited"; loving couples came to it by means of quite different cars, beginning romances in the surrounding woods clear of the hurried life of the capital city in the Alpine foothills. During the night of April 2nd 1962, an engaged couple stopped in a car near the Rivoli hill called Pozzetto, but certainly not to talk about enigmatic astronautical problems; but nevertheless they had to think of such things a little because towards eleven o'clock they saw a lens-shaped object coming down from the very dark sky. It had a diameter of about 15 metres and was sending out a green and clear light. This light was pulsating and throbbing with a regular rhythm and only when the machine touched the ground did it go out. A slit appeared on one side of the vehicle and two figures emerged, who then walked around for a few minutes as if they were talking. Then one of them pointed to a nearby wood and the other disappeared into it. The figure left behind jumped on board again, closed the door, and then the green light started up once more. The machine rose unsteadily, gained the crest of the hill and plunged into the sky like a lamp upside down.

So much for the account by the engaged couple. Even if our friends had been stretching it a bit they came of their own free will to report what they had seen, stating the facts under oath. Nevertheless we feel justified in considering their story albeit with a good dose of scepticism, as we should for all tales of this genre. But if we want to add a touch of the fantastic we can try to answer the question: how did it come about that in the night of April 9th 1962 a furious fire broke out in just the area indicated by the two lovers, *while there was a torrential down-pour?* is there perhaps some connection between the fire that flares up so often—today just as often as at the beginning of the last century—in the environs of Turin and the inexplicable light phenomena which appear in the sky? Is there perhaps some truth in the very old fable of the district that huge caves open under the slopes of the inhospitable Musiné, that stone slope a few steps from Turin with its forbidding alien look?

CHAPTER SIX

DOORS TO INFINITY

"The pass was by this time in front of us, swept clean by the wind between its harsh, gashed columns and spiteful contours. Beyond the pass, the sky became clouded over with whirling vapours lit up by the low polar sun; the sky of that mysterious realm which we thought human beings could never have set eyes upon ... I think a shout of awe, wonder, terror and disbelief escaped us when, having conquered the pass, we saw what lay beneath us ... all sorts of expressions came to mind as we looked, stunned, at that incredible sight. I remembered once more the supernatural myths the vision of which had haunted me from the first contact with this old world of Antarctica; from the demoniacal plateau of Leng, and of Mi-Go ... of the pnackotic manuscripts with their pre-human implications; of the cult of Cthulhu and of Necronomicon; and finally of the Hyperborean legend of Tsathoggua, that nebulous figure, and the stellar origin associated with it ...

"The buildings were very varied in size: there were enormous complexes of the beehive type, with much smaller, separate ones. The shape was usually pyramidal or in terrace form; but there were also perfect cylinders and groups of cubes, with others being rectangular, arranged in a way characteristic of buildings with many corners so that the plan resembled that of a fortress in a modern style. All the surfaces had been terribly scarred by time and the sheet of ice from which rose towers were strewn with blocks of stone and the rubble of countless ages past. In some places in the ice we could see through to the inside of huge buildings; and there were stone bridges preserved in the ice linking together the various towers at different heights above the ground. On the exposed walls we could also make out the marks left by still other bridges of the same construction. The examination finally revealed a very large number of rather big windows, some of which were wide open in a sinister and threatening way . . .

"That could not be a town like any other. It must have been the primitive centre of some archaic and incredible chapter of Earth's history, the outside connections of which, remembered only vaguely in the most obscure and devious myths, had completely vanished in the chaos of Earth's convulsions well before any human race we know had emerged from the ape level of evolution. Here was indeed a megalopolis in comparison with with the fabled Atlantis and Lemuria, Commorion and Uzuldaroum, and Olathoë in the land of Lomar are all phenomena of the very present, not even of yesterday; a city which could have rivalled those godless ones they whisper about, such as Valusia, R'lyeh, Ib in the land of Mnar, and the nameless city in the Arabian Desert . . ."

These extracts are from a fascinating book by H. P. Lovecraft called *The Mountains of Madness* which is the story of the discovery in the heart of the Antarctic regions of a fearful city built millions of years ago by a non-human race from the stars. It dabbles in fantasies of course, but of a "restrained" type such as to make his critics write: "Lovecraft brings a solid and accurate scientific knowledge to the utmost limits of the imagination. The reality of daily life and science become part of a vast world full of cosmic pressures and the power of myth". And this Antarctic world does indeed bear the stamp, invisible but not for this reason any less grand and terrifying, which the American writer has understood surprisingly well, although he has never been there himself.

Oases among the Ice-sheets

One afternoon in 1958, in the course of the International Geophysical Year, the United States geologist and a friend of his (we shall refer to the former as "W".) were with one of those caterpillar tractors called weasels, a short distance from their base camp on Knox coast in the Antarctic. The two men were talking and taking various scientific measurements when they suddenly saw, hardly one kilometre away in a northerly direction, an abrupt and violent whirl of white. They were rooted to the spot with amazement and almost asked each other what was going on. It could not be a meteorological effect since the day was splendid and in any case an atmospheric disturbance was out of the question in an area so limited and clearly detailed.

The men thought of the Japanese and Russians who had established camps nearby and were engaged that day in a series of measurements; but as they could not imagine what it was they could be doing they decided to go and have a look—also because they were afraid that their colleagues might have met with an accident. When they reached the spot the Americans noticed that the whirlwind was not crystals of snow but a kind of hot white steam with a sharp smell not easily defined. In the middle of the cloud now dissolving they saw a dome-shaped structure, no more than two metres high, but with a diameter of about 8 to 10 metres and shining like glass.

"The first thing I thought of," said W. "was of something unknown below the ground, perhaps of volcanic origin. Being both fascinated and frightened at the same time I ran towards the dome. At first I thought someone had got there before me when I saw two moving figures; but immediately afterwards my blood froze as they were not human at all but round 'things', yellowish and with a height of hardly more than a metre, like balloons but clumsy on the ice and only half inflated, tottering and wheeling around.

"Near them or on them there was a light which seemed to me like an oxy-acetylene lamp. A little ball seemed to explode in front of me, spreading a crackling rose of blue sparks. I started to run as I was in a real panic. 'Get away!' I shouted to my friend who had stayed behind, 'Get away, quick!' and we only turned round to look when we were back in the safety of the weasel. For a few moments we saw the reflections of the dome and then another white whirl. There was a reflection in the sky but scarcely visible, and when the cloud faded there was nothing at all on the ice."

This is not the only odd story we have heard about the Antarctic; particularly during the Geophysical Year when the sixth continent was invaded by scientists from 11 countries who built 60 research stations there, 33 of which were permanent camps. From the workers around the Argentinian stations there came at least a dozen stories about seeing unidentified objects in the sky or on the ice, most of them having oval shapes. Various Russian and American investigators flew over areas full of structures odd enough to make them think of open spaces with gigantic walls and buildings covered in heavy slabs of ice. Some attached to the Soviet bases (probably Vostok One, Two or Sovietska-ya) said they had seen structures which were "too geometrical" to be accounted for by weathering; and even "things moving", among them being a squat, dark, creeping mass of something and a white shape similar to that of the bear or human being.

It is known that the Antarctic plays all sorts of jokes and creates optical illusions and hallucinations found nowhere else in the world; and the fact that the people involved in these phenomena (published in due course in various papers and reviews) have refrained from giving their identity or persisting in their descriptions of such things is easily understood. Sightings of unidentified flying objects in Antarctic are anything but rare. In June 1965 there was an uproar among the scientists, technicians and sailors of three countries (See *Shadows across the Stars*) concerning which there was an official communication from the Argentine government as follows: "The naval garrison in Argentinian Antarctic (Deception Island) noticed on July 3rd at 19.14 hours (local time) a huge lens-shaped flying object; it seemed to be solid, of a reddish-green colour chiefly, sometimes changing to a yellow, blue, white or orange shade. The object moved in a zigzag towards the east, but changed course several times toward the west and north at varying speeds and quite silently, passing at 45 degrees over the horizon at a distance of 10 to 15 kilometres from the base. In the course of the movement completed by the object itself it was possible for the eye-witnesses to get some idea of its enormous speed, and not only because it was poised motionless for about 15 minutes at a height of around 5,000 metres."

As for other sightings the lack of such numerous and qualified observers has helped to cover up everything in silence; but for years Argentina was flown over by mysterious objects, several of which dashed off in a southerly direction beyond the Drake Straits and towards the huge white desert.

"Once again somebody has something to look for down there," says journalist P. Deville. "But what? Perhaps a fantastic astroport, maintained for countless millennia in what was once a marvellous continent and now a chaos of ice? Let us remember that for centuries prior to the discovery of Antarctica an unknown number of bold adventurers, navigators and dreamers pushed down southwards seeking the 'southern paradise' . . . not simply following some personal fancy but being guided by records of a myth surviving for hundreds of thousands of years!"

Most likely this "southern paradise" cannot be identified with Antarctica since the latter was at very different latitudes (it has actually been proved that the

Poles have changed their positions many times as a result of a world cataclysm which changed the Earth's axis). But the real "white continent" was certainly not the one we know: its huge ice-shield which in some places is three or four thousand metres thick has squashed flat some large islands, perhaps a peninsula with a sub-tropical climate, on the bottom of the sea. This is confirmed by the discovery of fossilized trees and giant ferns as well as by the presence of vast carboniferous layers. In 1947 Admiral Byrd saw on the sides of a mountain in the Queen Maud massif a coal seam which he declared to be "enough for the needs of the entire world". But this is only poor quality lignite, though it does supply us with precious evidence concerning Antarctica's past geology.

"Lands which nature has condemned to everlasting cold, that will never burn under the sun" James Cook wrote about the places he passed by in the years 1772 to 1775 "lands whose frightening and savage appearance cannot be expressed in words: these are the regions discovered by us. And we have seen only the best, those more to the north. How will those of the extreme south be? Should anyone have the intention and strength to push on down there I shall not envy him the glory of a similar discovery."

This description by the famous British sailor is on the whole true: but the ice, oddly enough has left a piece of that buried paradise in the open air, to leave us with a sight which if somewhat modest is nonetheless amazing in that strange white scenery. The first ones to talk about this sensational discovery were the members of the expedition, Schwabenland, from Germany, led by Captain Ritscher in 1938–39. A few hundred kilometres from the ice wall stretching to the east and west along the 70th Parallel from Long. O the pilots of the two German seaplanes saw a hilly region which was not only free of ice but was studded with sheets of water! The announcement was greeted with a certain reserve but in 1947 Byrd's airmen made full confirmation of this and revealed to the world the existence of what was baptized as the "Garden of Queen Mary

Land": a succession of hills covered in dwarf conifers and musk deer and dotted with lakes. The Americans counted 23 of them and alighted on the water of the three biggest.

Seen from above the sight was amazing: below them stretched sheets of water—intensely blue, red or green. After landing they realized that the phenomenon was due to microscopic algae, vividly green on the bottom of the lakes. But they were in for another surprise; by dipping their hands in the waters of that marvellous country they found it lukewarm; and not only that: in some parts of the lake nearest the iceberg Ferrar the water was actually hot! What is the cause? There can only be two answers: either volcanic action (which in those parts seem unlikely) or radioactivity: if this second hypothesis should prove true then we would be certain that fabulous layers of uranium must exist down there. Thus far does science go: but beyond this there are the collectors like William Bennett of oddities of this nature; and according to him these hills and lakes are part of a "garden city" belonging to space-men who have been settled there for thousands of years. The true metropolis would extend under the Antarctic ice, with the most powerful machines to supply the energy and keep the areas threatened by ice quite clear at the same time. Our unknown guests would have a huge cosmodrome in the sixth continent and extremely rich mines for supplying their needs in the way of metals, etc.

The fact that Bennett at the time of his revelations (1956) may not yet have had information concerning the Antarctic's unknown flying objects is not important, and the references to layers of ores quite accidental (it will be known only much later if the subsoil down there is rich in chrome, gold, molybdenum, graphite, uranium, coal and petrol). But we must not ignore the fact that the whole matter is not just an invention of this bizarre student: his work has been an attempt to try to interpret certain Tibetan texts which refer to the mythical plateau called Leng. And Bennett, like Lovecraft (and most likely without knowing the latter) declared that Leng could not have been in Asia but in Antarctica![1]

However that may be, the sixth continent offers such puzzles, and so many of them, that it gives us the feeling it must be an extraterrestrial island; and contrary to what one would expect normally the atmosphere becomes warmer the higher we go. The atmosphere has itself a density of only half that in the other regions of the world—so the Antarctic fauna is immune to bacterial effects.

What is the reason for this amazing immunity? The sea from which the animals, directly or indirectly, get their nourishment is extremely rich in plankton; and some scholars think that the vegetable plankton contains a universal antibiotic—sufficiently powerful to arrest any infection.

Perhaps it will prove so: but the fact that the air down there seems to be completely antiseptic (or aseptic, rather) would appear to suggest that the antibiotic is spread all over the continent. And some people believe it is in a host of micro-organisms as yet undetected which have come from unknown worlds and survived solely in Antarctica because only there did they meet conditions similar to the planet they left. Do we want to follow Bennett? We could build fantasies about space travellers busy in the remotest ages on problems of making the atmosphere of their new home as similar as possible to the one on their original planet, in order to protect themselves from the bacterial dangers by building an efficient antibiotic polar cap.

So the Antarctic world keeps it secrets in its own inimitable way. Excavations are in fact extremely difficult since the ice shell moves slowly but continuously towards the sea, away from the centre of the continent, and full of imposing icebergs like Beardmore which is 18 kilometres wide and several thousand long. This too

---

[1]"The students of mythology," wrote Lovecraft, "have placed Leng in central Asia; but the racial memory of a man or his forefathers is long and it can be said that certain fables have had their origin in lands, hills and temples of horror which are the oldest in Asia and predating any human world known to us" (from *The Mountains of Madness*).

is moving towards the sea, changing the shape of the terrain it crosses. "But," William Bennett predicts, "one day we shall see in all this many things about the remote past of our world which not even the boldest investigators dare to suspect."

The Men without Faces

"Rival factions fought for the dominion of China, helped by celestial creatures who took part on one side or the other and employed spectacular weapons": Raymond Drake is speaking to us about legendary oriental conflicts and says that the situation as described by Asiatic legend is identical with that of myth all over the world; and what Homer depicts—to give one example only—when speaking about the Trojan wars, with gods assembled on either side of the battlefield, is also the same. And from this it is no great step to the idea that the extraterrestrial astronauts have not always been together harmoniously but on the contrary have been cruel fighters on Earth. If we accept the theory that the landing of spacemen on our globe was a fact then we shall straightaway be brought to the point of admitting that it must have been a racial matter between ways or forms of life having little in common with each other. And now let us consider once more the disembarking of commandos on this or that planet and of encounters with other space colonialists: to bet that all would be settled in the best of manners, that the occupants would immediately find means to understand each other, that their interests would be reconciled—this could only be our view if we are pitiful optimists. So let us imagine, then that the two conquering races from space are as different from each other as we are from the bees or from the apes and then we shall be fully aware of the possibility of comprehension and the difficulties involved.

Our remotest forefathers could have regarded their guests as divinities good or bad, as friends or enemies: this will clearly depend not only on their attitude but also on the mentality and objectives of the strangers.

If we look at Ireland we find a good sample of weird creatures with the most varied intentions: fairies who are not fairies (at least not in the usual sense) but shapeless beings gifted with supernatural powers which are often hostile ones; gnomes spiteful or friendly, elves with whimsical, unpredictable behaviour. They all have their counterparts in the remotest corners of the world; the monster with the flat head, almost cylindrical, with a powerful forehead and enormous ears inevitably puts us in mind of the enigmatic statues on Easter Island, the "man with neither mouth nor eyes" who makes us think of the sculptures and masks they could produce (according to the scholars we have quoted) like space-helmets; and the tusked devils with slanting eyes remind us with amazement of the closely similar emblems and drawings which stamp the obscure past of central-southern America. In connection with the New World it is interesting to note that some Mexican populations tell us when they are referring to the monstrous statuettes of jade which represent their distant ancestors—thus reminding us of remote traditions—that the stone used for such work was done so for a very specific reason: because its colour was just like that of the legendary man-like race. However, Irish literature is again rich in creatures with green skin. A genuine case? Or fantasies due to the fact that this green pigment is entirely absent among people everywhere? It may be so, but we must remember what the scholarly writer John Macklin tells us in an article of his which appeared in the magazine *Grit* in December 1966:

"One afternoon in August, 1887 two children came out of a cave near the Spanish village of Banjos. They held each other by the hand as they walked, crossing a field in which some peasants were busy with the harvest. It took place, as we said, eighty years ago but there are still people living today who can remember it. Certain accounts are distorted but the basic facts are not to be doubted: the two children came timidly out of the cave speaking an incomprehensible language and wearing clothes made of a substance never seen before.

And their skin was green! It is a strange, illogical and inexplicable story which could suggest researches into the fourth dimension of a world existing side by side with our own: a world of fantasies from which the children could have escaped. In this sense one could give credit to the theory which would see them as being cast into a 'spatial vortex', like a man who had fallen through ice into a cavern and could no longer find the way out. Ridiculous? Perhaps: but it is the only hypothesis capable of throwing a glimmer of light on this appearance of two green children. A monk arrived from Barcelona to investigate. He saw the children, listened to witnesses and then wrote, much later: 'I have been so convinced by what I heard that I felt obliged to accept the fact even if incapable of understanding it and of making any explanation with the power of intellect'.

"The harvesters were resting after their meal when the two children appeared suddenly from the cave. Not believing their eyes the workers hurried towards them; the frightened children fled but were brought to the house of Ricardo da Calno, a magistrate who was also the largest landowner in the village. He took the hand of the child and stroked it: the colour stayed green, so undoubtedly it was part of the pigment. He offered them food but they did not eat. Instead, they simply took the bread and the meat and looked at it with a mixture of suspicion and stupidity. The magistrate observed that the facial features, although regular enough, seemed rather like those of the negro; the eyes were almond-shaped and deep in the sockets. The children stayed five days in Da Calno's house without eating and were clearly growing weaker, as it was not possible to find any food which attracted them. In the end, says one report, 'they got the chance one day to eat some beans which they both devoured madly . . . and after this they refused to eat any other food'.

"But the starvation had seriously harmed the boy: despite the beans he grew weaker and died a month after his appearance. The girl, however, grew better and became later a domestic servant in Da Calno's house; the green colour got less noticeable and the curiosity surrounding the case diminished somewhat. After some months she was able to say a few words in Spanish and even give some explanation of her arrival —but this only served to deepen the mystery. 'She explained that she had come from a land where there was no sun, a country of eternal twilight: but she added that there was a country of light not far from her home but in between there was a large river.' How had she reached Earth? She said that the 'only thing she could remember was a very loud noise after which she was taken up by a spirit and found herself with her brother on the harvest-field'. The girl lived another five years and was then buried with her brother. It is indeed a strange story; is it a fable or a joke or a story handed down from generation to generation? The documents concerning the case exist, together with all the evidence given under oath by witnesses who saw, touched and questioned the children . . ."

William Butler Yeats the great Irish poet and Nobel prize winner for literature tells us a great deal about such nightmare people as we have discussed. In *Caterina* for instance: "I have heard people speak of a creature like a bird (a pigeon or seagull or whatever it might have been) waving a stone or a stick and making a noise with it as if it were made of copper." And again in an address to the mysterious inhabitants of the woods "What does it matter if you carry your head under your arm, whip yourselves with a horsewhip or have feathers on your heads instead of hair?"

Here then is the "metal bird" used in world-wide myth to represent the unknown cosmic ships of prehistory; and here too the crown of feathers on the heads of the leaders of all states worn to symbolize authority and divine origin, together with all those ideas about flight which derive from the spacemen! The mention of the "tail" does not necessarily mean that men were adorned with something similar, even if we see them thus in Saharan rock drawings. It could easily be a mythological corruption of a common enough item, such as part of a portable tank or space respirator which when not in use might be pushed to the back; and it is worthy of note that some Arabs in North Africa have used the nickname of "soldiers with the tail" (because of the handle of the small spade carried on the belt at the back) to describe the teutonic warriors of the last war.

So we must proceed carefully concerning these fabled creatures who carry their heads under their arms: we could be dealing with cosmic monsters, it is true, but another and far less fantastic explanation is possible. How would a primitive man define the long antennae mounted on a space-helmet? It would be not at all unlikely to hear him talking about "arms" (which is really the case, it seems, with the Japanese "kappas"). And what if the Celts or their ancestors were to see a cosmonaut with his helmet under his arm?

Flying machines are certainly not without their legends; we do not meet them solely in "Roth Fail" and the "dome of silver" (see page 55) but also in pre-columbian traditions where we hear about "antigravity discs". With all this we have sufficiently outlined the connections between the Irish traditions and the American. We cannot claim any completeness but it would be unpardonable not to mention the mythical hero of the green island: "the typical hero of Homeric proportions vigorous in any game of war or peace; generous, invincible and the protagonist of a thousand undertakings," as Umberto Eco says.

This hero is called Cu Chulainn. Yet Kukulkan is the name of the white god of the Maya, the one who "came to teach laws and sciences" and who is represented by the symbol of the plumed serpent and the flying dragon! And the Irish too have their prehistoric astronauts: there is the so-called giants' causeway not far from Portrush, an impressive stretch of large blocks of stones both hexagonal and pentagonal. It is thought to be of volcanic origin; the blocks would have been set solid as soon as exposed to very cold winds which would have shaped them in cylindrical or almost round fashion; and being squeezed together afterwards they got their polyhedron form still obvious today.

Naturally there are those who see these huge boulders as being built by a race of giants living on Earth thousands of years ago and whose tales the Irish have kept. But the supporters of the "space hypothesis" maintain that this could very easily be the result of an explosion and the later cooling of the fused rock. An explosion of a space-ship or an entire fleet perhaps? There would have to be confirmation of the myths favouring an apocalyptic battle between beings resembling demi-gods, but we do not feel justified in arriving at this conclusion if we go on legends probably imported by the Celts and then spread across the country.

Other scholars maintain that it is not a giant's causeway or at least not the only one since other parts of Ireland and Iceland bear the imprint of what could seem to have been bursts of flame from interplanetary cruisers of enormous size. It is strange to see how the extreme north of Europe joins on quite naturally to central America if we draw a line across the northern part of the Atlantic. Does this line follow the disposition of a chain of "gateways to the Infinite"? Some people do not doubt it and they assert that there are the remains of a stellar civilization under the Atlantic of an incredibly high level: a culture which would have made its mark all over our world and impressing other invaders from space before huge catastrophies came to convulse the planet.

Polar Zombies

"Someone or something stopped up there in the Far North," say the students of the occult who have searched those regions for the presence of spacemen; and they tell us of strange events not so difficult from those of the Antarctic; of amazing mirages which always show ruins covered in ice, and complexes of buildings, squat edifices that nobody ever thought could be in the Arctic. "Does it not mean anything that in the thirteenth century the coasts of Greenland were covered in vegetation and that at least 300 large family units might have lived there; and yet when the

Danes arrived two centuries later there was not the slightest trace of their houses and works?" This fact is one of Europe's biggest mysteries: people have talked about emigration, epidemics, fights and Eskimo raids but all the hypotheses have been shown to be without foundation. No event we know could cause the disappearance of 300 small communities spread across a vast area—together with everything they had managed to create. If we were to study the folklore of the people living around the Arctic Ocean we would find no shortage of explanations; the Eskimoes believe they were deported from regions which today are tropical by the use of 'huge metal birds'. Another legend among them just as current is that some of their forefathers now dead or 'carried off into the skies' returned afterwards with magical powers they never had before. It is true that there are hosts of such tales of people who come back favoured with divine gifts and are venerated afterwards by their companions. But the Eskimoes do not talk about them with any admiration or satisfaction; on the contrary they think of them with terror, saying that they 'would not belong any more to their people' and that they would recognize neither relatives nor friends but acted in a cold manner like hostile supermen."

"They no longer hunted the bear but belonged to these animals, talking to them and to the devils" is what we learn from Eskimo legend of the Far North in Canada. And the cult of the bear, together with the belief that the plantigrade is gifted with mysterious powers, such as to enable him to communicate with the "higher spirits", is spread all over the Arctic from America to Asia and Europe. Even the Lapps from the time of their conversion to Christianity cultivated it alongside their Shahmanism and totemism and the vestiges of a sun religion concerned with the descent of beings from the sky.

What is behind all this? Is it just a vague tale about the bringing back to life of men and animals afterwards enslaved by the perpetrators of such sombre marvels? We would be almost inclined to believe it if we listen

to certain sinister accounts and think of the complete
terror which the Sirenians experienced regarding their
dead; these Finns living right at the top of the Kola
peninsula burn everything which belonged to the departed, so as to leave no records and also to avoid
trouble in case the body should be resurrected amongst
them. But let us rather ignore ideas about supernatural
beings dragging corpses away to use them later as
slaves only half-alive or even exchanging bodies with
them according to the most impressive of the horror
fantasies. (Do you remember the colonies of highly
intelligent micro-organisms who manage to build astroships with the help of which they shower Earth with
creatures having prehensile organs—who then haunt
the best mortuaries in order to get corpses if not too
badly decayed so that they can re-activate them?)
There is one little race reduced to the minimum by an
isolation perhaps not altogether voluntary—that of the
Yucaghiri (between the Siberian rivers Kolyma and
Yana) which boasts of descent from space visitors
transformed by magic into human beings. If we accept
the theory of temporary abduction of animals or people
would it not be more reasonable to think of some cruel
technique of remote control used on people and bears
by the supposed invaders? A mad idea? Quite the contrary. We too, if we insert a very thin electrode into a
certain part of the brain, can change people into mere
automatons of flesh as has been shown by the experiments of Walter Hess, Erick von Holst and José
Delgado (see *Shadows across the Stars*) and this is
solid fact.

CHAPTER SEVEN

MAGIC FIRE

"In the times of great forests and flourishing meadows there were demons who kept our people in slavery and sent the young to die amongst the rocks and below the ground. But then came the thunder-bird and our people were liberated and learnt about the marvellous cities of the thunder-bird which rose beyond the big lakes and rivers". This would seem to be an extremely sketchy précis of the history of the Canadian redskins as told to the ethnographer Baker by one of the wise men belonging to the many secret societies based on totemic cults. We could regard the demons as the first white settlers in Canada, always ready to exploit local labour in mining and building; while the thunder-bird might be the clamour of a new epoch in which the Indians were no longer slaves but could see new horizons and gates opening to the cities of the south. Everything might seem clear, therefore: but it is not quite so and for the best of reasons. In the first place the tradition is spread around the Far North where the ice prevents the trees etc. from flourishing; and it refers to

88

the remotest period of Canada when it was covered in luxuriant growth. In the second place the sage's account has a sequel: "Many of us went down there and saw the shining cities and their marvels such as the grand homes and the men who flew into the skies to meet the thunder-bird. Then the demons returned and there was terrible havoc everywhere. The few of us who had gone down there and managed to get back declared that the cities and the life there had all gone. There, where once such cities stood there is nothing but ruins now."

It is completely useless to ask old Indians about these ideas; they cannot explain them, since all they know is this and if anything is added it is simply the result of their imagination or based on religious sources no more than about two centuries old. Not even about the "devils" can anything specific be known, the features portrayed being so varied as to render any classification impossible. But the totems representing the thunder-bird or the "bird of fire" are, at any rate in the eyes of scholars convinced of spatial influences in the past, eloquent enough: they would represent space-vehicles, as the same characteristics of the mythical flying bird would tend to confirm; and it must be confessed it is difficult to perceive anything else in a "bird which flies with the sound of thunder"; which goes up "in a big flame" and roosts in "a nest of flames".

The astronomical allusions of the Canadian Indians, then, would not stop here; like the Egyptians they consigned their kings to eternity with their "solar boats", just as many North American tribes bury their dead in "canoe-graves"; and the latter were not meant to cross the skies in mere symbolical fashion: their builders fixed them on high supports just as we would if we wanted to carve an aircraft in flight.

The oval masks of wood which the Nootka Indians decorate with feathers and wear on their heads like a crown seem to be connected with the significance normally associated with the diadem of feathers and the hypothetical copies of space helmets. On some cloaks other plumes signify the wings and refer us to the

richest plumed cloaks of central-south America and to
the symbols still alive in New Mexico, even if the tradition of what inspired them is now lost or corrupted; the
Apaches wear for their famous "dance of the white
eagle" a cloak which represents the head, wings and
tail of a flying bird to perfection.

The Kingdom of Death

Let us return to Canadian tradition. Noting that the
"fire-bird" is linked in nearly all American myth with
the "white men", we come to the question: What is
the meaning of the reference to the terrible havoc south
of the present frontier? Not to a universal flood which
it is said brought about the disappearance of Atlantis,
which certainly happened in much later times. Perhaps
it was a conflict like those referred to by the Indian and
Chinese writers and to a frightful encounter between
humans or semi-human beings and the indescribable
creatures referred to as demons?

It is impossible to give any answer: we know only
that something apocalyptic must have convulsed the
territory now occupied by the U.S.A. "These lands,"
the Maya tells us directly, "are the Kingdom of Death.
Only the souls which will never be reincarnated go
there . . . but it was inhabited a long time ago by
ancient human races." Only a huge disaster, however,
can explain the sudden disappearance of cultures present in the most distant epochs of North America. A
million years ago in the Canyon of St. Mary in the
Bronco Mountains there were cave dwellers who had
already learnt how to fashion weapons of stone, to rear
animals and to bury their dead in jute baskets. Why
did they do so? And where have the builders of the
famous mounds gone, those huge tumuli scattered
across Wisconsin, Illinois and some valleys in Ohio
and Mississippi? Some people think the mounds are
tombs or sanctuaries while others feel that they are defence works; though actually we do not know anything
about these very odd structures which often reproduce
animal forms in which the shapes of reptiles and even

of human beings can be distinguished. Near them were discovered blocks of stone which could be altars, knives made of opsidian, terracotta objects, pipes, cusps of bronze weapons and finally bone fragments which on analysis showed that the unknown builders of the artificial hills did not belong to the red-skinned races but to the white or, at least, to a race similar to ours.

"Discoveries have been made there," says the paleontologist and archaeologist J. Montez "which lead us to believe that the mound builders were in touch with the representatives of the ancient civilizations of the South; and near them other instruments of an astonishingly crude level which induces one to think they were made by troglodytes with just a glimmer of intelligence; while others again, those bronze ones, appear to support the existence of a culture totally alien to both the Stone Age and the Archaic period of central and southern America."

In view of the fact that the discoveries for the most part were all mixed up when they were brought to light we can only think that various human groups of different origins were encamped at the foot of the tumuli; it also seems most logical to think that such communities were sufficiently far advanced to be able to maintain contact once with distant countries but afterwards isolated and forced to make use of crude implements for survival. If we survived a shipwreck by reaching an uninhabited island but had managed to scratch a few things together before leaving the ship might not we too find ourselves left with nothing but an ultra-modern alarm-clock, a razor, a comb of fish-bone and a bowl patiently carved from a big stone.

Some remains looking just like horse bones have been discovered not far from one of these artificial hills in Illinois. Nothing extraordinary, since it is now known that the horse is of North American origin. But let us remember that it was reintroduced into America from the Old World. Why had it gone? As a result perhaps of that same force which shook the United States back into barbarism and killed off its original inhabitants? But did this orgy of destruction really take place? There are geologists who maintain that those immense areas have not been brought into their present queer forms by natural causes; and the mysterious ruins dotted across southern California to the Colorado show traces of marks which could not have been made by natural cataclysms but only by weapons of incredible power.

"The whole region between the rivers Gila and St. John" wrote a friend of the adventurer William Walker "is covered with ruins. The remains of cities are to be found there which must be most extensive and they are burnt out and vitrified in part, full of fused stones and craters caused by fires which were hot enough to liquefy any rock or metal. There are paving stones and houses torn with monstrous cracks which seem to have been attacked at times by a giant's fire-plough."

A Starry Festival

We now move from these mazing ruins towards the northwest across the desert where our road ends at the foot of Mount Shasta, which some writers say has been populated directly by men from space. An astronomer, Edgar Lucin Larkin states that he has observed a large gilded dome surrounded by curious structures on this superb volcanic cone; while a local tradition (known also in Mexico) mentions a gallery dug under the eastern slope which leads to a city under the ground. Have the "sons of the thundering-bird" established one of their secret bases here? Some people are ready to swear to it, saying that they have seen mysterious lights shining on the mountain and odd creatures nearby. From the north part of Shasta to the Mexican borders, however, all sorts of bewildering apparitions reveal themselves: creatures "dressed in a kind of close-fitting metal breastplate" go around near Lake Tahoe; and small, shining spheres dash about noiselessly in the National Sequoia Park as far as the borders of Death Valley, while shadows without any object to cause them are found flickering across to the Mohave Desert.

"Throughout California and nearby regions (Oregon, Arizona etc.)" writes Serge Hutin, "there are odd ruins. Off the coast of Santa Barbara there are islands with the remnants of fortifications erected by a vanished race, that of the Chumash, which had a brilliant scientific and technological level . . ." And among these ruins things happen which are usually talked about quite freely. They say, for instance, that even in the Mohave Desert huge circular or polygonal places exist which are covered by a very hard substance like opaque glass. And if one remains there a feeling of anxiety and sickness attacks one . . . as if there were something there which would not tolerate the presence of human beings. But what are the colourful flames which sometimes shine on the sea? and off the southern islands? What can we believe of these reports which assert that some of these light effects are just like those in Japan? In the night between July 31st and August 1st, according to the ancient lunar calendar, and to be more exact it is towards dawn, there occurs at Kumamoto (East of Nagaski, on Kyushu Island) a very strange thing: countless orange lights rise above the water, offering a sight which is astonishing. All the theories which have tried to account for it so far have failed to do so. It cannot be due to fishermen's lamps since the light is also present when there are no boats on the sea; and neither can it be any natural phenomenon seeing that it recurs with amazing regularity whatever the atmospherics are like; and has done so for about a thousand years.

Students of spatial phenomena assert that the shiranui (unknown fire) admits of only one explanation: that some cosmic race intending to celebrate across the centuries in some such inexplicable manner its landing on our planet. Kyushu seems to hold several "stellar imprints": "Tombs," wrote the Japanese daily *Japan Times,* "decorated with strange circular marks which one can find nowhere else and cannot be compared with any other design. They seem to be discs . . . and the brilliant colours in which they are painted would suggest the same for the 'unknown fire' . . .

added to which there is the fascination of the Jomon plate, of the strangely modern figures suggesting prehistoric astronauts (see photo insert for the Jomon costume. There is also the mysterious pre-Ainu language, the vocabulary of which refers to nature which itself came with cosmic visitors, some believe."

There is an abundance of such legends which appear to support these theories, and it is significant that some of those spread around the bay of Yatsushiro (to the south-west of Kumamoto) may have not a few features in common with folklore situated right at the other end of the Japanese Islands at Hokkaido, where they talk about travellers having come from the sky in shining boats, and of extraordinary beings from whom the natives learnt countless numbers of useful things. Of such creatures we find traces everywhere in the realm of the Rising Sun: in a design of unknown date, for example, we can see seven figures holding each other by the hand and dancing in front of a spiral;[1] while in another one we see an odd silhouette from the head of which rises an antennae-system. Near this there seems to be a shaft and an indefinable construction (a missile and a launching-pad, say the really bold ones) with seven shining discs on a black background.

In times close enough to ours an important chapter of Japanese history seems to have cosmic echoes; it is the one which in the sixth century sees the rise of the great Kamu (the Manchurian conqueror who became Yimmu Tennö) and his invasion of the Japanese islands to force the bearded and barbarous white race called Ainu to take refuge in the extreme north. The Kamu—the myths tell us—was guided by the Raven of the Sun sent to help by the divine great grandmother

[1]This symbol, which is a drawing from the remotest antiquity, can be seen everywhere in the world; it represents the Creation and thus of the Universe. But the Universe stylized here is in its cosmic form, with the galaxy in the shape of a spiral. It is clear that to obtain this considerable astronomical knowledge would be needed and this our distant forefathers did not possess according to modern science at any rate. As a consequence it is asserted that the symbol must have come "from outside" and that our ancestors used it as much for the expression of the Infinite as for the spacemen.

Amaterasu. It may be noted that the Ainu, living on the island of Sakhalin and now reduced to a primitive level worship the bear, just as many Siberian and Arctic tribes do; and the serpent which one legend explicitly says "came from the stars" is also venerated by these people. Are we here dealing with the final conflict of the "birds of fire" and the "celestial serpents" perhaps? The hypothesis is not an established one, and it is most likely that this fable of very remote events has been grafted on to the stormy history of the sixth century.

Returning to the shiranui we are obliged to add that it is also revealed in the waters of Oshima, south of Tokyo; and likewise to point out that this could be simply a coincidence, but if so, an impressive one: the apparition of the magic flames is often accompanied by the appearance—confirmed by genuine photography—of unidentified flying objects.

"The unknown fire," writes the Japanese review *Brothers,* "could be caused by magnetic radiation coming from space and from an unknown 'basilary essence' existing in the zone and thus making it visible. This 'fire' makes a circle around Oshima; and when that happens UFOs are seen going towards the ancient tombs and towards the centre of the region where these phenomena always take place. According to the course taken and the colour they assume it would appear that they completely control the fire . . . the tombs to which we have referred carry the 'sun sign' and around them one can still see the ruins of the 'kingdom of the sun'."

Invisible Cannons

When, in the summer of 1965, the members of a Japanese ship sailing to the east of the island of Sakhalin heard detonations during almost the whole of the final part of their journey they thought at first it must have been caused by a Soviet unit exercising a short distance from their own steamer; but then they realized that there was no ship at all in the place producing the explosions and thus concluded it must be some new type of aircraft breaking the sound barrier, which would produce a sound similar to that of jet planes.

A couple of months later, after having heard similar detonations when sailing along the western coast of the island of Hokkaido and off the eastern Siberian shore, the commander of the ship demanded confirmation of his theory from a friend in the Soviet fleet, a Vladivostok official. "No," the latter said, "it is not a question of aircraft or of bombs." The two were on holiday and made use of it by travelling to the banks of the lake Khanka on the Chinese borders: there the Japanese sailor had the chance to hear several times a day noises just like those which had struck him before. His friend said the phenomenon was anything but unusual, adding "We haven't the slightest idea about the origin. It certainly cannot be any machine—unless it's flying saucers." The Soviet official spoke perhaps with a smile but when his explanation reached the ears of the dedicated they welcomed it as if it were some long sought key. These mysterious explosions have puzzled scientists since before the invention of the jet plane; and even the British Defence Minister proposed an enquiry, only giving up the idea when persuaded that there would be no worthwhile result. "It is probably a natural phenomenon," a scholar stated, "but it is very hard to decide if its cause is on land or sea or in the air."

Some people believe, as we said, that they have found the solution and the most reasonable one at that: the subterranean transit of space vehicles from a moderate speed to an exceptional one—which would bring about acoustic phenomena like those caused by breaking the sound barrier. This would have to happen with remarkable frequency in the regions where the UFOs may still have their secret bases. It is of course an arbitrary deduction; but we must say that the explosions are heard regularly near the regions considered for a long time to be the scene of events for one reason or another inexplicable.

The phenomenon is scientifically known as "invisible Cannons" or the "Cannons of Barisal"—from the name of a village to the west of the chief mouth of the Ganges, about 70 miles south of Dacca; the first people to describe it were actually some English travellers going across the Sundarbans (or Sunderbunds) that enormous stretch of swamps and lakes through which the sacred Hindu river finds its way to the sea. Colonel Godwin Austin talked a great deal about it when he heard the detonations in the spring of 1865 in Bhutan, on the southern slopes of the Himalayas; so also did Colonel H. S. Olcott in 1895 at Barisal and Chilmari, on the Brahmaputra. But the most famous account is still that of the explorer G. B. Scott.

"I heard the 'cannons of Barisal' for the first time in December 1871, when I was sent from Calcutta to Assam across the Sunderbans. The weather was calm—not the slightest sign of disturbance. During the day the noises were so loud on board ship that other sounds were drowned. But at night while we were moored in one or other of the narrow canals near Barisal, Morelgunge and others far away from villages and surrounded by thousands of green plains everywhere—there, where the only sounds were the rippling of sluggish waves and the splashes of lumps of soil falling in the water, we heard a noise at regular intervals, a hollow rumbling similar to that of gunfire: occasionally only one but sometimes two, three or more in succession; never near, always in the distance and seeming inaccessible."

Although nobody has made a list as yet of all the places in which the sound has been heard, we know it often occurs in English, Scottish, Irish and Icelandic regions; also off the Belgian coasts, in various parts of the United States (in one case in Montana, on the Rocky Mountains and on the Black Hills of Wyoming and Dakota) and in different regions of Siberia; also at Haiti where it caused superstitious terror.

In Australia they were heard perhaps for the first time by Charles Sturt during his great journey which brought him in 1828–29 to the discovery of the rivers Darling and Murray. "It was not a terrestrial sound, although it might have resembled a discharge of heavy artillery." And another account which should encourage our supporters of the spatial theory was given in June 1908 by H. L. Richardson of Hillsprings, near Caernarvon in Western Australia: "I heard three explosions in the air, at a great height, followed by a noise like an escape of steam, lasting several seconds . . ."

Several groups of redskins living on the edges of the desert regions of the south-west in the United States tell us even today about thundering birds and hearing other rumbles (very easily explained as being caused by rock falls in chasms). What would they think if they heard the "cannons of Barisal"? We would like to know.

CHAPTER EIGHT

THE GENTLEMEN OF THE DEEPS

"The 'things' had come from space to Earth, still without life upon it, and then many other strange creatures arrived . . . who had lived a long time under the surface of the seas where they had built fantastic cities and fought against indescribable enemies, assisted by engines driven by motors based on principles quite unknown to us. It is clear that their scientific and mechanical knowledge was very advanced with regard to the present-day level achieved by human beings . . . their supernatural health and the simplicity of their natural needs made it possible for them to live at a high level without the aid of artificially produced objects and even without clothes, except as an occasional protection against the elements".

Once again we are quoting Lovecraft (see *The Timeless Earth*) who in his fascinating account proceeds as follows: "It was in the sea that the first forms of life were created, using materials already existing and applying methods which had been practised for a long time—at first for obtaining food but afterwards for other purposes. After the annihilation of various cosmic enemies the experiments became most elaborate. They had succeeded in doing the same thing on other planets, not only producing food but also protoplasmic masses capable of making their own tissues under hypnotic influence, in such a way that they would fashion a temporary limb and thus prove ideal slaves for the society's heavy work. These sticky masses were undoubtedly the 'Shoggoth' of which Abdul Alhazred hardly dared to whisper in his frightening book *Necromicon,* though even this mad Arab had never hinted at the fact that such might exist on Earth. With the aid of the 'Shoggoth', whose ability to grow made them eminently suitable for the lifting of fantastically heavy weights, the small submarine cities grew into vast and imposing labyrinths of stone. Volumes could be written about the life of the Ancient Beings, either of the period in which they lived under the sea or of that during which they were partly established on land. Their strength was unbelievable: not even the terrific pressures of the sea depths could disturb them.

"But another race, consisting of beings resembling the octopus and probably corresponding to the fabled pre-human progeny of Cthulhu, began to slip in from the cosmos and begin a monstrous war, during which the Ancient Beings were for some time beaten back into the sea where they had to face new perils—an invasion from space of creatures which were partly fungi and partly crustaceans, probably the same as those recorded in some northern legends such as the Mi-Go in the Himalayan regions . . ."

A Reich made of Water

Creatures rained from the stars, to hide in the depths of our seas? In support of this, the boldest of all hypotheses, we could quote numerous mythological elements; as long as one can speak of support as such since here more than anywhere else reality and fantasy are inseparable up to this point and undoubtedly the latter dominates the former, corrupting it irremediably.

According to some detectives of the occult real submarine astroports would exist, built to receive amphibious spacecraft. Mr. René Fouéré even offers us a detailed map, according to which the chief bases of the flying saucers are between Sicily and Malta, in the Red Sea, in the Persian Gulf, off Bermuda and in other places we shall not consider listing. The idea of machines able to plunge through water, sail on it or go up in the air is anything but absurd—as shown by the United States which has had a plan for an aircraft of this nature but it was later considered useless. It is clear that to seem versatile enough the cosmic explorers would be used to the underwater life of their own planet or sufficiently inclined to obtain inaccessible shelter on the planets singled out for their attention.

We are of course in the field of pure theory here: but although we do not want to indulge in wild speculations we must admit that in our seas things go on which defy all analysis. Taking first place in importance are the submersible craft which mysteriously appear with a disturbing frequency. They ususally escape us because newspapers do not trouble much about them; but all the great powers have voluminous counter-espionage archives and these are full of unanswered questions concerning such matters.

It is said that after the settling of the Cuban crisis the United States and Russia might have arrived at a secret agreement whereby both would renounce all special missions linked with undersea craft which until that time had been sent to operate in the territorial waters of both countries. This seems reasonable not only in connection with the need to put an end to the cold war but also because such operations have less effect in an age of reconnaissance robots and satellites. But there would be treaty violations by both sides and a period of months in which lively Notes would fly between Moscow and Washington until the whole affair would be settled by both sides authorizing a search and destroy mission under the waters along their coasts.

In different circumstances a similar communication had been already sent by Khrushchev to the military authorities in Argentina; in the letter he questioned the bombardment of a mysterious object calmly lying in the Gulf of Nuevo (a real trap, as it was enclosed between the southern tip of the Valdés Peninsula and the Punta Ninfas) by which means the Argentinians hoped to make it emerge. The object was located precisely on January 30th 1960, the Gulf being blockaded in such a way that nothing would succeed in leaving it, no matter how small. As words were useless the authorities began to drop depth-charges. Nothing rose to the surface; on the contrary, rumour had it that two other submarines had gone to rejoin the first one; there were heavy underwater explosions, dark shapes (frogmen, it is thought) were seen darting about under the waves and between the keels of the warships. And then just when a second massive bombardment was about to take place the sonic devices showed that there was no longer any unknown object in the depths of the Gulf.

In 1960 there were many such cases in the seas the world over. On February 14th the Americans were driven beserk by an object moving with unbelievable speed in the Caribbean Sea. The day afterwards tons of depth-charges were uselessly unloaded in the Mediterranean around a submarine which seemed to be following the yacht belonging to President Nasser; and on March 5th a "metallic object, perhaps jointed" (though it might have been a large cetacean) was in the waters off Seattle. Half-way through May something similar to the Gulf of Nuevo incident took place at Sydney. For several days a mysterious object was found calmly lying at a depth of about 150 metres until it suddenly disappeared; and on the 25th of the same month numerous Americans tried to identify and dislodge an unknown object off Florida. An American spokesman, overwhelmed with questions, declared that "it is not any submarine device", but he eluded the question about it possibly being an animal. In New York harbour the petrol tanker *Alkaid* collided in July with "an unknown semi-submerged object" and received a frightful gash. And in September these mysterious things turned up along both Pacific and Atlantic seaboards of North

America; also in the Philippines, and in the Arctic. In October and November they emerged at Hawaii, Bahia Blanca and off the Terra del Fuego.

1960 is the year chosen here because in that year the phenomena followed each other with a most powerful rhythm. Consider, for instance, the 1965 chronicles and even if we limit ourselves to Oceania we find a whole series of inexplicable events.

On February 12th—the New Zealand review *Spaceview* says—a pilot K. was carrying out a test flight on a DC3 from Whenuapaj, the Auckland airport at Kaitaia. He kept low along the west coast and when near Porto Kaipara (north of Helensville) he saw something he took at first to be a stranded whale. Going down he realized that it was not an animal but "a metal structure with the following distinguishing marks:

1. It had a perfect symmetrical shape, suitable for sailing;
2. It had no outside controls or protuberances of any sort;
3. It seemed to be certainly of metal and high up above halfway there were lines suggesting portholes;
4. It was on the bottom of the gulf and its shape suggested that the bows were facing south;
5. The form was not that of a normal submarine;
6. Captain K. estimated its length at about 30 metres and the width at four and a half metres over the widest part;
7. The object was in not more than 9 metres of water and was thus very clear."

On April 11th 1955 two men were on the Wonthaggi rocks south-west of Melbourne, looking at the wreck of a fishing boat when they saw two strange metal objects emerging at about 800 metres from the beach. "We looked at them for a quarter of an hour," said Mr. R. Banks, "and we watched as they went out into the open sea and disappeared. We could only infer that they must have been submarines of which we had seen the turrets." The Australian naval authorities were at once informed but the result of the inquiry was that there was no submarine in those regions and that what the men saw could not have been turrets or any other part of a submarine.

From April 15th to the 19th three odd devices were noticed north-west of Brisbane. On July 6th a pilot, C. Adams, and a television worker, L. Hendy, flew right over a group of five hulled objects, equally unknown to the experts, near Fraser Island—also north of Brisbane. November 13th saw two fishermen from Bluff (near Invercargill in South Island, New Zealand) staring at an amazing sight: at a distance of barely ten metres a cone and a dark cube rose in front of them which was evidently part of the superstructure of a type of submarine unknown to them. The things were visible for a few seconds then disappeared, leaving a trail of bubbling water.

It could remind one of what happened on August 5th 1958 near Brioni in the Adriatic; or of the Cuxhaven incident on April 21st 1959 when huge columns of water spurted skywards as if there were a bombardment in action. The Germans actually thought it was a Nato naval exercise and protested about not having been informed. But their supposition was wrong: no explosion had been heard either in the Brioni incident or the Cuxhaven one and a later examination dispelled the idea that natural phenomena were involved. So the two episodes are still shrouded in mystery.

What enigmas do the "adventurers of the green depths" still hold? Some people attribute the cutting of telephone cables under the sea to such creatures. This happened off Newfoundland on February 21st 1959. The sinking of the atomic craft *Thresher* on April 10th 1963 in the Atlantic is likewise held to be due to them, and if we ask the people who believe such things to be true they will reply by quoting the words of Robert Charroux:

"Among the plans of the 'Horsemen of Poseidon' (a secret neo-Nazi society of about 15,000 men) would be found one aiming at the establishment of a practically invulnerable underwater city, from which they could dominate vast maritime areas; and if the day should come when they can sink a French, British, or American atomic submarine they would then have a nuclear capacity sufficient for the needs of their entire city for a virtually unlimited (5,000 years) length of time. Such a thing is not excluded from their scheme."

This then would be the purpose of such a criminal undertaking as the capture of an atomic submarine. But would not someone else have thought of such an idea before the fanatical defenders of the "Aquatic Reich"? This question is asked by those who follow the appearance of mysterious objects in oceans all over the world; whereupon someone comes along to talk about underwater cities from which a monstrous race is preparing to subjugate the world after having captured innumerable people and put them to horrifying experiments—intending to use them as slaves never again to see the sun.

"Let us consider riddles like that of the *Mary Celeste* or the *Bluebird,* of the scores of ships found without any crew on board and in blood-curdling circumstances," says one writer, following a colleague A. Iribarren, "and we shall convince ourselves that these theories are not just the result of fantasy."

Floating Nightmares

On December 4th 1872 Captain Moorhouse of the three-masted English vessel *Dei Gratia* made a strange discovery east of the Azores: he encountered the *Mary Celeste,* an American ship which had left New York a short while before he did to take to Genoa a cargo of oil and alcohol. And he met it without a living soul on board—if one excluded the cat which was fast asleep. The case shook public opinion like few others, and especially because absolutely nothing could give a clue as to what happened to the crew and their only passenger, Mrs. Mary Briggs the captain's wife. She seemed to have left it perfectly dressed while her husband and the other sailors had left behind clothes and shoes in their quarters. The theories were rejected as soon as formed: an attack by pirates? Impossible, as the *Mary Celeste* had not been raided; an epidemic which had sent them mad so that they had all jumped into the sea? No, because everything on board was in perfect order and there was not the slightest sign to suggest the presence of disease. A fire, a storm, an attack by someone suddenly gone beserk? All this seemed quite absurd since there was nothing to support such ideas at all. So what had become of the fourteen sailors, of Captain Briggs and his wife?

The solution to the mystery came thirty years later when Wellighan, a former cabin-boy on the *Dei Gratia* decided to state under oath that one Pemberton, formerly a cook on board the *Mary Celeste* had been considered as having perished with his companions. Thus it was known that the first victim had been the captain's wife, crushed by a piano against a bulkhead. Her husband had gone mad with grief and had thrown himself into the sea; meanwhile the crew, left without a leader, got continually drunk. Some died as the result of bloody quarrels and others deserted when the ship reached Santa Maria in the Azores. There were three men left on board whom Captain Moorhouse had lent (while still in New York) to his colleague Briggs; these men, by means of a false name and a sum of money, were declared to have absconded; while the swindler Moorhouse collected the rich reward due to anyone who helps a ship in distress. A hoax had thus created the sinister legend that for thirty years had made even the toughest seadogs shudder with horror!

All sailors know the story of the *Flying Dutchman,* of Captain Van Straaten, condemned to wander for ever on the sea without reaching land. As everybody knows, the story was put to music by Richard Wagner. Although we do not know where or how it arose there is reason to think that it had a true origin, because in every age we meet ships abandoned in mysterious circumstances, ghost-ships which never fail to excite the imagination. The story of the American yacht *Bluebird* is just as well-known as the *Mary Celeste,* discovered by the authorities in Ponta Delgada in 1884 and also in the Azores. The men who went on board only found a big cat. The whole world became interested in the event and for weeks the newspapers published appeals to any possible survivors to come forward and explain the mystery. Nobody did so and the problem looked as if it would never be solved. But in 1956—72 years afterwards!—the death of one Lovat Nicholson, an eighty-six year old innkeeper at Manhattan (New York) explained everything: in his will he had arranged to hand over to the metropolitan police an envelope enclosed in a strongbox or safe containing the horrifying story of the massacre he had committed himself (being a sailor then) on board the *Bluebird* with the aid of other members of the crew. They had all escaped after having assassinated both the rich captain of the yacht and his guests. But the criminals had not got off scot-free: they had all died violent deaths, while Nicholson, the only one to survive for many years was plagued by misfortunes and oppressed with remorse as he himself wrote.

The fact that the ghost-ships can wander for years on the seas without being detected is proved by a case which arose towards the end of the last century, when the French yacht *Vengeance* collided with a sailing-vessel without a crew. The state the boat was in was such as to lead to the conclusion that it must have been abandoned about 25 to 30 years ago; the old-fashioned clothes left on board suggested this too. The records were illegible but it was believed to be a Brazilian vessel on the Rio de Janeiro–Cape City run which disappeared in 1860; but nobody will ever know the truth.

A similar episode though even more peculiar took place in 1921, when the sailors on the Peruvian cargoboat *Francisco Moreno* leapt on board a deserted ship discovered in the Pacific. The ship had certainly been drifting for years, and yet the stove fires were still burning as if the last sailor had only left them a couple of hours ago! The experts who made the examination could only conclude that a deadly epidemic had broken out on deck. One man had survived for years but not being able to control the boat had resigned himself to his fate. Just before meeting the *Francisco Moreno* a wave had probably seized him and hurled him into the sea or perhaps he had gone mad and jumped into the waves.

The skipper of the sailing-boat from Samoa—the *Taoofo*—had met exactly the same fate in 1913: for five years he had been navigating, after which cholera had exterminated his crew. When the mail steamer *Friedrich Karl* (a German ship) approached him he threw himself into the sea as a result of the nervous crisis inevitable after years of solitude. But fortunately he had been saved by a German official and had thus lived to talk about his tragic odessy. It seems impossible but even today there are still "Flying Dutchmen": on board the fishing-boat *Jóyita,* an old American yacht which set out from Apia (Samoa) on October 22nd 1955 in a northerly direction and was discovered off Fiji on November 10th. "It was half sunk and there was nobody on board. For some weeks the yacht had gone adrift, a grim wreck buffetted by the waves. There were still some provisions in the cold-store but the ship's papers had vanished and the instruments, which had been dismantled with care, had gone. The dinghy was missing, likewise three life rafts and the cargo. And what about the twenty-five men who had left Apia? Not the slightest trace."

In this case, too, many theories were propounded. People talked about pirates and marine spies, volcanic eruptions etc.—even about the possibility that the captain was guilty of fraud (though it was known at the time that the ship was not even insured). How near could one get to the truth? What an old Samoan sailor said is worth hearing: "This is only the work of the Ocean. A small typhoon which can cast water into the skies: I mean what the Polynesians call 'the wind which kills'. The Pacific can be extremely calm in one place and a few miles further on it can show its teeth and sink them into the sides of ships. And do you know why? Underneath, five, six or seven hundred metres deep a small volcano has woken up. Anyway we shall be able to solve the mystery only when we find a survivor, and it is highly likely that we shall come across something: it takes years and years before we discover a shipwreck on some small unknown atoll but it does happen. Here the man can get enough to eat; the cannibals will not eat him because they don't exist any more there. Only the storms have maintained their old ways . . . and all we can do is hope."

The "Thing"

Some disappearances have nothing peculiar about them; however, for some months or years they are considered as being inexplicable. The real mysteries are elsewhere: in those ocean depths still inaccessible even in an age when cosmic vistas open before our eyes; in traces which have been photographed 4,000 metres below the Atlantic. Sir Anthony Laughton, a well-known scholar, has said in a report to the Royal Institute of Oceanography that the marks seen "remind us of the footprints of a biped". A creature which can walk erect on the bottom of the sea, burdened with a frightful pressure? The idea certainly seems strange, but what is *not* alien to us down there amongst the animals which seem to be plants and plants like mythological monsters? And where the fish are fantastic beacons and waterfalls of light? No, the image of some hypothetical "biped of the deeps" is familiar enough to us; more familiar—let us confess—than the "thing" stranded in March 1962 on one of the deserted beaches in Tasmania. Its body was a most unusual shape, 7 metres long by 6 wide, covered in a kind of downy fur and having neither eyes, nor mouth nor skeleton; and yet extremely tough, resistant to both fire and chemical agents. "It's flesh is ivory-colour and like gum" Bruce Mollison, a naturalist, tells us after an examination, "but it is not rubber and not even flesh in the standard sense of the word, and neither fruit pulp. It is something which escapes all classification."

"It was odd," writes Lovecraft, "to notice how Cthulhu and Mi-Go seem to have been made from different materials to the ones we know, to judge from battles portrayed by their cultures . . ."

PART TWO

IMPOSSIBLE DIMENSIONS

CHAPTER NINE

BEFORE THE TIME OF ADAM

"He has unusually long skin-bones, like a sprinter. He was certainly a man, with shoulders much wider than those normal to individuals of his height, which was 175 centimetres. His head is still more interesting: he does not have any trace of the ape about him at all. His brain must have been very large as he had a high forehead and his pronounced chin fully corresponded to the modern type."

These statements are from Professor Georgij Debets, of the Ethnographical Institute, Academy of Soviet Sciences, and he was talking about the skeleton found near Vladimir by Professor Otto Bader of the Archaeology Institute of the same academy. It is the skeleton of a man about fifty, who lived about 52 thousand years ago by hunting reindeer and mammouth in the heart of Europe. It is undoubtedly a most interesting discovery, considering the fine state of bone preservation, but not really a sensational one, since we already know that the men living 52 thousand years ago might have been exactly the same as we are if we leave out of account his enviable physical stature.

But one particular thing is surprising: the "Vladimir Man" used to dress much as one does today, with a large pair of trousers and a very practical jacket. Nothing is left of his garments but it is not difficult to reconstruct them if we go on the ivory badges (found intact) of his coat, sleeves and trousers. This is not really very strange seeing that the men of even 15 thousand years ago, whose existence is recorded in the rock drawings of Lussac-le-Château (Department of Vienne, France) wearing hats, jacket, trousers and petticoat, together with boots and shoes; and the Americans of the unknown Archaic culture, which the most recent studies tell us began at least five thousand years ago, covered their heads with hats almost the same as sombreros, while the women practised an elaborate and elegant hair-do.

"Of course," the anthropologist G. Holm says, "even 52 thousand, 15 to 5 thousand years ago men existed who went around naked or at best covered with skins which he did not bother to fashion in any way. But don't they exist in our own times too? Are there not races today totally different from our own (the pygmies for example?) As long as certain scholars persist in denying the hard facts of evolution from ape to *homo sapiens* we shall never succeed in building an acceptable picture of human evolution."

And Professor Giuseppe Montalenti, of the University Genetics Institute in Rome, goes on: "Until recently human genealogy was thus delineated: apes, Australopithecus, Pithecanthropus, Pre-Mousterian, *homo sapiens*. It was thought that from forms like Australopithecus, which lived in Asia, Pithecanthropus could have originated and men from the latter . . . then everything was turned upside down by other discoveries."

Year by year, or month after month we could almost say, we see confirmation of what we explained at the beginning of *Terra senza Tempo (The Timeless Earth);* we see official science forced by successive discoveries to take note of what has been called "vague theories based on discoveries which cannot be taken into consideration." Today, all the dogma built up on the most fragile of supports by scholars who are more darwinian than Darwin himself has gone miserably to pieces, though some still refuse out of sheer pride to admit it. And finally there is Professor Louis Leakey, who already has contributed so much to anthropology, to deal yet another decisive blow at them.

Darwin did not know it

Olduvai Gorge, south-west of Lake Victoria, has proved to be a surprising chest of treasures for science: after the discoveries we have already mentioned (see *The Timeless Earth*) Leakey brought to light with the help of his wife and sons the remains of "Zinjanthropus", an Australopithecus capable of using the antlers or bones of big animals as clubs, but unable to make weapons or instruments himself.

"There was another Hominid living at the same time and in the same region," Professor Montalenti wrote, "who was much more like people today, and who knew how to make rough tools from stones and fragments of rock, such as axes and scrapers. Therefore the name of *homo abilis* has been given to this man (in 1964) and it is likely that he contributed to the extinction of Australopithecus. In fact the latter is no longer found in the higher strata: *homo abilis* is king of the castle. In still more recent strata there is yet another type of advanced man, whom some scientists say is like Pithecanthropus; *homo erectus* and finally one arrives at *homo sapiens* who belongs to the Acheulian cycle. The discovery of these fossils is important for various reasons. First of all homo abilis can represent the famous missing link, or at least one of the links of the chain connecting a simian form (still prevalent) like the Australopithecus, with the Hominids. And it is likely that Australopithecus who lived at the same time as *"abilis"*, and the latter himself, are both from a common progenitor living in Pliocene. Besides this the scientists have been able, by using radioisotopic techniques for dating the soil, to estimate the age of the various strata in the Olduvai Gorge. It ranges from about two million years for the deepest beds to half a million for the highest."

As we have seen, other finds appear to have pushed back the origin of human evolution still further. But there are those who would doubt the existence of the common ancestor in the Pliocene to which Leakey refers. "There is nothing to prove," says one French writer, "that man came from apes. The species are so little alike that human and gibbon blood-transfusion or chimpanzee and orang-utan carry just the same risks as those between animals of totally different species."

According to the Darwinians, then, our hand would have gained its present features through a long series of transformations; it would, in other words, merely be a simian hand specialized; gradually changed by the change of its functions forced upon it by time. But it is not so, and science has now proved it. Our hand is not old in respect of some animal-extremity compensation but, on the contrary, rather young and still has unpredictable possibilities of development.

These are just as varied among the mammals: the hoof of a horse, for instance, when compared to our hand, seems rough and primitive but it is actually most elaborate, and is the result of a long evolution which has brought a foot of quite different appearance into its present-day specialized form. The extremities of all the animals resembling men are highly developed so that they can climb in agile fashion whenever necessary. Similar observations could be made concerning the teeth: those of the reptiles tend to point outwards but mammalian ones generally inward—clearly a sign of adaptation to the animals' needs. Yet human teeth are not specialized but absolutely straight!

"Darwin did not know these things," the German student Walter Dohmann wrote, "or else ignored them. Yet his own researches led to a series of scientific investigations concerning the origin of man. Nevertheless he used expressions like 'primitive', 'specialized' and 'original' without realizing that things were indeed so varied.

The extremities of a primate Darwin would probably have called primitive but we know today that they are highly specialized. It is completely adapted to its surroundings and could never become universal like our hand."

Here, then, is a very simple but extremely important consideration: the human skeleton when compared with that of all other animals has a meagre number of mineral components; but an abundance of such components is a sign of ageing, of the decline of the race. Or again; the bodily growth of a man is slow from birth, extremely slow if compared with that of other animals—which shows itself also in a condition much more "specialized" than in us. If men had descended from monkeys then, he would have to be still more perfect than the latter— he would have "learnt" to become adult in a few months! Remains found especially in southern America complicate the matter further; they are certainly human or humanoid but belong to races unknown to us. Which of our more or less distant ancestors will it be? Of creatures similar to us, but come from space, as some of the defenders of the cosmic migration theory believe? Or of beings which lived in the most remote ages, swept away by some huge disaster that also convulsed Earth?

The *Maya Bible*, the *Popol Vuh*, seems oddly explicit about these problems. It speaks of ancient races being annihilated by divine powers because the former were incapable of worshipping the latter. This is certainly worth considering. Is it not obvious that this incapacity is caused by lack of intelligence perhaps, which would no doubt have doomed our unfortunate Zinjanthropus-type forefathers who were scarcely able to use a club, just as he stopped more gifted animals from getting the upper hand as the dominant species?

" 'Earth' they said.

This is the testimony.

The Universe was quiet. No breath. No sound. Still and quiet, the world. And the space of the sky was void.

This is the first testimony, the first word. There was no man yet, no animal. There was neither bird, nor fish, nor crustacean, no tree or stone, no cavern or abyss. No grass, nor forest. There was only the sky. The face of Earth was not yet revealed. There was only the sweet sea and the vast space of the sky. Nothing was yet united.[1] Nothing gave forth a sound, nothing moved or shook, nothing broke the silence of the sky. Nothing was yet erect. Only the water, the sweet sea, deserted and silent. Nothing else.

Motionless and silent was the night, the darkness . . .

'Let the void be filled! (the Creator ordered).

'Waters, withdraw and give space, that the Earth may emerge and be firm!'

Thus did they speak.

'Let there be light! Let Earth and sky be bright! There will be neither glory nor greatness until Man shall appear, unless a Man be created.'

Thus did they speak. And they created the Earth. The Truth is that they created the Earth. 'Earth!' they said. And it was created instantly. From fogs, clouds and dust creation came, and the mountains rose above the waters, and the mountains grew . . ."

These passages are from the *Popol Vuh* where we are told that, at the beginning, Tzakól the Creator and Bito the Shaper seemed intent on populating the world only with animals. But they must have undergone a great delusion, as it goes on: "When the Creator and the Shaper did not know how to speak they said: 'They cannot call each other by name . . . and this is not well.'

They said to the animals: 'We shall replace you, because you do not know how to speak. We have changed our minds. You will have your food, your grass, your lairs and your nests, you will have them in the gorges and in the forests. You have not been able to worship us and call to us, therefore we shall create others who can. This is your destiny: your flesh will be devoured. Let it be thus. Let this be your destiny.'

[1] It is curious to note how this expression reflects the state of matter and energy, according to genuine scientific theory, before the Creation: everything would have been concentrated in a kind of primitive atomic nucleus. Here, so dense that no other combination could arise, and thus "not yet united", would be found the protons, neutrons, electrons and photons.

Thus they announced their will to the animals on the face of the Earth, to the small and the large.

To escape their fate they made a new attempt to worship their creators.[2] But they did not understand even amongst themselves and vain were their efforts. Thus was their flesh sacrificed and the animals on the face of the Earth were condemned to be killed and eaten."

Here then does the Creator start to give to our globe its authentic masters. But a great deal of time will be needed before the work is to succeed. Let us consult the sacred text of the Mayas once more:

"Of earth, of clay the flesh of men was made. But they saw that it was not good. Because it dissolved, was too soft, without movement and strength, fell, was soft, and did not move their heads, the skin hung from their sides, their glance was shaded, they could not turn round. This being could speak but did not possess reason. Soon the waters soaked it and it sank there . . . Then the Creator and the Shaper destroyed and shattered their work."

Which semi-inchoate monsters are being dealt with here? Of the very first beings to have a vague resemblance to man, the tottering biped capable of emitting some guttural sound but unable to think? Perhaps we shall never know; their fragile remains lie buried who knows where—in the depths of the planet broken and re-formed by those primordial cataclysms still recorded so vividly by the Maya, connected with the fates of those races that preceded ours.

". . . and the beings were made of wood. They resembled men, spoke like men and populated the world. They lived; populated the Earth, had sons and daughters, those creatures of wood. But they had no soul, no reason and did not remember the Creator and the

[2]The period outlined here is perhaps the one in which the animals were not the only undisputed masters of the planet, since other species specially equipped tried to climb the ladder to power —to "speak with the gods" showing themselves to be intelligent in this way; or it might be a question of so-called social insects.

Shaper. They walked without destination and crept on all fours.

Since they did not remember the Heart of the Sky they were cast out. At the beginning they spoke but their faces did not move. Their feet and their hands were without strength. There was neither liquid nor solid in them, neither blood nor flesh. Their cheeks were dry and dry were their feet and hands, yellow their flesh.

It was only a rough copy, an attempt.
Therefore the Creator and the Shaper forgot they had created them and taken care of them.

These were the first men; very many lived on the face of the Earth. Then they were destroyed, annihilated, these figures of wood and death came to them. The Heart of the Sky caused a flood and vast waters were cast down upon these beings of wood . . . Resinous liquid[3] fell from the sky, the face of the Earth was hid in darkness and black rain commenced by day and by night . . ."[4]
Most likely we are concerned here with a simian race, as the *Popol Vuh* would have us understand: ". . . and it is said that their descendants are the apes which live today in the forests. In them they can recognize those whose flesh is yellow and who were made by the Creator and the Shaper. Therefore the ape resembles man, as a record of a human reaction, and of those men who were nothing but puppets of wood."

If Saurat and Bellamy (see *The Timeless Earth*) are right in some respects when they tell us about the disaster which shook the globe (brought about by collision with a moon preceding the present one) the cataclysm associated in Maya tradition with the end of the simian creatures caused the advent of the giants. In the *Popol Vuh* the extermination of the "men of wood" is an exact reflection of the Greek mythological struggle

[3] Lava, it is thought by the translators.

[4] These passages, like the preceding and following ones in this chapter are all drawn from the *Popol Vuh*.

between the Titans and the gods. Uucubk'aquix[5] is the name of the leader of the rebels sent into the regions of darkness but his sons give no end of trouble to the divinities: Cabracán, who "shook and beat down the mountains" is killed by two bold twins, Hunahpú and Ixbalanqué, who also proceed to deal likewise with Zipacná. The latter however had sent into the darkness four-hundred youths who became changed into the Pleiades, so these stars shine, too, over the myths of the "Greeks of America"; and it is interesting to note that the Maya called them "Motz", a term shortened from "momótzli", a noun indicating a sacrificial altar. Thus the Pleiades represented sacrifices sent to the skies. Why the Pleiades exactly? Is the answer to be found in the cosmic references we have alluded to in the first part of the book?

Many people believe that the death of the four hundred youths symbolizes the end of an entire race caused by volcanic eruptions and other disastrous tellurian phenomena, represented in the *Popol Vuh* by the giants. But this does not convince us in one respect: the death of the Titans, beaten by men or, if we like, by supermen. We could still think that the other and earlier moon had caused further upheavals and that in this period the Titans themselves had been swept away from the surface of the world. That the forefathers of the Maya might have seen in such natural phenomena the final tremors of the giants is not something which should cause us to marvel.

The apes appear in the limelight again in the deeds of Hunahpú and Ixbalanqué, who are regarded by some as Neanderthal men, unexpectedly pushed forward on the evolutionary road when their satellite was ruined by cosmic conditions. But from now on it is the advent of a new race we are concerned with, one which is destined to rule the world. The gods shape them first from maize, yellow and white maize. And thus the perfected creatures arise:

[5]The spelling of the Maya names is that adopted by the chief translators of the *Popol Vuh*: H: always aspirated; Qu: like K; Y: like I; X: like Sh.

"They looked into the distance and could discern everything which was in the world. When they looked they saw everything around and the dome of the sky and the inside of the Earth. Without moving themselves they saw everything hidden in the distance. They saw at once the entire world, from the place in which they stood. Their wisdom was great. Their eye reached every forest and mountain and lake, every hill, sea and valley. Verily, they were wondrous men . . ."

Sometimes the note of divine dissatisfaction is varied but nonetheless pronounced:

" 'Let us satisfy their desires a little, for what we see is not well. Must they resemble us in the end, their creators who know and see all from the distance?

Thus did they speak, the Heart of the Sky Huracán, Chipì-Cakulhá, Raxa-Cakulhá, Tepeu, Kukmatz, Alóm, Caholóm, Ixpiyacóc, Ixmucané, Tzakól and Bitól. Thus did they speak and soon changed the nature of their works and their creatures.

The Heart of the Sky cast a veil over their eyes so that they grew dim as when the breath touches a mirror; they could see only that which was near at hand and clear. Thus was destroyed all the wisdom and knowledge of the four men concerning the origin and the beginning. Thus were our forefathers created and formed. From the heart of the sky, from the heart of the world."

What brought about the birth of these supermen and the consequent limitations they had to suffer? An intense stream of cosmic rays, the last effects of which only ceased after the lunar catastrophe? The coming of their ancestors from the east, from that terrain distinguished by a very high level of culture—perhaps Atlantis—and the following unions of its individuals with Indian races? Or what if it were the direct descent from space of these wonderful beings? In the *Popol Vuh* the hints which could lead to some fantastic interpretation like this are anything but rare. And would not these supersensed creatures really be the fruit of scientific achievements afterwards lost?

many parts of the world there are ancient rock draw-
gs which show a remarkable similarity to astronauts in
ace-suits.

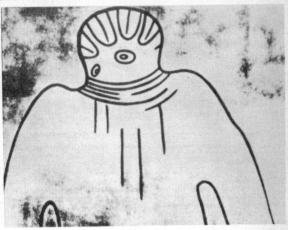

1. This is the so-called "big god of the Martians"
found in the Sahara Desert.

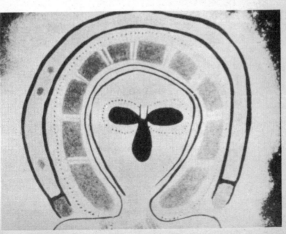

2. An ancient Australian rock drawing.

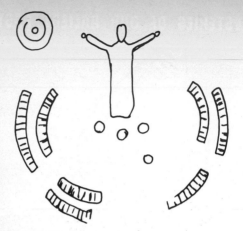

3. This drawing was found at Woomera and might indicate "a great white man who has come down from the sky" Top left is a space-ship while the circles represent the elders of the tribe and the semi-circles the people being instructed by the stranger.

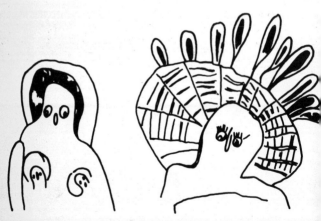

4. These two, also found at Woomera, are called "Creatures without mouths" by the aborigines. The one on the left shows details on the breast which could perhaps be connectors for items of equipment.

5. This comes from the antique astronomical observatory of Merowe and has been thought to be a missile.

6. Are these space-helmets with the external appendages? On the left is a photo of the rock drawing found 40 kilometres south of Fergana in Uzbekistan (USSR); on the right the "spacemen of Val Camonica" Italy, with geometrical symbols in their hands.

7. The famous Roman money coined in A.D. 193. On the left, at top, an object strikingly like one of our artificial satellites.

8. The coffin cover from the Mayan Temple at Palenque. When it was found space-travel was hardly a possibility. Today could it be interpreted as anything but a man at the controls of a space-ship?

9 and 10. Two Japanese "Dogu" statuettes. Several scientists think they are drawings of beings in space-suits who landed on Earth in very remote times.

11. A piece of unknown substance which fell from a "flying disc" at Laigueglia in April 1963. Similar objects have been mentioned in ancient Roman sources.

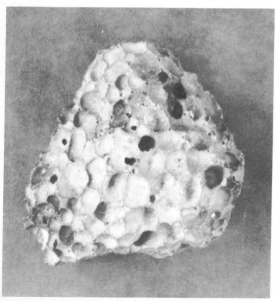

12. A mysterious fragment of a coral substance which fell from the sky and was collected by an American, Donald Bunce.

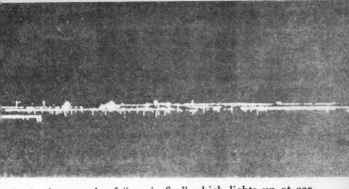

13. A photograph of "magic fire" which lights up at certain times on Japanese seas, often in conjunction with the appearance of "flying discs".

14. Archaeologist Roger Grosjean during restoration work on the Corsican menhir discovered by him.

15. View of the famous megalithic complex at Stonehenge which has been shown to be virtually an astronomical computer.

16 and 17. The "Blair Cuspids" discovered on the moon. ABOVE: the photos taken by artificial satellites. BELOW: their triangulation.

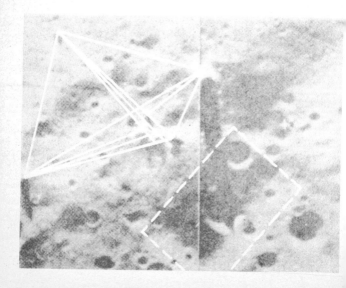

18. The "sleeping Buddha" of grotto 58 at Tun-huang. Among the various human figures behind the god, there are some which seem to belong to unknown races, while others have features like the American Indians.

19. These tablets were found in Mexico by the archaeologist Niven. They are extraordinarily like Asian graffiti.

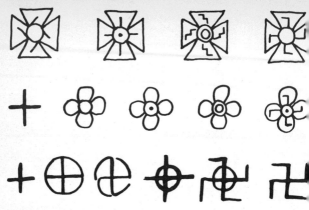

20. Development of the cross in Central America; the second row shows the lotus flower form, while the third has the swastika shape as in India.

21. Design from the North American mounds: the first shows the sun rising in the west (before the presumed cosmic catastrophe); the second the sun as it is today; the third is of the sun in a drawing found near a mound in North America. The fourth is a Mexican drawing with the west-east movement.

22. Three spiders with the cross or the solar symbol discovered on pottery found by the mounds.

3. This strange being with a flat head may have been one
of the unknown inhabitants of pre-historic America. How
could such vast monuments of stone have been transported
across the difficult terrain of the Cauca Valley, Columbia?

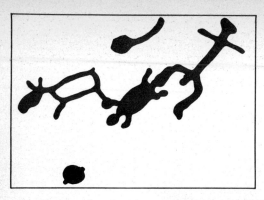

24. Prehistoric cinema from Lake Onega, Carelia. The figures appear to move at sunset.

25. A feline Mexican creature. Just artistic imagination or could it be a memory of pre-historic inhabitants?

26 and 27. Two views of Chan-Chan in Peru. These imposing ruins cover an area of 18 square kilometres and include pyramids, reservoirs and enigmatic palaces.

28 and 29. Two views of the "Great Wall of Peru". It was discovered by the Johnson expedition and its function remains completely unknown.

30. ABOVE: The reconstruction of the "Castle" of Chavin de Huantár. This marvellous building of three floors, each of which has its own system of ventilation, has neither doors nor windows. This suggests it represents a space-ship with its occupants, the mysterious "cat-men". 31. BELOW: Another Peruvian enigma—a chain of dark shapes which run along the flanks of inaccessible mountains.

32. Two amphitheatres found in Peru, with a close resemblance to those of the Mediterranean.

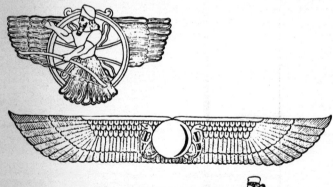

33. Men within winged circles are familiar in the mythologies of several Mediterranean peoples. TOP: winged Assyrian disc. MIDDLE: winged Egyptian disc. BELOW: the god Ahura-Mazda.

CHAPTER TEN

THE CYCLOPSES AND THE COSMONAUTS

"There were crickets. cockroaches and spiders . . . Burl knew them very well, those spiders! his grandfather had been a victim of a ferocious tarantula which had emerged with incredible speed from a vertical shaft about one metre in diameter, extending into the ground for several metres. And there, at the bottom of that lair, the monster waited for the feeblest sounds which would tell it that some victim was near its hiding-place.

"Burl's grandfather had not been careful enough; and Burl could still vaguely recall the terrible shouts uttered when the seizure took place. He had also seen the web of another species of spider, threads of dirty silk thick as a finger; and keeping himself at a safe distance he had watched as the monster sucked a big, half-metre grasshopper which had got caught near its snare. He vividly remembered the yellow, black and silver lines across its abdomen. He was both fascinated and petrified by the blind struggle which the cricket had vainly put up

123

against the sticky coils of the net before the spider began its feast ...

"The day before, crouched behind a mass of vegetation he had watched a duel between two enormous horned beetles. They were very long and could reach Burl's chest when they stood up. They had seized each other with their sideways-opening jaws and one could hear the grating noise produced on their impenetrable armour. When they hit each other their legs echoed like so many plates ... and when there was a breach in the shell of the smaller one it was followed by a loud cry, or at least it seemed like that; the noise was caused by the shell chiefly, which was cracking in the conqueror's jaws ..."

Scenes of this sort appear on a "lifeless" planet colonized by spatial voyagers who from some trivial error have then lost sight of it.[1] But the same sort of thing happens on Earth, too, according to an American explorer John Perkins, who says, for instance that a valley with an incredible landscape can be reached by a subterranean waterfall, where the grass grows as high as cypress trees, flowers are gigantic and the bushes are so large each would form a small forest by itself. Perkins said he found it accidentally and only managed to leave it after unmentionable hardships. According to him there are also forms of animal life but ghastly ones: phosphorescent flies as big as hens, and spiders the size of pigs—mutations caused by radioactivity.

True? We cannot guarantee it but we must point out that gigantism resulted from the eruption of the volcano Pelé in Martinique—which led to the discovery of large veins of radioactive minerals. And according to Saurat and Bellamy a lasting animal and human gigantism was caused when cosmic rays in intense numbers were showered on to Earth—also helped by the increased gravitational pull of the earlier moon on its disastrous approach to our own world.

[1]These quotations have been taken from *The Forgotten Planet* by Murray Leinster.

Facts from Rocks

In 1577, at Willisau in the canton of Lucerne, an impressive skeleton saw the light of day. The authorities hastily convened a commission of experts, led by the most famous Swiss anatomist of the time, Doctor Felix Plater of Basilea. Scholars were doubtful but faced with this show of experts they had to keep quiet. Plater said they were undoubtedly human remains but their bulk was such as to make this assertion seem rash. The skeleton was not complete but the anatomist modelled it in clay, thus obtaining a direct outline of the man to whom it must have belonged. The result was a giant 5.80 metres in height, which was immediately dubbed the "giant of Lucerne", whose bones were proudly displayed in a large hall of the town. Attracted by this sensational discovery another anatomist, this time of European renown, Professor J. F. Blumenbach went to the scene from his University of Göttingen. After a glance he burst out laughing because the bones were obviously those of a mammoth—a fact which the angry people of Lucerne eventually had to accept.

Thirty-six years later France had to have its own giant, this one from a cave near the castle of Chaumont (St. Antoine) and found in a tomb with a lid bearing the words "Teutobochtus Rex" in Gothic characters. The money and the "medals" found inside left no doubt that it was the king of Cimbri, defeated and killed by Mario. When the lid was uncovered the spectators gazed breathlessly at a skeleton more than 7.60 metres long! A certain Doctor Mazurier who lived nearby hastened to write a description of the bones after an examination, enthusiastic enough to arouse harsh words among the scholars concerned. Finally some other gigantic bones were found in a ditch near the castle which turned out to be of the same species as that of the bones in the tomb—which brought the swindle to light. Doctor Mazurier had plotted it in order to obtain the glory and the money involved. The

remains are now in the Paleontology Museum in Paris
—the bones being those of a mastodon!

Other giant-sized bones came to light about the same
period at Gloucester. The great English physician and
physiologist William Harvey said that they belonged to
some large animal, perhaps an elephant, but nobody
paid any attention; yet at the court of James the First
furious discussions went on about burying the remains
in consecrated ground when they were marvelling about
a tooth which was supposed to weigh more than 3½
kilos. People must then have had a curious knowledge of
mathematics because if it were so the body of the giant
to which it belonged would have had to weigh not less
than one hundred tons! It was shown in fact that the
bones were indeed those of an elephant. Does the story
of the giants belong, then, to the realm of fairy tale? The
things quoted here do not allow us to think so, if only
because people the world over have kept records of
them. They speak about such fables so eloquently and
clearly, in the Bible as in the Mahabhárata, in the sacred Thailand texts as in those of Ceylon; and in
Egyptian, Irish and Basque.

A Caucasian legend also tells us about "rock-facts"
—which is probably a reference to their physical
strength. It is interesting to note in this connection that
there are very few "good" Titans anywhere though we
do find bad ones at all latitudes most of them being involved in ruthless war against human beings: which
becomes explicable enough if one thinks of these two
races contending for the mastery of the planet. Herodotus tells us in his *Histories* about the adventures of a
certain Lica di Sparta who went to look for the wife of
Orestes, son of Agamemnon. At Tegea, an ancient city
in Arcady, Lica meets a smith who shows him an open
space behind his house, saying: "When I was digging a
well behind here I came across a long coffin seven
cubits (3.25 metres) long. Not wanting to believe that
such big men could exist I uncovered it and saw that it
contained a body of the same length."

Neither is America short of such traditions. We have
seen them by reading the *Popol Vuh;* while the so-

called Mexican manuscript of Pedro de los Rios states: "Before the flood which took place 4,008 years after the creation of the world the land of Anahuac was peopled by the Tzocuillixeco, a giant race, one of whom bore the name Xelua . . ." Which is not just a myth pure and simple, because when the Spaniards landed in America some of the local sages told the chronicler and almoner Bernal Diaz del Castillo how once upon a time "very tall men and women lived in that land; being evil they were slaughtered in large numbers and the survivors died natural deaths". But they were shown monstrous bones, one of which Hernán Cortés sent to his sovereign, as it was "a femur itself as high as a normal man".

Around Lake Titicaca legends abound, some of which clearly state that the last of these monstrous creatures fled to the south. Their descendants must have populated Patagonia until some centuries ago and Magellan found the land, sometimes coming face to face with them. In June 1520 there was another encounter when the ships of this great Portuguese sailor were at anchor at San Julián and about this Pigafetta writes: "That man was so tall that our heads would hardly reach his belt and his voice was like that of a bull". Magellan captured two of these huge natives, intending to send them to Europe but both died before the ship reached the Equator. Drake too, in 1578, saw at San Julián men about two and half metres high and after him other travellers such as Pedro Sarmiento, Tomé Hernandez, Anthony Knyvet and Sebald de Weert also did: the last two encountered them, separately, at a height of 3 to 3.60 metres, while Jakob Le Maire and Wilhelm Schouten must have been rooted to the spot in 1615 when they saw two skeletons of similar length.

At the beginning of 1700 the giants had gone from the coast, but the Spanish authorities of Valdivia, in Chile repeatedly mentioned in 1712 a tribe of men about three metres high situated in the Patagonia interior. And in 1764 Commodore Byron, grandfather of the famous English poet, met them again near Cabo Virginies. "One of them," he said, "came towards me. He was huge and seemed to express all those legends about monsters with a human face. I was not able to measure him but he was certainly not less than 2.10 metres . . ." Which was only a modest giant, seeing that some of Byron's men spoke of beings with a height of 2.70 metres if not more.

Do giants still exist in the heart of unexplored Patagonia? Some think they still do and the 1897 discovery is worth considering in this connection. In a cave at Consuelo Cove, on the west coast of Patagonia, the skin of a recent milodont was found. A milodont is a tardigrade or slow-moving animal thought to have been extinct since prehistoric times. The giants' remains (or their descendants', rather) have turned up everywhere, and it is not just a matter of mistakes or swindles as those at Willisau, St. Antoine and Gloucester proved to be. In Lampock Rancho in California in 1833 some soldiers discovered during excavations a skeleton 3.65 metres long and surrounded by worked shells, heavy axes of stone and boulders covered in unintelligible writing; and a similar one was unearthed on the island of Santa Maria, near Los Angeles. "In July, 1887," Ronald Charles Calais says, "four men looking for precious metals in Spring Valley near Eureka, Nevada, noticed an odd object projecting from a rock. The thing was a human leg, broken off neatly above the knee. After getting rid of the quartzite around it the leg was taken to Eureka, where doctors carefully examined it. The leg was undoubtedly that of a man—but what a man! From the knee to the heel it measured 99 centimetres, which meant that the man must have had a height of 3.65 metres.

"Near Brayton, near the source of the Tennessee River there are human footprints in what today is solid rock. Those feet had six toes and are 33 centimetres wide; and near them there are gigantic hoof-marks about 20 to 26.5 centimetres broad—which proves that both the man and the animal must have existed at the same time." Then there were two enormous molars which caused a great fuss in scientific circles as they were three times as large as present-day ones and found in geological strata at least 30 million years old (this discovery was in 1920 in the coal mine called "Eagle Number 3" at Bear Creek in Montana); but some people say that bones just as old and large have been unearthed in many other American mines, but were consistently ignored by science!

But let us recall the huge six-toed feet at the source of the Tennessee and remember that at Crittenden in Arizona a number of workers in 1891 uncovered a sarcophagus whilst excavating an old building and found it contained a human being three metres high and with six toes on the feet! We have mentioned other discoveries in *The Timeless Earth* so let us deal with the most recent skeletons with a length ranging from 2.80 to 3.12 metres discovered by Soviet anthropologists in the Caucasus Mountains.

Heroes in the Making

Whoever reads the *Popol Vuh* looking for references to astronauts will certainly not be disappointed; here the Creation already seems to be linked with unknown cosmic colonizers; and even if the theory of artificial pansoermia (insemination through space) seems too bold to accept it would not be difficult to think that the Maya might have attributed it to galactic explorers landing on the Earth much later and held to be of divine origin. The "American Bible" tells us in fact that creation itself was decided "in the night and darkness, by the Heart of the Sky called Huracán" and it goes on: "His first manifestation is lightning, Caculhá. His second is thunder, Chipí Cakulhá. His third the reflector, Raxa Cakulhá". Today, at the beginning of the space age, it would be hardly necessary to allow imagination full play in order to describe the universe as an immeasurable and dark abyss; or to attribute to an astroship the rays of light, the speed of lightning and sounds of thunder all of which it could produce. Let it be noted that the sacred text expresses just this and nothing more!

Do we want a fine cosmic ferry to shuttle between

Earth and some unknown planet or celestial body? Here it is, in the description of the Huracán messenger: ". . . there was Chipí Cakulhá (the thunder), Rexa Cakulhá (the reflector). And this hawk is never far from Earth, never far from the other world: in an instant it leaps into the sky, by the side of Huracán . . ."

Other space vehicles are seen by some scholars in the embassies of the "gentleman from Beyond": ". . . they were owls, known as Owl-Lamp Owl-with-a-leg, Owl-with-the-red-skin and Owl-Head. Owl-Lamp flew like lightning, Owl-with-a-leg had only one leg, Owl-with-the-red-skin had a red back and Owl-Head had nothing but head and tail".

Here it is already necessary to use a good deal of imagination and the same thing can be said in connection with the demons, thought of as beings from space and armed in deadly fashion. Some simply "spread blood" but others "made men swell up, causing ulcers in the legs and making the face yellow", while still others "broke their legs and skulls . . . ate men to the bone and bare skull"; or "made something happen to men going home or when inside their cottages", so that they "found themselves wounded, open-mouthed and dead" or else "made the blood run from men's mouths, causing what was called "sudden death".

In these sinister people we can of course only see the personification of disease and various fatal accidents, as in the "burning chairs" which the demons invited their victims to sit in (almost as a joke) but other scholars see them as burning blocks of lava. Such interpretations appear however to be more sophisticated and the experts confess that they face undecipherable myths; where for example they find mention of four "houses" in which the citizens of the "other world" subject the Maya champions to harsh ordeals; the first one is completely silent and deep in darkness, the second is glacial "with a freezing wind which clears the white walls", the third is full of jaguars and the fourth with bats; while the fifth has dangerous knives "which beat against each other". Without mentioning the "Maya Bible" a specialist in space medicine was asked where he would think of placing the first two: "Obviously in a training-centre for future astronauts" he replied; and when asked to explain the whole business he added that a primitive people could most easily talk about jaguars, bats and knives if, not having the slightest notions about space simulators they were asked to try them. Two other facts in the *Popol Vuh* are worth considering: only strong athletes were invited to undergo the tests; and two of them on leaving said to their relatives: "Do not grieve: we are going, but we are not yet dead." But they do not survive the ordeals faced and the legend tells how the head of one of them is placed on a tree and remains alive. Now it happened that the virgin Ixquic was looking for prophetic plants when some saliva from the head fell on her and she became pregnant. Her father, believing her to be a loose woman, ordered her out of the house and arranged to have her killed; but the hired ruffians fooled him and she gave birth to twins, Huhnapú and Ixbalanqué—the two who later eliminated the last two giants.

It is true that in the story of the brothers we meet elements of the myths most common in various parts of the world (the expulsion of the mother, the pretended assassination of the children, the placing of them—much later—on an ants' nest and on thorny bushes) but the amazing fertility of Ixquic has not failed to excite the imagination of the protagonists of "spatial hypotheses". They tell us that recent work in the field of artificial conservation of male semen has stimulated United States' interest in the possibilities of organizing gigantic "semen banks" in underground shelters so as to ensure the survival of the human race if decimated by atomic war. Also cherished is the idea of sending volunteers with a good supply of semen phials to distant planets, should they prove hospitable, so that a sufficiently numerous posterity is ensured from a very few individuals who prove to have the right physical and mental equipment; and the phials would save space on board the astroships.

If not already realizable such plans could probably

be so before long, if we recall what was officially stated in April 1966 by the Michigan Gynecological and Obstetrical Society after experiments by Doctors S. J. Behrman, D. Ackerman and Y. Sawada: "Various quantities of male sperm donated by men whose physical and mental characteristics were similar to those of the husbands of the women who presented themselves for the experiment had been frozen in suitable containers and maintained at temperatures well below zero for a maximum period of two and a half years . . . and when, with the consent of the husbands and guarantee of anonymity of the donors, 55 women were artificially inseminated, 9 of the first group of 11 had successful pregnancies and gave birth normally . . . All the babies born in this way are in excellent health and show no signs of malformation."

It is natural that we should be able to put forward only inconsistent theories about the possible donors and workers in pre-Columbian America; but the achievements of Hunahpú and Ixbalanqué are really astonishing; they had, for instance, hoes and axes which could work by themselves, without being touched, and they owned a dove of wood which could tell them when strangers were approaching. Are we dealing here with an attempt to mechanize agriculture and use pocket radar? To a modern mind the descriptions seem to be such as to strengthen this idea; but it is odd that, before departing for the Beyond, Hunahpú and Ixbalanqué should plant two reeds in the dry ground and say to their grandmother: "If these reeds wither we shall die; but if they sprout it will mean that we are alive." Is it too fanciful to think of long-distance communication devices here? Imagine being ignorant of technical matters, totally ignorant, and then seeing a tube with an intermittent spark revealing the heart-beats of an astronaut or some other vital function; could it not be that we might compare it to a germinating reed?

The twins must have had a marvellous knowledge of the tricks of those who invited them into a kind of death kingdom (with no trace of souls, however!); they refused to sit on the chairs of fire and used ingenious expedients to overcome their trials in the "house of silence" etc. Finally, however, a "vampire of the night fell from the sky" to snap off the head of Huhnapú. But immediately Huracán, the "Heart of the Sky" rushed in and replaced it temporarily, after which the twins sacrificed themselves, only to rise again (some of see in this a most advanced form of surgery) and return to the void they had victoriously left to perform a series of marvels like bringing a dog back to life and instigating a fire which burnt nothing (". . . and no-body—of those inside the building—burnt, and even the house became as it was before"; is this a trick of the light?) after which they would unhinge joints as though they were those of a robot, operate on the chest and finally kill off a goodly number of the "devils".

They would be willing to revive the father and the uncle, left in unthinkable state between life and death but they do not succeed; so they leave them, saying: "You will be called. You will be summoned as the first of all and as such the sons and daughters of the light will honour you. Your names will not be lost". The epic concludes with the scent of the twins into the sky: one becomes the sun, the other the moon.

Nothing but fable? No; once again Agrest, the famous Soviet student tells us: "Here we face unquestionable reality,[2] reality such as to show us that the ancient races kept records of facts which struck their imagination profoundly and then became veiled in a halo of myth."

[2]Regarding the appearance of the sun, for example, the *Popol Vuh* expresses itself in a perfectly scientific way: "Today we see only the reflection of the sun, not the original sun . . . of which the heat was intolerable."

CHAPTER ELEVEN

MONUMENTS ON THE MOON

When the giants dominated Earth they demanded that the little men should build monuments worthy of them. And our forefathers of the distant past, set to work more unwilling than willing to construct them. Thus arose those enormous stelae, the primitive menhirs, a Breton word meaning long stone. But for the ancient Irish fortune seemed to arrange it so that some good giants were on the spot too; and these who did not have the tyrannical nature of their fellows and were devoted to men considered the cult very foolish and suggested to their protégés a plan for putting an end once and for all to the arrogance of the giants. "Build big tables and make our fellows think it is for banquets in their honour. The tables will attract the people of the night who will protect us and hold their evil in check".

So mortals did this and built rough megaliths—the dolmens, Breton for table of stone, consisting of one slab placed over two uprights fixed in the ground. This is not from a genuine text but is simply an Irish legend: the people of the emerald island could have kept a vague tradition of it seeing that their land is very rich in such buildings and other odd ones. In 1898 W. C. Borlase listed 780 dolmen there—including the Legananny unusual in its large size—and 50 room-tumuli (of which the burial-chamber of Mycenean type at Newgrange is typical, and decorated with the famous galactic spirals) 68 monuments of uncertain classification and countless menhirs, together with tomb niches of all sorts and stone circles suggesting Stonehenge and Avebury very closely.

If the legend in question had any truth in it there would be some agreement with the French cosmologist Saurat who regarded menhirs as giants and dolmen as their altars. We said some agreement because as we have seen the stone tables would only have *seemed* to be meant for giants' banquets. We certainly cannot say that the Irish legend is completely true but it can be considered as true in a different way. Even today the menhir and dolmens are veiled in mystery and although under the latter may be found human remains the tombs could at best be much later than the constructions themselves; that is to say, these last—which were no doubt built for a totally different purpose—could have been utilized as funerary monuments by the people who discovered them.

But even so, what would the "night people" have had to do with the megaliths? According to the boldest speculators one could see in these an interplanetary race of explorers; but if it is thought that the menhirs might indicate landing places, as some suggest, the distribution of the stones would hardly encourage such hypotheses. Still, the megaliths one meets all over the world have not been put up at random: their builders must have known the positions and courses of various heavenly bodies very well, which is the impression we get, too, from drawings on the rocks.

"On the 'Hi-zpgée' dolmen of Castellet (Fontvieille, Bocche del Rodano) there is the symbol of the sun-horse" says Serge Hutin, "yoked to a chariot portraying the star. Snake pictograms can be found on various megaliths and an underground chamber-tumuli at Gravrinis (island in the Gulf of Morbihan) which brings to mind the awe-inspiring crypts described by Lovecraft. Contrary to widely-held opinion it is not a tomb but a small temple: spiral snakes, horns, human feet and a goddess are also shown there. One can see the snakes in graffiti in England, in North America (Bush Creek, Ohio), in Brazil ('Pedra Pintata') and elsewhere."

The Mystery of Stonehenge

In a similar manner one could perhaps explain several prehistoric monuments the meaning of which is still a mystery. It is interesting to note in this connection what one dedicated man, Mr. Douglas Chaundy, has written about them: "When I read *Man among Mankind* by Brinsley Le Poer Trench, I was struck by what he said about the Somerset Zodiac discovered by Mr. Maltwood. Curious to know more I got a detailed map of Salisbury Plain which showed among other places of historical importance the so-called long barrows. Even without any archaeological knowledge I realized that it dealt with prehistoric constructions and I marked with a cross those I managed to trace. When I joined up the crosses I was surprised to see that they tallied with the constellations nearest to the celestial North Pole: Great Bear, Little Bear, the Dragon, Triangle and Andromeda. I also noticed that in the places where the tumuli were missing and would have completed the constellations cities had been built in many cases. My theory is that the long barrows represent the stars as they were at the time of the barrow building. Who can say, then, that the round barrows might not have symbolized the distant planets orbiting a fixed star? I also think they were built at the same time as the Temple of the Stars or The Zodiac of Somerset and Stonehenge."

Stonehenge: the most famous magic circle of them all, built a few kilometres north of present-day Salisbury. Three articles were given over to this "stone puzzle" in December 1966 by the best-known English review *Nature* one of which was signed by Professor Hoyle, unchallengeable in the field of astronomy.

What is Stonehenge?

"An open-air sanctuary, as it has been thought from the start" Giuseppe Tagliaferri tells us, "or was it an astronomical observatory as many think? Perhaps a bit of both but here we must point out those studies which tend to strengthen this idea *ante litteram* or the idea that it was a digital computer for forecasting solar and lunar events.

"The monument went through a number of building phases and we can say that the same plan has not always been kept to. At present the most salient features are:

(a) The Aubrey ring (diameter about 90 metres) concentric and with an earthwork outside, marked with 56 holes.

(b) The "Saracen" circle (diameter about 30 metres) concentric also, and with 30 stones of which some are missing today.

(c) The Hele stone, situated outside the earthwork and on the approaches.

(d) Several hollows, also on the avenue and arranged in six perpendicular lines.

(e) Two stones and two hollows connected with the Aubrey circle.

"In 1901 Locker was the first of the moderns to work on this plan and he tried to estimate the age of the building. By using astronomical calculations he tried to confirm popular belief that the chief plane of the Avenue points towards the rising sun in mid-summer. No other attempt of serious astronomical interest was made until 1963 when Hawkins thought of entrusting to an IBM 7090 computer the problem of certain measurements and reported the results in *Stonehenge Decoded* (Souvenir Press). Hawkins chose certain pairs of stones and hollows, estimated their azimuth and declination and finally compared these alignments with the position of some celestial bodies. The calculation of the deviation was made within a minute; and while no correlation of importance came to light concerning the stars and planets it was truly surprising regarding the sun and moon. The rising and setting of these at different times of the year were clearly indicated by the alignments of the stones. Hawkins then suggested other data—e.g. forecasts of eclipses—which might be obtainable by means of the Stonehenge structure.

"After recent criticisms of the work of Hawkins we see the intervention of Hoyle and Newham. Professor Hoyle concentrated on the Aubrey ring and worked out a whole theory according to which the circle would predict lunar and solar eclipses—*also the ones invisible from Stonehenge*. Newham worked on the Hele stone and the six rows of depressions on the Avenue in connection with the rising of the moon. Though we cannot go into details these studies explain how the 56 Aubrey hollows can indicate the lunar regression periods and thus anticipate the eclipses; and explain how the 30 Sarsen stones (to be exact 29 stones and one very small one) may represent the 29½ days of the lunar month, etc.; and a number of correlations between lunar-solar events and the Stonehenge structures which it is most unlikely are just accidental, even if the English of 1500 B.C. 'had not yet invented fixed homes—let alone the Royal Society' as the magazine 'Nature' amusingly pointed out."

But were the English really the builders of Stonehenge? Some people say they were from Crete and that they used Egyptian techniques at Stonehenge: a notion which could be supported by the remains of swords and bronze axes found near the monoliths in 1953. But those who study and encourage Celtic traditions, although conceding that Stonehenge is much older than the Druidic religion say that the latter's priests received fragments of a most ancient science, now lost, which would have been brought by beings from space. Here, then, is a link with the enigmatic "night people" of Irish tradition!

There are certainly many things left to discover at Stonehenge: we have heard serious students talking about boulders showing strange forms at certain times of the day, still discernible although eroded by time; and incredible light-effects seen only at intervals of months or years, besides amazing sound waves which must have been due to sudden leaps in temperatures, thus challenging the skill of the unknown builders. We have been asked not to give names—a request understandable enough if we consider the mass of esoteric speculation under which Stonehenge has been buried. It is a pity that things have turned out like this; and it is equally unpleasant that fantastic doctrines get so established that it is impossible to separate the various threads. It seems that this is the position adopted by the brilliant amateur M. E. Carey, of whom Jimmy Goddard writes in his *Enigmas of the Plain.*

"One evening in September," Mrs. Carey says, "my daughter Merilyn was entertaining two guests . . . we spoke about Stonehenge and I told them about things which had happened to me down there. A few days later my friends came back saying they wanted to go to Stonehenge to see if there really was a fish carved on those stones. We found the symbol of an elephant's head and discovered something else rather surprising; it seemed to be a bull—but when we took a photo it turned out to be a man who was taming a horse. We also found "my" fish which we likewise took a photo of and this turned out to be a canoe full of fish, with the head of a bear and a hunter!"

"One night," she wrote later about a further visit, "a stone began to shine and look like a snake with flaming eyes. It appeared to wriggle and a man came from its mouth. The body disappeared but the head stayed there and beyond I could see big fires burning. There was also the smell of burning wood. Around me there were people: not primitive Britons but the representatives of a highly civilized race . . . The temple was lit up . . . All these impressions only lasted a moment but they stayed in my mind . . ."

However strange it may be this sort of thing is not at all uncommon and even genuine scholars talk about them: like Professor Marcel Homet who saw the "Pedra pintada" of the Amazon. But Mrs. Carey adds confusing details, saying that she had "known" (by heaven knows what mysterious emanations from Stonehenge) how a great disaster might have befallen humanity in the remotest ages and how a few would have been able to save themselves from a submerged continent by reaching Great Britain, and America, assisted by the generous "people from the stars".

"We have found," she goes on, "three figures which would have referred to the celestial race: that of an individual with a helmet . . . a tunic, boots and knitted trousers: is he perhaps a member of a space crew? The second one . . . wearing a fur jacket, gloves, light tunic, belt and trousers fixed to the boots . . . There are many carvings at Stonehenge: who were the men who wore thin moustaches like pencils and a variety of headgear, including some with cow-horns?"

We could for curiosity's sake go back to Prince Rohotep of Egypt (2500 B.C.) who, portrayed together with his beautiful wife Nofret (Nefertiti) is one of the few characters of ancient times to wear such moustaches "thin as pencils". But this is not important: more interesting, perhaps, is the sequel to Mrs. Carey's tale:

"When we went to Avebury we almost had a shock . . . we were walking among huge statues with the heads of men and animals and then we stopped near the statue of a "king" on a throne. It seemed impossible to me that archaeologists could have ignored this statue. The stones at Avebury are still more wonderful than those at Stonehenge; and it is clear that the work was done by a civilized people who wore clothes and shoes. I do not know if there have ever been men here who according to legend were clothed in skins, but it is obvious that they could have built neither Stonehenge nor Avebury. To have linked these places and Tiahuanaco in Bolivia . . ."

Will it ever be possible to find the truth between the rigid attitudes of ordinary science and the bold deductions of the space theory fanatics? Will a day ever come when the bewildering world of Druidic legend shall be at least a little clearer? There are some who believe, for instance, that they can deduce from work already done that the Druid's lunar cult might have had an origin little enough connected with fantasies: or the supposed cosmic newcomers would be from the moon or have had a base on the satellite! What Flammarion writes is odd in any case: "One strange item has been left to us by Hecataeus (a Greek historian living around 500 B.C.) about the religious customs of the Britons . . . he said that the moon, seen from that island, appeared much bigger than from anywhere else and that one could even see mountains there, as on Earth. *How had the Druids made observations of this sort?* Plutarch, then, in his work *Concerning the Face on the Moon* tells us that the Gauls, in agreement with traditional science, thought that the moon contained several Mediterranean regions, likened by the Greek philosopher to the Red Sea or the Caspian. [The Gauls] had thought, however, that they could see huge chasms . . ."

The Guardians of the Seal

There are peculiar menhirs in Corsica: not just rough masses fixed in the ground but stones carved with human features. In July 1964 the archaeologist Roger Grosjean, commissioned by the CNRF to study the relics of Corsica's prehistoric past, found them first on the plateau of Cauria in the extreme south. The two finest dug up were about three metres high and they revealed harsh features underneath helmets of an odd make, with long swords hanging from their belts. Grosjean was impressed with one detail particularly: on the helmets two identical holes were made, it seems, for the horns with which many ancient warriors adorned themselves. The archaeologist went to Paris and studied all the similar ones in the museums until he found what he was looking for: this was the warlike headgear worn by the Shardanes, a maritime people from the eastern Mediterranean with whom the Egyptians were at war between 1400 and 1200 B.C. Grosjean then managed to find out that the Shardanes had invaded and conquered Corsica 35 centuries ago, exterminating the inhabitants.

The latter had no knowledge of metals; which meant
that it was the invaders who brought bronze weapons
recorded in the stone carvings. "The key," Grosjean
thinks, "is perhaps in one of Aristotle's writings when
he mentioned Iberians who erected around their tombs
as many obelisks as there were enemy dead. Perhaps
the Greek philosopher made an error only in the attribu-
tion: as is proved by archaeology the Iberians had never
had such practices—he had meant the Corsicans."

The writer Marc-Ambroise thinks of menhirs as
"quite unique"; but although his report is excellent he
is wrong in this respect—the carved menhir can be
found all over the world. The Irish ones at Cardonach
are odd, so too are those Siberian types called "baba"
(see page 10), which are funerary monuments having
much in common with those of Corsica. The way they
have been carved is curious; mostly on long masses of
stone rounded in the upper part, which has brought
about in certain archaeological circles the opinion that
this feature is a representation of virility; a view which
is untenable for various reasons but especially because,
if this were true, the sexual parts would also have been
delineated, but this does not happen.

On the other hand a valid parallel could be drawn
with the Maya stelae which according to Schmidt would
be "the logical development of the menhir". That is to
say, a "perfected" menhir; and it is a fact that the
chief characters are not portrayed in the whole figure
but symbolized in the anterior part of the monolith. The
clarifying attempts on the part of the supporters of space
hypotheses could be accepted if this is so and backed
up by the presentation of figures which have so little
of the Earth about them. "Whoever built such things,"
say some scholars, "must undoubtedly have been under
the influence of factors unknown today; why, in fact,
does no primitive population make them any more?"

A further confirmation could come perhaps from
Greece: there are not a few archaeologists busy on
Greek soil who maintain that the most remarkable ruins
often appear on the evidence of much older civilizations; and thus the Pelaggians, a people of unknown

origin in times we call prehistoric, would have settled in Greece, in Caria (Asia Minor) and in Italy—central and southern—such a people coming originally from Atlantis according to certain authorities.

Hutin attributes the oldest mining for iron on the island of Elba to the Pelasgians. The excavation revealed huge subterranean canals—like those connecting Livadia to Corinth—already known to the ancient Greeks and blocked up thousands of years B.C. so that they are of no use any longer. On Easter Island several galleries or passages linked with the sea appear to have been canals—which would explain how the water-supply system for the population of a strip of land may have been a burial-ground (as some think) of an archipelago now vanished. But how could such a supply have been achieved? Perhaps with a system like the one used three thousand miles away by the Phoenicians for supplying water to Tyre, conducted to the island by means of an underwater canal?

But there is something else on Easter Island: "At the southern end of the island," writes M. J. Thompson, "there are from 80 to 100 stone houses built in a regular line against a terrace of rock which in some cases is the basement wall of the buildings. Their walls are 1.52 metres thick and 1.20 metres broad; they are made of irregular stones and painted red, white and black, with bird emblems, human faces and various objects. Near the houses the rocks have been carved in a strange manner and portray tortoises, fish and mythological animals; but above all birds."

Alfred Métraux says in *The Marvellous Island of Pasqua* "The biggest religious festival on the island, the only one on which there are exact details, was that of the bird-man which was intimately linked with the cult of the god Makemake. This long mystical drama, performed every year on the cliffs at Orongo, not only had a deep religious meaning but profoundly influenced the social life on the island. The discovery and ownership of the first egg of "manutara", laid on the small island of Motu-nui, was the chief object of the rites every year and it caused violent emotions. The aim can seem disproportionate to the effort put into it and the risks run by those who hunted such a meagre booty; but only someone ignorant of the power behind the symbols can smile at such an undertaking. The egg was the incarnation of the god Makemake and the tangible expression of a religious and social power of great depth. The placing of stakes in the struggle for the first egg meant divine favours and the sanctioning of political power."

Métraux is certainly not indulging in theories foreign to those outlined by official science, for whoever follows the legends linked to the mythical bird all over the world, whoever stops to consider even out of sheer curiosity but without derisive smiles all the rites and legends with the "fire-bird" or the "thunder-bird" as the centre-piece—for him the festival on Easter Island assumes a significance much more than merely suggestive. *Getting possession of the egg meant becoming a man-bird oneself, like gods descended from the stars; it meant gaining the illusion of being for a whole year near the fantastic creatures whose record is still fixed deep in texts inspired by ageless traditions?* "Behold, the flying men arrive . . . the men with the hat flying . . ."

As is known, the present-day inhabitants of Easter Island are of Polynesian extraction—yet in Polynesia there does not exist—and has never existed any contact with the man-bird festival. But by contrast rites similar to the Easter Island festival still take place everywhere in America even if most of them are cloaks and coronets of feathers, symbolical wings and tails to represent the fabled bird!

But returning to the carved menhirs we shall be reminded of those people who see them closely related to the Easter Island statues; and even think of some of them as not being entirely unrelated to the positions of certain stars as observed from the island! In this connection certain South American legends see the giants of this peculiar island one day being able to live again with the aid of magic. Only a legend, agreed, but we should like to know if the writer Donald Wandrei has used it for his book *Cimitierre de l'effroi*[1] in which is imagined a mysterious lineage that would unite Stonehenge and Easter Island to indicate the coming of some universal catastrophe.

"When the stars are in the positions prophesied then the Titans will wake up and return. Earth will open wide and from an abyss deeper than the clouds are high the Guardian of the Seal will become as big as the Titans and will place himself on Crltul Thr. The waters will boil, the Earth will open and the stars shall rise in a sky of flame. From their Universe, beyond the stars, the Titans will descend. They shall reclaim for themselves every living thing, they who have made us of the dust and the fire that consume us. This will be fulfilled when the giants shall awaken, when the stars will arrive in their appointed places unless there comes one to confront and defeat the Guardian of the Seals. Then the Guardian will turn to stone and the Titans will wait in the great sphere until the stars shall no more return again to the positions fixed by prophecy . . ."

Monoliths among the Craters?

Another account we have probably mentioned elsewhere speaks of the landing of the cosmic explorers on the moon and tells how they go through unimaginable difficulties to reach a strange rock formation and then stand amazed at the foot of a monument to a majestic, bearded man on which is clearly written "To the King of Atlantis, the first cosmonauts", or something of that sort. Of course people think that the moon has been explored or inhabited for centuries or decades. They are in excellent company, seeing that Lucian of Samosata with other ancient thinkers no less famous saw odd animals and other extraordinary beings on our satellite. And there are still some people who see ex-

---

[1] Let us note that the statues of Easter Island are extremely heavy, so it is unthinkable that they were erected by means of wooden rollers. The officials of the warship *Topaz* had to use more modern means and over 500 men in order to lift one only 2.5 metres high.

amples of space fauna in certain details of the photo taken by Russian and American probes like the shapes of unknown astronauts. It is clear that with the help of a little dose of fantasy one can see a bit of everything in these fascinating pictures when exposed to the tricks of light and shade. If, then, there had really been something to support the idea of a strange presence on the moon the scholars would not have failed to stress the fact, considering that the material collected has been subject to the most thorough examination. Unexpected proofs have arisen from these examinations, certainly not as sensational as the theory which maintains that there is life on the moon, but still amazing enough. William Blair speaks of this, and he is certainly no casual observer but a famous specialist in physical anthropology and archaeology occupying one of the highest places in the "Boeing" Institute of Biotechnology. What attracted the attention of Blair to these things was a photo taken by Lunar Orbiter 2 from the western edge of the Sea of Tranquility and published by NASA on November 2nd 1966. It was immediately nicknamed the photo of the cuspids for the very clear shadows on it had allowed the typical lunar landscape to stand out distinctly. The biggest of these shadows was like the one the Washington Monument throws early in the morning or late in the afternoon. The highest of the obelisks measured about 213 metres, while the lowest must have had the proportions of above-average size spruce trees.

These formations have struck several scientists who however had not risked any explanations: references to lunar buildings as shown by their natural formations are a good enough reason for caution, which Doctor Richard Shorthill exemplified when he spoke of the cuspids as the "result of some geophysical event" —a vague enough definition which seemed acceptable to most but not to Blair, who thought the argument could be nullified by the very simplest terms of reference: by turning to our own prehistoric monuments as seen from the air.

"If the cuspids really were the result of some geophysical event," he said, "it would be natural to expect to see them distributed at random: as a result the triangulation would be scalene or irregular, whereas those concerning the lunar objects lead to a basilary system, with co-ordinates x, y, x, to the right angle, six isosceles triangles and two axes consisting of three points each."

What Blair calls "a highly speculative analysis in its use of hypothetical co-ordinates" includes a "ditch" or rather a vast rectangular depression to the west of the biggest spire. "The shadow thrown by such depressions," he stresses, "seems to suggest four angles at 90 degrees, and the structure persuades one to think it is like an excavation whose walls have been eroded or fallen inwards."

Other students have asked, not without a certain degree of irony, if Blair means by these remarks that the cuspids are perhaps the work of intelligent beings, observation or navigation instruments, or a direct communications system? "Do you want me to confirm it so that you can discredit me?" replied Blair, "well, I will tell you this: if a similar thing had been found on Earth archaeology's first concern would have been to inspect the place and carry out trial excavations to assess the extent of the discovery."

The sceptics can only reply by suggesting that there could be special conditions where the structure of the natural phenomena is odd enough to make one think of symmetrical formations. "But if this 'axiom' had been applied to similar structures on Earth," retorts Blair, "more than half the Maya and Aztec architecture known today would have still been buried under hills and depressions covered in trees and woods . . . 'a result of some geophysical event'; archaeology would never have developed and most of the facts relating to human evolution would have remained veiled in mystery."

The moon still conceals innumerable enigmas, from the shining obelisks to the domes distributed everywhere; from the strange cross formations photographed by Robert E. Curtis, an astronomer of Alamogordo and shown by the *Harvard University Review*, to the very peculiar block photographed by Sond 3 in July 1965 and published by *Pravda* in an impressive enlargement. Nevertheless the Blair cuspids make one think. We consider them as natural formations: but we should still feel obliged to admit that they are the first of this type we have ever seen; because if they had been produced by chance we would find ourselves faced with something even more amazing than giving a piece of chalk to a monkey which then proceeds by mere chance to set out the Pythagoras theorem.

CHAPTER TWELVE

THE IMPRINT OF MU

An old Caroline legend says that one day long ago some white strangers arrived in shining boats at Ponape. They did not speak our language but there were people of our race with them so that we could make ourselves understood even if their terminology was somewhat different and their customs had for long years been adapted to those of the foreigners, who told beautiful stories about a land by the sea, with wonderful buildings and happy people. These newcomers taught us strange miracles and so there arose new islands on the ocean. Our ships sailed safely on the waves and no enemy, no matter how strong could defeat us. But one day a big storm began and managed to achieve what the enemies had failed to do. Superb buildings were swept away within hours; and once flowering islands full of songs were sent with their inhabitants to the bottom. Though the strangers survived to urge our people to begin all over again the latter were too lazy and ignored their masters' exhortations.

Thus the island people fell and brother no longer knew his brother.

This legend is from Carolina and appears to refer specifically to Ponape Island in the Senyavin Archipelago. Just a bit of land like any other? Hardly, since here there existed gigantic ruins, amazing ones, among which was a basalt temple with ten-metre high walls still existing today, encircled by other ruins and a labyrinth of canals and terraces; and it was in Ponape itself that Churchward thought he could identify one of the seven legendary cities of Mu. "Huge buildings constructed on artificial islands, square or rectangular and with parapets on top" wrote Jean Dorsenne at that time, "enormous basalt blocks made it a gigantic Venice."

Who were the strangers that could not speak the language of Ponape? The white men of tradition accompanied by Polynesian workers already technically highly developed? What were their "shining boats" and "magical works" and "ships that flew on the waves"? We could here indulge in flights of fancy but let us remember that present-day ship builders are dealing with glass boats and hover-craft; and that while we would think of our marvellous achievements as the products of a most advanced system we, too, would be judged with like criteria by a primitive population.

Ponape is however not the only island with fascinating riddles: at Mangaia, south of Cook, ruins like those of Easter Island have been found according to Serge Hutin. Tongo Tabu has a stone tomb weighing over 170 tons; while Kuki in Hawaii has vast ruins and Navigator a very lovely redstone "platform". The Mariana Islands have pillars of truncated cones which cannot be explained. "In November 1938," Hutin records, "the brothers Bruce and Sheridan Fahrestack returned to New York from an expedition lasting two years, during which they found in the island of Manua Levu in the Fiji Islands, a monolith of 40 tons bearing an unknown script. This was an archaeological riddle which the papers spoke of as evidence of the vanished continent of Mu."

As for Tinian, in a part of the United States Oceania, Baron D'Espiard of Cologne says: "The island is literally covered in columns and pyramidal formations on a square base which could never have been used for building anything . . . These pillars are made of sand and other material which has been compressed and then topped with a hemisphere having the flat side uppermost . . . At Rimatara there are remains of high columns one of which measured 20 metres and was placed above a base now virtually vanished. On all the peaks on Rapa, further to the south-east, hardly thirty kilometres in circumference, there are remnants of huge forts . . ."

Is Ponape one of the relics of the legendary Mu continent? If as some people think Mu was a vast continental mass in the Pacific or a huge archipelago it seems to us that the Caroline legend refers not to its "envoys"; the allusion to a land situated "where the sea now is" and to sunken islands of a vanished empire but rather to a polynesian region which, according to the American archaeologist McMillan-Brown, had Ponape as its capital city. If this were in fact so then we could think of the "white strangers" as survivors of Mu who were trying to restore at least the semblance of ancient splendour.

The last sparks

One speaks of Mu and of James Churchward at the same time, since this traveller and scholar has certain remarkable merits in the scientific world, but his theosophical digressions must be set aside and ignored. Churchward was a colonel in India in 1868 and thus came in contact with several monks who revealed the secret of the vanished continent to him. The problem fascinated him, so he left military service and undertook long journeys looking for factors which would support what he had been told. He visited the Carolines and all the archipelagos of the southern Pacific as well as Tibet, Burma, Egypt, Siberia, Australia, New Zealand, U.S.A. and central America. He collected some very interesting facts but not such as would confirm his theories completely that Mu would have played a vital part in the creation and evolution of this planet's greatest civilizations.

He might thus have had information about the discoveries brought to light by the American geologist William Niven in Mexico: the latter studied the ancient ruins here and without knowing anything about Churchward at the time reached the same conclusions. Afterwards the two men together examined more than 2,600 stone slabs and found themselves in full agreement in their view that the vanished continent had played a part of prime importance in the Earth's unknown past.

Unfortunately we do not know at what stage Churchward was influenced by these odd, esoteric ideas; but with Serge Hutin, a serious student of the problem, we can still say, contrary to what certain irresponsible and prejudiced people would have us believe, that Churchward's and Niven's ideas are not just humbug. The famous stone slabs existed, and Doctor Morlay of the Carnegie Institute, who had studied them for years, asserted that they were "authentic objects with symbols absolutely unknown in Mexico and other regions of pre-columbian America" and that they were "linked with a totally unknown civilization". According to Churchward it was precisely from Mu that the culture spread out to cover the world. The continent had occupied a large part of the Pacific and would have been sunk about 12,000 years ago; its remains could be seen today in the islands Marquesas, Hawaii, Mariana, Caroline, Gilbert, Marshall, Tongas, Samoa, Tahiti, Cook and Easter. To support this the scholar brings forward Niven's stone slabs, documents discovered in India, Burma, Tibet and Cambodia, besides Maya inscriptions found in Mexico and Yucatan; also traditions typical of various islands in the Pacific and traces found in southern parts of America—and finally Egyptian and Greek writings.

Hutin refers again to Mu—which other people confusingly identify with the mythical Lemuria or even

with Gondwanaland: "Among the Madagascans we
find ancient allusions to the fabled city of Cerné in
the Indian Ocean. The peoples of Oceania have also
kept their records of a great deluge as a result of
which human beings would have found themselves "at
the bottom of the waters, there where the white gods
sleep". All the legends of Hawaii, the New Hebrides
and New Zealand talk about a white-skinned race with
fair hair who might have preceded the polynesian
sailors. An Easter Island tale describes how Hotu
Matua, the great legendary law-giver of the island,
came from a nearby region sunk by a vast cataclysm.
And other fables tell us how the same Polynesians
originated from a continent now largely submerged.
Among the Bushmen's rock drawings in South Africa
we do find at last some which are undoubtedly not
theirs but were carved by a highly civilized maritime
race from Indo-China or Malaysia."

Churchward says that the Mediterranean cultures
would have arisen from the death of Mu, first the
Egyptian and Babylonian. Others see these as coming
from Atlantis while still others from an encounter or
confrontation between the representatives of the great
empires now lost—and the southern Mediterranean
would have been the theatre of such meetings.

French students of the problem think that the Gobi
Desert ruins, discovered by the Soviets when using aircraft in their researches, may conceal one of the biggest
secrets of Mu if not the capital itself. Others who
base their opinion chiefly on the term Naacals, share
the view of the French historian Jean Roy: "In the
Indus valley there once flourished a great civilization
3,500 years ago of an ancient Dravidian race which
several centuries later absorbed the white-skinned
Vedas and the dark-skinned Melanides. The latter were
originally from the Tarim basin near Lob-Nor in Sinki-
ang, and they penetrated all the Indus valleys by crossing the Karakorum Pass, bringing a knowledge of
decimals to the Dravidians—usually called 'Arabic' because it was much later brought to the West by
Arab incursions and trade. The Dravidians gave the

name Naacals to the Melanides which meant high
brothers the origin of which could be explained from
their coming down out of the Karakorum, where there
are peaks 7,000 to 8,600 metres high. Among the
Naacals only the wisest knew about the decimal system
which they did not claim as their own invention, however."

But other people think that the inheritors of Mu
had founded the first Chinese dynasties and consider
Yao to be the most illustrious, whose reign would
have started around 2357 B.C.—he is the king to
whom Confucius ascribes kindness, wisdom, sense of
duty, etc., quoting the famous words: "If my people
suffer from cold it is up to me to provide for them; if
my people are hungry it is my fault; and if my people
commit crimes I alone am responsible." Shun succeeded
Yao, and followed the wise policy of his predecessor,
building a vast network of roads, bridges and passes
through the enormous land. Because of these works
some scholars attribute the silk road to him, stretching
for about ten thousand kilometres from Si-An-Fu,
capital of the Chinese province of Shensi, to Palmyra
and Antioch; and from the Pacific to the Mediterranean. It is thought by some that this most famous road
was built later—though the scientists object that at first
it was intended for trade in general and not just
for silk; besides which it seems that fragments of silk
date from an extremely remote period and not from
the time history usually gives it—such fragments having been discovered near Tun-huang in Turkestan. And
even on the south-western and south-eastern shores of
the Mediterranean we have references to the breeding
of silkworms, according to the elucidators of ancient
texts, in a time much more remote than the one
usually assigned to silk from that area.

On the silk road

Entering Turkestan at Kashgar this road goes at 1,500
metres above sea-level, according to Ivar Lissner,
through a fertile oasis of the Red River, the Qyzyl Su.

From here, across the Terek Pass at 4,000 metres it reached the legendary Ferghana. There are more earthquakes in the maritime zones as a rule but here in the heart of Asia they have been recorded at Kashgar and handed down from generation to generation. Passing from Khotan at 1,406 metres in the Tarim basin the caravans pushed on towards Tun-huang, the famous oasis of temples and caves. A northern route led to Turfan, 15 metres above sea-level in the region of Uigur, where fields of ruins had been brought to light . . . From Tun-huang to Sian-Fu, the capital of the Shensi province, it proceeds direct. As the great Swedish explorer Sven Hedin said, it is an unforgettable experience.

The road revealed an amazing and quite unexpected panorama: "Instead of a Turkish-speaking country the investigators discovered Indo-Germanic peoples along the silk road till the eighth century; Iranians and even Europeans. Many manuscripts contained their idioms but some were unknown. These were translated and scientifically examined at London, Paris and Berlin. The Indo-Germanic and Turkish scholars found they had to deal with 17 different languages and 24 varieties of writing."

On March 28th 1900 Sven Hedin found near the drained Lopnor Lake the ruins of the city of Lou-lan containing manuscripts of the greatest archaeological importance. "These fragments would have spoken about the age in which Lopnor flourished and about the men who lived here—also of their links with other parts of the Asian hinterland and the name of their country. The latter was engulfed by seismic phenomena but would have been brought to light with the peoples long ago forgotten and not mentioned in the manuscripts . . ."

The Lou-lan documents were written in clear, excellent Chinese while the wood carvings showed obvious Hellenic and Indian influences—evidence that these peoples of A.D. 300 had many Mediterranean contacts and with India. Much later some corpses from a cemetery were exhumed and found to be perfectly preserved both physically and in their clothing, though it is not known how. But some of these bodies did not belong to any yellow race or any other one along the silk road of those days: *they seemed to be a cross with an unknown race!*

The strangest legends circulate about the oasis at Kashgar—just one of the road's many deep mysteries. Genghis Khan and Marco Polo stayed here; also the famous first century A.D. Chinese warrior Pan Chao is buried there. The spot may also conceal the "man of jade", a legendary hero who could "walk in the sky" and "let loose green thunder-bolts"—expressions which are inexplicable unless one refers to the "space hypotheses".

For more than 200 days of the year Kashgar is enveloped in a huge cloud of sand, raised by winds from the Takla Makan desert. Another tale says the "demons from the sky" set up house here as they could not be seen by human beings. Indeed, whoever wants to hide himself and yet find conditions where life could be maintained would have discovered in Kashgar an excellent refuge. If Shi Huang Ti, the builder of the Great Wall and founder of the Ts'in dynasty had not been so foolish and arrogant as to want to destroy the past so that he could be "the first lord of earth" he would not have destroyed all the documents of wood, bamboo and parchment and we would have known a great deal more about remote Chinese history than we do at present. This despotism lasted only twelve years, from 221 to 209 B.C. but it was enough. The anarchic Han dynasty followed, during which Buddhism came to China; years afterwards, probably from A.D. 357 to 384 there arose one of those great monuments to this religion, the one represented by the completion of the artificial cavern 16 kilometres to the north of the city of Tun-huang and known as the grottoes of the 1000 Buddhas. "There are several similar places in central Asia," said Lissner, "for instance the caverns of Yun-kang, those of the Lung Men near Loyang and the Lou Lan ones of Qyzyl. At Tun-huang the strange caverns had a corridor leading to an entrance hall, behind

which were several large rooms. The caverns lying at
the same height were linked by a kind of stairway so
that one could go from one sanctuary to another. In the
inside wall of the basement there were niches with clay
figures in them, with marvellous scenes painted on the
walls".

At Tun-huang too there were strange legends—unfortunately not verifiable. It was said for instance that
the first caverns were not actually built by Buddhist
monks but by someone who had preceded them by
thousands of years; and such structures must have
hidden the entrance to the labyrinths stretching under
vast areas of central Asia. They are the tunnels of the
legendary kingdoms of Shambhala and Agarthi (or
Agartha or Agharti) which kept the secrets of an extraterrestrial race . . . perhaps the one which brought
Mu to an extremely high level of culture. It is also
said that the first section of the galleries would have
been blocked up by the priests to stop bandits getting
inside and stealing their hidden treasures.

And who knows if there may not still be something
concerning Mu in the caverns of Tun-huang. When in
1907 the great English archaeologist Sir Aurel Stein
went there he discovered several manuscripts and silk
paintings which were unfortunately weathered to fragments; others were taken away the next year by the
Frenchman Paul Pelliot and those which could be slowly restored are now kept in the British Museum or in
the Louvre and the National Library in Paris. Several
could not be restored and among these unfortunately
were some astronomical and geographical charts, one
of which showed an area of the Pacific which could
even have been a part of the submerged continent.

But there is one certain thing about Tun-huang: in
the grotto numbered 58 by the archaeologists there is
an altar showing a sleeping Buddha, behind whom are
crowds of the faithful, together with good and bad
genii. We can ignore the latter as being unknown or
simply due to the artists' whims—but there are some
which clearly show by their clothes and facial features
that they are just like the American Indians! It is also

odd that in a previous expedition (1900–1901) Sir Aurel Stein found a number of letters and documents in the deserted city of Khotan, in eastern Turkestan about which Lissner wrote: "They were in an ancient Indian language, fixed to wooden tablets, tied up and sealed. The seals were Grecian and one could see in them an Athena, a Hercules and other divinities. During the second expedition Stein then found at Miran, a site of some ruins near Lop-nor, some Buddhist sanctuaries with wall paintings of the 4th century A.D. and in greco-roman style".

Does this explain the silk road? Perhaps, although somewhat difficult to piece together in view of commercial influences so deep and frequent. Some people who think of Mu and Atlantis as the mothers of all cultures consider there has been a separation of the various elements instead of associations which, if they had happened would have continued in view of the fact that communications were improving with the passage of time. But Lissner says in connection with the other end of the silk road: "The road went through Palmyra, the Aramaic Tadmor, the city of Queen Zenobia, who for a short time ruled over an empire which today still shows traces of Far East influences in its ruins. The road led across Ctesifon, chief residence of the king of the Parthians and so of the Sassanides, to Ectabana, now called Hamadan. Here we find in the capital, Media, a strong fortress with a row of palaces, columns and cedarwood or cypress houses on a low hill. This was estimated by the Parthians and the Archaemenidians so highly that they had covered the wooden parts of their buildings with sheets of gold and silver. Rhages, the Elamite city was mentioned in the Book of Tobias: the summer is wonderful here in what today is called Rej, south of Teheran and it is not hard to understand why the kings spent part of the year, March, April and May there. When the caravans crossed Bactra they traded in gold because the gold of Bactra was as highly prized as Chinese silk . . ." So here again we find a culture which kept and probably still does keep many secrets.

Palmyra is the city which under Zenobia spread its influence, while she reigned in place of her son from A.D. 267, from the Euphrates to the Mediterranean and from Arabia to central Asia Minor. Lissner thought it showed influences from the Far East; and yet it is different basically from all the others and as fascinating as the legends around it. One of these says Palmyra was the heir of the "secrets of Ugarit", the city of Canaan of which nothing at all was known before 1929. We know little about such secrets, only that Ugarit had, 3000 years B.C., streets, houses, fortifications and hygienic establishments acknowledged to be incredible by the archaeologist concerned and that objects originating in Crete had been found in one of its tombs. These dated back to 1900–1750 B.C. and some had unknown functions. Electricity is sometimes held to be one of the secrets: though we can say nothing regarding this it is odd to note that the Sirenian women used amber spindles in the remotest times.

"Such spindles," says de Agostini, "would attract small threads and straws and make them stick on the clothes of the spinners: hence the name 'electron' (Greek) giving the word 'electricity' for the physical phenomena observed for the first time in amber." But if we follow the silk road we pass across Ctesiphon (or Ctesifon) a few kilometres to the south-east of Badgad. Ctesiphon was the home of the Sassanides and during this dynasty (A.D. 226–630) the electric batteries were made which were recently discovered, in a Bagdad museum, to be still capable of functioning.

As for Ectabana the chief legend to note is that which says the city was not founded by human beings but by those who "came from the sky on metal steeds". Is this perhaps one of those impressive "gryphons" as symbolized at Persepolis? Or one of the "winged wild beasts" which are said to be still sleeping under the ruins of Rhage? Or even one of the flying Afghan horses uncovered in Ghaban province which are perhaps still erect, imposing and threatening, on the fabled Bactra road?

Minotaurs from Space

Maybe the key to all these legends is written in some indecipherable characters somewhere along the branch of the silk-road which leaves Ctesiphon and goes down east of Babylonia and Seleucia to the Persian Gulf, among the mysterious remains of cities found here which used to rule the whole of Mesopotamia: Ur, Eridu, Larsa, Uruk, Lagash, Suruppak, Kish, Eanunna, Upi. It is not too risky to imagine a presumerian culture, since four thousand years before Christ, when this mysterious race (neither Semitic nor Indo-European nor of any other known people) settled between the Tigris and the Euphrates, it already possessed a considerable culture. But it was subject to barbarian invasions which caused great havoc and introduced human sacrifices with its pillaging. But towards 2600 B.C. the country rose again, thanks to the wisdom and greatness of King Gudea, as related by a splendid epitaph: "Under his reign the slave was the equal of all men and the weak could rest in peace by the strong". But immediately afterwards the Elamites came down from the north and began with Hammurabi the Babylonian culture; but, as Lissner says, "from the entire Assyro-Babylonian culture and the clever Semites only the ancient Sumerian forms rose again". And once again these factors let us have a glimpse of the most unexpected links.

From the ruins of the Sumerian cities we watch the shadows of the cat-men whose emblems of stone look at us from the ruins of pre-columbian America. At the Berlin Museum there is a statuette dating back to about 3000 B.C. showing, some people assert, the king Lugal-Kisalsi; but others say it is the goddess Mammu. The false beard seems to accentuate still further the cat-like ears and eyes, while the mouth and nose seem to have both feline and human features. Just as in America the "cat-god" is portrayed as a wild beast, here are the lions of the goddess Ishtar and the discoveries of Tell Ugair, of which Harmut Schmöckel wrote in *Discoveries in Mesopotamia:* "whichever divinity wanted to be honoured in such a way we have not been allowed to know; and we still do not know if the leopard—some think it is a lion—has any connection with the cult of the divinity as it stands there seeming to guard the stairs. Then there is still the question whether its beauty and aggressive attitude, and it is an animal which no longer exists in Iraq and only rarely met in the mountains of Kurdistan nowadays, might have some symbolical significance. It is thought by some that the statues of the cat-men spread all over central and southern America represent an ancient race the tradition of which, handed down from generation to generation, might have brought about the origin of the jaguar-cult. The animal would have been a reminder of the features of a vanished race, symbolizing agility and power at the same time.

And what about the creatures with the excrescent horns on their foreheads who hover between science and fantasy every now and then, to emerge from the myths to be considered by the boldest scholars as representatives of a race long vanished from the face of the Earth, or the minotaurs, satyrs and demons of medieval traditions?

The origins of these horned helmets must be sought, they say, in some such direction, where the forefathers of the ancient warriors would have known how to equal the strength of the bull-men. Whilst not agreeing with such theories we ought at least to mention that even in fairy-tales beings of the sort we have mentioned have been connected with cosmic legends. Among the last Columbian natives, descendants of the Muisca who gave platinum to the Old World[1] there were still vestiges of the epic of the "horned god who descended from the sun". And it is precisely in Lavapatas that we see the horned head of a man! In Columbia itself!

Returning to Mesopotamia we cannot fail to be

[1] F. de Agostini: "When the Spaniards discovered Columbia they found the Muisca Indians purifying silver so that it shone like gold and, like gold, could not rust. Martino d'Ulloa found it in the gold-bearing sands of Columbia and gave it the name of platinum. This metal was sacred to the Muisca sun-god whose great festival was celebrated every fifteen years."

amazed at the bull of Assurbanipal and gaze in awe at
its human head with beard, horn and feathers, the
wings sprouting from the shoulders and the figure
(which has a fifth leg invisible from the front but seen
from the side gives the illusion of walking) which brings
to mind at the same time the powerful bulls deified
by very distant populations; and the "fire-bird", the
creatures with the feline features. What, then, are we
to say about the winged lions, the bulls with the human
heads and the amazing monsters of Babylonia? "From
this series," writes Schmökel, "we shall choose the
eagle-lion motif which the Sumerians called Imdugud
. . . It was at el Obed, near Ur, that R. F. Hall found
the model in 1911 of the eagle-lion on the animals.
The eagle, with its wings spread in all its majesty and
with the lion head rising above the cornice, stands
threateningly suspended above two red deer . . . With
his claws Imdugud seizes the deer, his prey . . .

"There is now the question of how this fascinating
and most effective Sumerian motif (together with
others) disappeared for years or, let us be cautious
here, not come across by us, and then newly emerged
from obscurity and may have undertaken a triumphal
career in a world totally different. In fact we do meet
the eagle-lion again, likewise with two animals seized
by its claws on Byzantine and Moorish silks of the
ninth century A.D.; and in the twelfth we encounter it
as a "basilisk" on flocks of animals on the façade of a
pillar in the cathedral at Autun (Saône-et-Loire) and a
century later on certain Sicilian brocades!

"We see it again as a picture in the vault of the
Clermont cathedral crypt (Puyde Dôme, France thirteenth century) and with a surprising likeness in one
of the capitals at St. Pierre ad Aulnay (Charente In-
ferieure). But we also find this Persian symbol in the
portico of the Borromeo Palace on the Bella Island in
Lake Maggiore, where the eagle is hung on two uni-
corns antithetically arranged . . . Then there are the
embroideries of the Greek islands (seventeenth and
eighteenth centuries) which show us this virtually immortal motif. Finally they are also kept up by the pop-

ular art in northern Russia. Let us marvel at this pervasive effectiveness of a Sumerian symbol the original significance of which has not been understood for a long time."

But does it really deal with a symbol of the remotest antiquity, adapted to express the descent on to Earth (by the wings, i.e. flight) of creatures from space? Unfortunately we cannot go beyond conjecture: the witnesses of our presumed continent of Mu spoke a language too confused and too fragmentary, but let us however make at least some attempt to interpret it.

CHAPTER THIRTEEN

THE COUNTRY OF THE BLUE MEN

When Doctor Ulrich Schmucker, now teaching at the University of California, occupied himself with terrestrial magnetism he had a disturbing experience: when examining two basalt domes very close to each other he found that they had been magnetized in completely different directions. The first had been formed in relatively recent times while the second was around the 20 million year mark. For Schmucker it was like consulting two different compasses, one showing North as it is today and the other the North of 20 million years ago!

Furthermore the North of that remote epoch was lying in what today is a southerly direction! There was no doubt about this and for the simplest of reasons: the basalt rocks (of volcanic origin and by far the commonest on Earth) are directed on cooling by the magnetic field existing at the time; if, for instance an eruption were now to take place the measurements would show that the solidified lava would be magnetized in the compass needle direction—that is, North.

164

Before Schmucker's work a great study of the subject had been undertaken by the famous German geologist Hermann Reich of Göttingen, who wrote: "Lava streams solidified during and after the glacial age up to the time of 500,000 years ago show normal magnetization; but rocks of volcanic origin and antediluvian sediments are magnetized in the opposite way. In Pliocene rocks formed from 2 to 12 million years ago the magnetization shown is partly the normal and in part the opposite, while in the Miocene rocks (still older) of 12 to 26 million years of age there must have been a great change in the direction of magnetization. In the recent geological past there must have been four alterations of this nature at intervals of about 500,000 years."

Researches into the so-called fossil magnetism were begun in 1895 by another German scientist, Professor Folgereiter, who worked on earthenware, which is always somewhat magnetized. This is because it contains in its clay some particles of magnetic oxides of iron which in the course of the heat process are aligned along the existing magnetic field. Folgereiter's studies led to amazing results, since some Etruscan terracotta revealed a quite different magnetization from the one appropriate to it for the Christian epoch! It was said at first that the pottery examined dated back to about 5–8 centuries B.C., but today there is some doubt about the date, since one should rather think of it dating back thousands of years rather than centuries. The same can be said of certain statuettes of the archaic central-American culture, thought by some to be from 3000 to 1000 years B.C., though a date of at least 12,000 years has been put forward. But we can be certain that in the course of the millennia the Poles have changed their positions several times. One such was confirmed in March 1968 with a communication from the National Science Foundation of the United States which reported the discovery in the mountainous central Antarctic regions around 525 kilometres from the South Pole of the jaw-bone of an amphibian extinct for a very long time—one which seemed much like a crocodile. This was part of the skeleton of a Labyrinthodont brought to light by an expedition organized by Ohio University and led by geologist Peter J. Barrett. "It is clear," said the *Associated Press* in this connection, "that an amphibian of this type could only have survived in a hot climate, or at least a warm one, and that therefore the Antarctic must once have been absolutely free of ice. The animal's jaw-bone found by American scientists could be an extreme demonstration as convincing as could be of the theory of the polar shifts." One of the polar shifts, we should point out; many factors tend to show that the most important mutation as regards human history must have taken place between 20 and 6 thousand years ago.

When East was West

Logically the Earth's axis cannot be displaced as a result of phenomena on our own planet: such a thing could happen only as a result of events which would not be limited to such a displacement but would have caused the destruction of the entire planet. The catastrophes must thus have been brought about by external forces —by events capable of making such a shift but not one which would fatally affect the planet. To take a rather hackneyed but convincing example we might think of a sphere of glass or crystal illuminated by a powerful lamp, hanging from the ceiling, as we cannot imagine it suspended in space. What could cause it to shift? Either the explosion of the lamp, which would probably destroy it, or a collision of some violence. Thus it would be right to admit that a phenomenon of this sort might well have befallen Earth. But what can have caused it? One thing only—another celestial body. In the case of Mu the tablets found by Churchward at Lhasa there is mention of a vague "Bal" star which "fell where today there is only sea" and would thus have caused the sinking of the continent about 12,000 years ago. But it is most likely to have been an asteroid rather than a planet or star: an asteroid which passing very close to the Earth would have pulled it out of its own orbit and made Atlantis sink—something which world-wide tradition calls the "universal deluge".

Charroux refers to one such theosophically unacceptable one when he talks about the Egyptian god Toth, or Hermes Trismegisths as the Greeks called him, who was law-giver, inventor of writing and initiator of the arts and sciences. He foresaw the deluge and probably had all human knowledge written on stelae then in Syrian territory.[1] And he refers to another version of the same story when talking about a Chaldean tradition according to which the god Chronos warned the king Xisuthrus about a deluge coming and the sovereign commanded that the writings concerning the beginning, the middle and the end of all things should be hidden at Sisparis, the sun-city. He then had them put on board a ship "which landed like the ark in Armenia but on Mount Kurkura".

But the French writer was certainly right to stress that amongst all peoples a legend spoke of a flood which only one man would survive; the Lithuanian Mannus, the Hindu Manu, the Egyptian Menes and the Greek Minos. "Eskimo, Lapp and Finnish traditions, among which is the 'Kalevala' all speak about Earth being convulsed and 'the low becoming the high' or a world fire breaking out, to be followed by the deluge. In America, too, there is a tradition similar to the Biblical story and even the redskins remember very old tales connected with the Flood."

Becoming steadily more wide-spread is the idea that Egyptian civilization has its source in times much remoter than those usually assigned to it. Herodotus says that from its birth till the time in which he lived (490/480–431/421 B.C.) 11,340 years had elapsed (*Histories* Book Two). The calculation is not exact as it is based on number of generations; but this does not exclude the possibility that Egyptian history—including the unknown part—occupied a period of time equally remarkable as the one given. Let us quote Herodotus.

[1] It seems that Egypt may not have been disastrously affected by the devastations that touched all other regions of the world.

He says in his *Histories*: ". . . the gods of Egypt's past had not yet appeared but the sun had risen four times in the sky in places different from the one where it now rises; twice it rose where now it sets, then setting where it now rises . . ."

This is clearly a reference to a change in the Earth's axis. Charroux observes that the Harris papyrus speaks of a cosmic cataclysm "of fire and water" following which "the South became the North and Earth turned round"; and that papyrus Ipuwer speaks of the world "turning as on a potter's lathe" and that the Hermitage papyrus refers to a similar event.

Other papyri found in the Pyramids state: "The sun has ceased to dwell in the West and shines again in the East". This according to Charroux who continues: "The Polynesians, Chinese, Hindus and Eskimos have equally witnessed the events. In the end a number of facts at one time too much for archaeologists came to have an odd value after the discovery of two astronomical charts painted on the ceiling of the tomb belonging to Senmuth, architect of the queen Hatshepsut. One of the maps is normal, with the cardinal points placed as they are today; but the other one shows from the stellar position the east on the left and the west on the right. This is clearly of great significance, especially in a tomb of someone who was professionally skilled in geography and astronomy".

As is known, the hooked cross, the famous swastika derives from the very ancient sun wheel of India. It represents the life-giving star but was once meant to symbolize something quite different: the apparent movement of the sun. Why then do its arms turn to the right—from the west to the east? It is thus shown as a rule and considered to be a bringer of luck. It was a mystery to everybody until solved by Churchward, who found the exact symbol on a number of tablets. Not only this, he also found a vase near one of those artificial North American hills called mounds and on it there were paintings of both the signs: a swastika with the arms turned to the right and a sun-wheel (the counterpart of the hooked cross) pointing to the left. The former must thus have emblemized the sun which in a very remote age rose in the west to sink in the east; while the latter was for its present-day east-west movement. This would also explain the Indian belief according to which the swastika turned to the right would bring good luck while the other one was a harbinger of grief, etc. The superstition probably goes back to traditions so ancient their very meaning is lost—to the records of a happy age before the deluge and the terrible conditions in which the survivors had to fight for life.

Queen Antinea

"When in 1873 the excavations of the ruins of Troy at Hissarlik were going on I discovered in the latter city the famous Priam treasures, among which there was a special bronze vase of large size. The vase contained various pottery fragments, a number of figures made in a special metal and several objects of bone. These were embellished with Phoenician hieroglyphics which read: 'Of Chronos of Atlantis' . . .

"In a collection of objects from Tiahuanaco now at the Paris Louvre there is an old vase identical to the one I found at Troy. It cannot be mere chance, finding two vases so far apart and having the same size and shape and the same odd owl-head arranged in the same way"

This was said to have been written by Heinrich Schliemann, the famous discoverer of the Trojan ruins, adding that the vase contained a square plaque of white metal like silver. This was fixed to the bottom inside the vase and was inscribed: "From the temple with the transparent walls". Other discoveries were listed but it was said that "they could not for the moment be described in detail".

There was a further observation: "In the Petersburg Museum in Russia there is one of the oldest papyri known, written during the reign of the Pharoah Sent in the second dynasty. On it there are the words: 'The Pharaoh Sent dispatched an expedition to the West in search of the traces of Atlantis, from where, 3,500 years earlier, the Egyptian forefathers had come, bringing with them the wisdom of their homeland. The expedition returned five years later, saying that they had found neither people nor objects which could give a clue to the vanished land'.

"Another papyrus from the same Museum, written by Manetone, the Egyptian priest and historian, gives a period of 13,900 years to the kings of Atlantis; and according to this papyrus the zenith of the Atlantis culture coincides with the beginning of the Egyptian, about 16,000 years ago."

As we said, all this was supposed to have been written by Schliemann but the extracts quoted together with others did not appear until October 20th 1912, signed by "Doctor Paul Schliemann" nephew of the archaeologist who disappeared in 1890. These are clearly sensational revelations supported by Schliemann's name and by the paper he published, the *New York American*. Or, rather, they would have been sensational if there had been the slightest truth in them: but "Doctor Paul Schliemann" never in fact existed—it turned out to be a huge piece of journalistic swindle!

If we add to such nice things all the esoteric speculation, the noise of "discoveries" which from time to time circulate, and the obstinacy of those who stick to the idea that Atlantis must have been in the places *they* say it was in and nowhere else—then we shall see how necessary it is to go extremely carefully when collecting facts which allow us to form a plausible theory. But leaving aside all the foolishness let us consider the position given to the fabled continent by several theories recently returned to the limelight and which may not seem unjust.

After the discovery of the Sahara rock-drawings there is a link again between Atlantis and North Africa; again, because Herodotus himself had spoken about its people and the mountainous region from Morocco to Tunisia. The French geographer towards the end of the last century took up the discussion in earnest and Pierre Benoit borrowed from these for his romantic novel on the subject. The people of Atlantis are still spoken of as the "blue people" and the Tuaregs who live in the Atlas mountains actually wear blue clothes and are said to be descendants of the Atlantis peoples!

Oddly enough Benoit also refers to the Pleiades when quoting the verses of a Tuareg song; likewise when mentioning a precious manuscript he says: ". . . it was the *Journey to Atlantis* by the mythographer Dioniges of Miletus quoted by Diodoro, whose loss Berlioux had often deplored. It was a document with references to *Critias* and in fact reproduced the essentials of the famous dialogue. It established the topography of the Atlas citadel and showed that that site had not been submerged by floods as the timid defenders of the Atlantis theory imagine, although its very existence is denied by modern science. And it was called the "central Masinian massif". You know that there is no longer any doubt about the identity of the Masinians with the tribes of the Imoschaoch, the Tuaregs. Now the Dioniges manuscript establishes in an authoritative manner the identity of the historical Masinians with the Atlantides of the legend. Dioniges also told me how the central part of Atlantis had been the cradle of the Neptune dynasty and had not only not vanished in the disaster told by Plato —a disaster which engulfed the rest of it—but also how that part was really Hoggar Targui, where it was still believed that the noble Neptune dynasty had survived. The historians of Atlantis reckoned the catastrophe took place 9,000 years B.C. If Dioniges of Miletus, who was writing not more than two thousand years ago, is of the opinion that the laws of the time were still based on the Neptune dynasty you will understand that I had this idea at once: something which has existed for 9,000 years can also last for 11,000 . . .

"Sand can swallow a civilization better than water. Today, of that lovely island rendered so luxuriant by the sea and the winds there is nothing left except this dry massif. The only thing left in this rocky island home separated for ever from the world of the living is the marvellous oasis which lies at your feet with its red fruits, waterfalls, azure lake and sacred texts about the vanished age of gold. Yesterday evening when you came

here you crossed the five enclosures: three from the sea,
now dry for ever, and two land ones with a corridor
through which you went on camel-back and in which
the triremes once sailed . . ."

In 1925–26 Count Byron Kühn de Prorok found a
tomb in Hoggar which must have been that of Tin
Hinan, Benoit's Antinea, a woman of whom one knows
little or nothing but the Tuaregs consider to be in effect
the last queen of Atlantis. The explorer also brought to
light the skeleton of a girl lying on her side, with necklaces, precious stones and things made of gold.

And strangely enough there have been discoveries in
Hoggar itself of emblems of a spatial nature (see page
45) but it is still more peculiar to consider all the remains left in the Sahara and the legends surrounding
them. At El-Arish on the Moroccan coast southwards
from Tangiers there are the remains of Lixus, where the
ancient writers thought the gardens of the Hesperides
were, home of the Daughters of Night and of Ocean,
full of golden apples guarded by dragons. Whoever tries
to interpret this myth will find innumerable references
to "Night" and "Ocean" which could be symbols of
space—like the "dragon", regarded as an astroship. And
then there is the Gorgon appearing here and there
around the Atlantic as if to represent some monstrous
interplanetary explorer in its mysterious way.

The tribes south of the High Atlas no longer talk
about "dragons" but of flying "stones" and "towers";
could they not be associated with the "Gorgons", the
"terrible creatures with the hundred arms" whose at-
atavistic traditions were so strong they terrorized natives
to the extent that the latter refused even to reveal the
places haunted by them—in ruins which perhaps would
be of inestimable value to archaeologists?

Was Plato wrong?

It can be said, however, that the people from the vanished continent may have pushed across the Sahara once
when the latter was covered in vegetation: some scholars
think the Egyptians came from there, but to place the

whole of Atlantis down in those regions is certainly too risky—like the theory which recently placed the "reign of Neptune" in an ancient city of over 300,000 souls found at Thera (Santorino) 120 kilometres north of Crete on one of the finest Cyclades isles.[2]

However much its discoveries may exert themselves to show that Plato made a number of errors in placing and dating concerning Atlantis in his two dialogues *Timeo* and *Critias* their assertions cannot simply be rejected. Plato is extremely precise in fact about this subject: "There was, beyond the place still called the Pillars of Hercules, a great continent named Atlantis or Poseidonis . . ." But Professor Galanoupulos is of the contrary opinion and states: "This is the starting error. Plato perhaps went through Santorino, but apart from the fact that he was a philosopher and not a geographer he could only think that Atlantis could be reached by a journey through Egypt. Why? Think of Plato's time, three or four hundred years before Christ. More than a thousand years had gone since the time of the grand cataclysm and in one thousand years the sea had become infinitely bigger. Mysteries had grown too with the sailors' widening of the world's frontiers—an enormous extension when compared with that of the thousand years before his time. Plato's *Timeo* and *Critias* contain all the mysteries and memories of the Aegean of a thousand years old or more . . ."

We can say of course that the Pillars of Hercules were just the same one thousand years before as a thousand years afterwards and that without any doubt at all the Straits of Gibraltar were meant. But apart from this there is the fact that Atlantis is not for nothing the most fascinating legend of the remote period of the Aegean; the origin of the story can be found in Egypt, since Plato makes use of points dealt with by the Athenian legislator Solon in connection with his talks with the Theban priest Sonchis. The walls of the Medinet Habu temple show inscriptions about the deeds of the last peo-

[2] An interesting summary of this theory with details of two scientific expeditions is given by James Mavor in *Voyage to Atlantis*, Souvenir Press.

ple of Atlantis; and from this it is quite clear that the latter did not come from Egypt but from the "land of the Hyperboreans" near the North Sea!

Regarding the date given by Plato for the end of Atlantis (around 9,000 years before his own time) Galanoupulos is just as specific: "It is an historical extravagance. 9,000 years before Plato, who refers to stories already two or three generations old, no Greek or Egyptian could have had any ideas about the Gibraltar Straits. We know almost certainly that only five or six hundred years before Christ the Phoenicians explored the sea beyond Gibraltar—so about two hundred years before Plato's time . . ." So Galanopoulos starts with a virtual denial of everything Plato says in connection with Atlantis; and in doing so he unfortunately creates his own personal Atlantis, thus adding another one to a host of theories which is already far too large.

CHAPTER FOURTEEN

SATURN IN AMERICA

Plato describes with surprising exactness the islands which were supposed to be beyond Atlantis and can easily be identified with the Antilles, towards the American coasts. On the other hand Diodoro Siculo says, when referring to discoveries which in his time were only the vaguest notions and describing a big island many days' sailing distance from Libya, towards the west; "Its soil is fertile, wonderfully beautiful and traversed by generous streams . . ."

It is a picture of southern America, sketched in a manner similar to that of the Assyrian king Sargon (2750 B.C.) who when listing his conquests referred to "a country of lakes, lying beyond the Mediterranean", meaning of course that it was a land already previously known.

"The ancient Greeks," says Serge Hutin about some acceptable manuscripts, "had without any doubt established 'bridgeheads' in America well before the foundation of Carthage; and it seems the same can be said for the Egyptians: regular expeditions would have set out from Nile territory towards the West, that is, in the direction of America and bringing the gold needed for the manufacture of the necklaces and other ornaments required for the big temples and palaces."

The communications between Great Britain and the Mediterranean were still more frequent, the former exporting gold, tin, amber and pearls to the latter; a mutual trade, as the French scholar points out: "from 2500 B.C. the English probably had ships which could make long journeys, while other ships came to England from Crete and Mycenae—in some Wessex tombs objects have been found which are undoubtedly of Egyptian origin and date back to 1400 B.C."

The legendary island of Thule was not only known to the Greeks, Romans and Carthaginians but also to the Phoenicians; and has been identified by several authorities not with Iceland but with a land situated still more to the west which has now vanished. Looking through the dialogues of Plutarch it seems that we can deduce that the American coasts were settled by a number of Greek colonies and that this same land of Thule functioned as an important meeting-place. "Every thirty years," says Plutarch's Sylla, one of the questioners in his dialogues, "the inhabitants of Thule disembarked on the opposite shores where the Greeks lived, in order to celebrate the Feast of Saturn; and in that land during one of the months the sun sets for hardly an hour a day." Here, then, is a direct reference to Northern Canada!

Unknown Migrations

We have already pointed out the striking similarities between the American and Mediterranean languages; but let us now add that the Phoenicians must have settled in Cuba and Haiti, and then pushed further into central and southern America. We should note here, too, that the Ecuador language spoken by the Indians in Peru contained words similar to the ancient Hebrew. At the foot of one of the mounds at Grave Creek on the

Ohio River a mysterious white disc was found with some written characters on it very like those noted on some rocks in the Canaries; Professor Schoolcraft headed an international commission set up to study it and established the presence of four Etruscan letters, four similar to the archaic Aegean alphabet, five Scandinavian runes, six Druids symbols and some incisions like the Phoenician ones; besides fourteen of Anglo-Saxon origin and some close to the Numidian and Hebrew.

We may now add here in the words of Serge Hutin: "The Azores natives were well aware that there existed inhabited country to the west. Favourable winds could take a sailing boat in fifteen days from Africa to America; favourable currents would similarly assist men to reach California from China and Japan, which explains the discovery—wrontly thought to be only a legend—of the country of Fu Sang (most likely to be the Californian coast) by Chinese sailors around A.D. 458.

"Christopher Columbus is considered to be the discoverer of America less and less. The medieval Friesian expedition into the Dark Sea beyond Iceland has already been scientifically established and today quite a lot is known about the colonization first of Greenland and then of certain zones of North America, which took place A.D. 680 to 700 by Vikings already settled in Iceland. But the discovery by the Icelandic sailor Ars Marsson of the Viking expeditions to a land called Hvétramannaland (Land of the White Men)[1] or Irland-it-mikla (Great Ireland) seems to show that the Celts first colonized North America; or perhaps it was a still older race.

"The legends of the Redskins talk of a race of white men who came long ago from the East . . . and archaeological evidence of such expeditions still existed: it seems, for instance, that the Round Tower of Newport Rhode Island was a Celtic sanctuary."

But even admitting that the first European explorers

[1] An Indian tradition speaks of Florida as being inhabited by white men who owned tools made of iron.

may have found the New World by pure accident we can still use this to explain the successive expeditions of the Viking-type which landed with mathematical precision in the places to which they were directed. The magic stone which occurs in the saga of the Norwegian king Olaf 2 (995–1030) could be brought in here: an object which "could find the sun, even when behind clouds and fog" and could thus help the sailors to keep on course. This Olaf saga is very interesting, not only because it gives us an idea of the early navigation system of the Scandinavians, but also because it offers us a clear example of how ancient legends may conceal scientific reality. Renato Gatto says about this matter: "Pilots today have compasses with crystal polarization, capable of finding the exact position of the sun when it is not directly visible. It was when I was comparing the two systems that a Danish boy ten years of age was struck by an idea: what if the legendary stone and the modern instrument were based on the same principles since they had the same purpose? His father was persuaded by this original idea to consult the scientist Thorkild Ramskou, putting the theory to him so convincingly that he began to work on minerals in the natural science museum in Denmark—minerals which would have a molecular alignment parallel to each other like polarized crystal. "Ramskou was successful, finding that cordierite, a common mineral in the magnetic and metamorphic rocks in Italy, Finland and Norway whose fine clear crystals are better known as water sapphires, agreed perfectly with the characteristics looked for. But its most important quality is that of change of colour, varying from yellow to blue (not from yellow to red as some people say) when the natural alignment of its molecules forms an angle of 90 degrees with the plane of polarization of the sunlight.

"All they had to do now was to demonstrate the validity of the theory. Ramskou and Jensen flew towards Greenland on a particularly cloudy day, the one armed with ordinary flight-compass, the other with the cordierite crystal. When they compared their measurements of the sun's position they found the difference was only 2.5 degrees. And to think that we have tried for thousands of years to invent a precious instrument which already existed in nature and already exploited by our primitive forefathers!"

The Empire of Crete

But let us return a moment to Galanopoulos, stopping briefly at Thera to consider this new stage, which is without doubt very important to archaeology. Readers may remember that in May 1967 the excavations carried out here by a Greek-American expedition[2] brought to light the first remains of the big centre, which turned out to be a most precious find: whole houses intact, with two or three floors, utensils and amphorae, skeletons of domestic animals etc.; everything was submerged under the lava of a volcanic eruption which took place 3,500 years ago and lasted about fifty years, thus forcing the inhabitants to find shelter elsewhere. But the slow burial allowed the surprisingly good state of preservation found.

These could be looked at, however, from another viewpoint, the one conjectured by the experts of the London *Times* in 1909 who wrote: "The recent excavations at Crete force us to reconsider on a new basis the entire plan of Mediterranean history before the classical period. We now know without doubt that Crete was the centre of an extensive empire while Egypt was in the Eighteenth Dynasty."

And this empire was probably linked with Thera, but as the Cretan puzzle is far from complete there may well be other surprises. One such came in 1964 from the Desert of Salato, in the heart of Turkey about 300 kilometres south of Ankara. The British archaeologist J. Melleaart has been conducting most interesting expeditions down there and the digs have brought to light a centre called Katalhujuk—already inhabited by several thousand people in the seventh millennium B.C. Among the finds there were oriental-style statuettes and

[2]Described by James Mavor in *Voyage to Atlantis* (Souvenir Press).

designs of bulls, even a chapel dedicated to the cult of this animal, besides skulls and heads of bulls in terracotta and stone figures of leopards in fight. There were also vases painted with several motifs suggesting other ancient cultures yet at the same time were without equal.

Those of Katalhujuk have a direct relationship with Crete, yet the latter has links with the Maya culture, as surprising as they are authentic, seeing that the Maya culture stems, some think, from Atlantis! And what about legendary Baalbek? Did it likewise undergo Cretan influences and those of the unimaginable world to which it was connected?

Churchward thinks so and says in this connection: "The story of Baalbek is a closed book. These ruins have aroused the amazement and admiration of visitors for thousands of years—who built such monuments? We do not know but one thing is quite certain: their grandeur and grace have not been equalled by any other human building in the last twenty centuries. These buildings are of blocks of stone as big as a bus . . . and there are tunnels in the walling large enough for a train to go through. With such a structure it is not at all marvellous that Baalbek has lasted so long."

In his book *The Marvels of the Past* Richard Curle asserts that Baalbek was built in the time of Antonio Pio (A.D. 86–161) but Churchward says in allusions to the work of other scholars: "It is difficult to think of a more mistaken idea. Neither Roman, Greek or Egyptian history contains any reference to the building of Baalbek, although the chronicles of these peoples faithfully registered the chief events and works carried out in the period of time mentioned by Curle. The Greeks, then, a few hundred miles away, carefully recorded the deeds, works and other constructions from 1,200–1,300 years before the period he gives for the building of Baalbek—yet there is not a word about this anywhere in their annals. Baalbek is not Roman and neither did the Romans build temples to the sun. Certain experts say that some of the marble columns came from central Egypt; this could be so, but why in that case is there no sign of this in Egyptian chronicles or in Greek and Roman? Two facts are clear: that Baalbek was never completed and that the works were suddenly earthed in." For what reason? Perhaps as a result of that terrible tellurian cataclysm, as Churchward says?

The legendary Hyperboreans

It is anything but unlikely that the offspring from Atlantis would have come very close to north-west Africa and thus influenced the Mediterranean world in which others see the traces of Mu or the junction of the two lost continents. Equally, the regions of north-eastern Atlantis may have pushed towards northern Europe. If so it it would give rise to the theory that Atlantis may be identical with the equally legendary Hyperboreans. "The central-American tradition," says Churchward, tells us that the Quetzal had skins white as milk, blue eyes and fair hair—all the characteristics of the modern Scandinavians. Some descendants of the Quetzal still live in America, their villages are in the almost impenetrable jungles of Honduras and Guatemala and it is there that I have collected the best legends ...

"On the other hand there is an old language called Quanlan, in which I have discovered certain words corresponding to some in the original Mu language; but still more surprising is the fact that many Quanlan words are the same as those of one of the American-Indian languages—they also have the same meaning."

Serge Hutin in referring to the Hyperboreans' land —identifiable with Iceland according to some and with a vanished country according to others—tells us the following: "It must have been a very fertile place seeing that the Ancients depicted it full of such wonders. Diodoro Siculo, when mentioning the Hyperboreans, talks of a big island like Sicily, which could very well be Iceland, but he continues: 'The soil of this island is excellent, such as to yield two harvests every year.' It is true that Iceland possesses a privileged climate owing to the Gulf Stream; and at the time of the Vikings in the tenth and eleventh centuries the corn ripened there but it is very likely that Eden, in its northern version, refers to an age in which the Earth's axis did not have its present-day position and the Poles were differently aligned."

"At that time," Roger Vercel says, "huge trees covered Greenland and Spitzbergen with their wide fronds. Under a burning sun the dense tropical vegetation was full of moisture but now there is nothing but dry lichens. Then the tree ferns rioted with giant catkins and the palms of the Tertiary, the lianas of the 'arctic' jungle. The summer flared up and the heavy clouds rained warm showers; and in the vastness of the 'polar' forest lived proportionately large animals: the woolly mammoth and two-horned rhinoceros, the lion of the caverns and the great stag with its antlers four metres across. Birds of fabulous size flew over the trees . . ."

CHAPTER FIFTEEN

ATLANTIS

Must we then place Atlantis where Paul Le Cour located it, thinking of it as a continent or collection of vast islands between the two Americas to the west, with Europe and Africa on the eastern side? It seems so; many western students are becoming more convinced of it and so are several Russian scholars, of whom Professor Zirov seems most interesting: "Plato has talked of Antarctica in his *Timeo* and *Critias*. In the first the legend is only an illustrative episode, whereas the second is dedicated entirely to it. The famous Greek sage said that a long time ago there was an enormous island called Atlantis. He quotes Solon (sixth century B.C.) as his source that it was in the extreme west beyond the Pillars of Herucules in the Atlantic Ocean. Its dimensions were like those of Asia Minor and of Libya put together, and a small sea separated it from Europe. To the west stretched a large ocean, beyond which was a vast continent (modern America). To the east Atlantis was sufficiently close to the Spanish coasts, a part of which where the city of Gades (now Cadiz) lay belonged to one of the kingdoms of Atlantis. Plato specifies the position of Atlantis exactly in his *Timeo*."

Zirov then stresses that Plato sought to support this by mentioning the mild climate of Atlantis, the powers of its kings and their intelligent leadership; also the temples and the ships which he depicted similar to the Greek ones. "Plato was a man of his times," said Zirov, "and of his people, so everything he dealt with was seen through a Hellenic prism: he could not imagine the Atlantis temples etc. as being different from Greek ones. Plato's Atlantis was nearer to the Aztec and Maya culture and the so-called pre-dynastic era of Egypt—fifth millenium B.C.—but even if we accept his version we must remember that Atlantis for some reason or other developed more quickly than elsewhere. In general such ideas are not unlikely, even if it seems more probable that Plato, by making use of sources unknown to us (as some believe) may have described the late Atlantis culture of the fifth to the seventh millennia B.C. But we do not actually know when exactly the last traces of Atlantis may have sunk. According to the famous Swedish biogeographer René Malaise it would have happened in the seventh century B.C.

"The question of the nature of Atlantis culture is purely speculative and perhaps of secondary importance; it could only be answered by discovering some of its remains. No historical, ethnical or philological research has given (nor will it be able to give) either a positive or negative reply. The first thing to do is to show the existence of Atlantis by some geological or geographical object; only by verifying the geological history of the Atlantic Ocean, especially in the glacial and post-glacial periods, will it be possible to solve this age-long riddle. If geology and oceanography definitely say 'No' then the problem of Atlantis will no longer exist and will have to be considered as pure fiction. But in this exposition we shall try to show that science already has many facts in favour of its existence."

Submerged Mountains

Zirov goes on: "There are two geological and oceano-graphical schools, diametrically opposed as far as the origin and nature of the oceans is concerned. Today there is an ocean of varying depth where Atlantis used to be; if it really had been here then clearly the oceans could not always have been in the same places and with the same dimensions as today—which is what most American students of the subject believe. If their view is correct then clearly there was never any Atlantis. But many Soviet scientists believe that there was once land in these regions; the Atlantic is thought to be the youngest of all the oceans and has been the scene of violent volcanic activity. Where was Atlantis exactly? Many people—also the author of this exposition, to-gether with E. F. Khagemeister—have put the idea for-ward that it could in some way have been connected with the underwater tableland where the Azores now are. Details of the last decade's oceanography bear a remarkable resemblance between the topography of these islands and that of Atlantis as described by Plato.

"He also said that Atlantis was a mountainous coun-try, so somewhere under the Atlantic there would have to be submerged mountains—which is just what the marine expeditions of the nineteenth and twentieth cen-turies have established: the existence of an enormous mountain system extending from one polar region to the other. In equatorial areas there is a break in the continuity so perhaps it is better to speak of two sys-tems, one in the North Atlantic, the other in the South. The author of these reports links Atlantis with the northern chain.

"The latter consists itself of two parallel mountain chains, separated by a narrow and deep plain. The latter can link up with a great irrigation system in the chief Atlantis region which ran around the edge of the kingdom's plateau, surrounded in the north, west and south by powerful mountain massifs. The irrigation canals were absolutely necessary for the drainage of the water which accumulated in the low-lying plain. On an average the North Atlantic chain is four thousand metres high. The eastern and western slopes have terraces covered in a thick layer of sediment indicating that the sinking of Atlantis would have been gradual and not deep at first. Plato also talks about this and says that after the sinking the sea was not navigable because of the huge quantities of mud. In the last decade or so the expeditions have collected material showing how the cessation of the ice ages in Europe and North America has been caused by the sinking of this mountain chain; an idea which had been put forward about the same time and quite independently by the Soviet scholars Vladimir Obrucev and Ekaterina, as well as by the Atlantic expert René Malaise.

"These workers have connected the beginning and end of the last glacial epoch with the direction of the Gulf Stream and with Atlantis. When the latter still existed in the North Atlantic and the Azores plateau it blocked the way to the European coasts of warm marine currents, but when it sank the Gulf Stream gradually caused the ice to disappear. The Russian hydrologist M. Ermalaev showed that the present Arctic water system was established around 12,000 years ago, this date also being that of the end of the glacial epoch in Europe and North America—a fact confirmed by numerous proofs based on the isotopic method of the atomic clock system. Other factors in favour of the link between the end of the ice age and the beginning of tectonic movement in the North Atlantic have been advanced by the French geologist Pierre Termier, who was of the opinion that a piece of tachylyte lava had been able to solidify only in the air—but it was found at the bottom of the ocean north of the Azores. René Malaise and the French geologist J. Bourcart have pointed out that two soil samples found in waters east and west of the northern chain were of a different nature: while the sample from the western slope was made of oceanic mud the one from the eastern side was glacial in nature, presumably brought there by icebergs. As a result, the chain emerged from the water during

e period of ice extension and marked out its limits
tween the warm Gulf Stream, which was moving
om the south along the western slopes, and the eastern
urrent carrying icebergs along the eastern side of At-
ntis. On the top of one of the submarine peaks of the
ain a number of strange, limestone discs were found
ith a diameter of about fifteen centimetres and a thick-
ss of about four. They were smooth enough in parts
ut elsewhere they were marked with rough indenta-
ons as if they might have been plates. Their strange
ppearance makes one think of an artificial origin
ather than a natural one. Radioactive carbon methods
f examination revealed that they were above water
2,000 years ago. Which means that this mountain of
Atlantis must have been an island at that time!

"It seems to us that Atlantis consisted of three parts:
he Poseidon island in the northern part; the Azores
lateaux and the narrow, central island of the Antilles,
ring more to the south; and thirdly the equatorial
rchipelago which almost reached the Equator near the
eefs of modern St. Paolo. It is also clear that even the
outhern part of Atlantis, until not so long ago, was
bove water. This is shown by the Swedish 'Albatros'
neasurements or a submarine plateau between the
North Atlantic chain and Sierra Leone, the plateau be-
ng a spur of the whole chain. In one sample of mud
liatoms were found which are normally sweet-water
lgae and thus not mixed with other marine creatures.
René Malaise thinks that they came from a lake of pure
vater, now sunk over three kilometres down.

"Perhaps the Carthaginian sailor Ganone (sixth cen-
ury B.C.) was a witness of the last traces of the south-
rn section of Atlantis, since he said his ships struggled
or not less than a week near the edge of a land lying
o the west of Africa, south of Senegal and with fiery
treams emptying into the sea; Ganone and his friends
truggled between the rivers of fire at not less than a
housand kilometres distance—so it must have been a
real cataclysm, not a volcanic eruption. We have compared more than fifty details of a geological, historical
and astronomical nature so as to find a link between

them and the supposed disappearance of Atlantis; an this has allowed us to fix the date of the catastroph very closely. In our opinion things of exceptional in portance took place between the twelfth and the eigh millennia B.C. in the history of the northern Atlant and of various people living on river banks in tho areas. These events were started by a huge geologic and volcanic cataclysm which was never forgotten native lore. All these facts are in agreement with th vanishing of Atlantis but for the moment its end can b put only very roughly around 9500 B.C. . . . Man Soviet scholars are of the opinion that Plato's Atlant really did exist and that the legend is not opposed t modern science. So the Atlantis problem begins to leav the realm of mystery; but the knowledge so far is no enough to dispel all the scepticism about it as yet. Sev eral other proofs will still be needed if we are to con vince the sceptics completely."

The disappearing islands

According to most theories Atlantis stretched almos down to the Antarctic beyond the 55th Parallel, whic to the west passes through the remote islands of th Tierra del Fuego and to the east is well below th southern tip of Africa. Until quite recently there mus have been islands there which have now vanished. Th most important were the Auroras, perhaps, abou 2,000 kilometres east of the Falklands, since there ar reports from the year 1809 concerning them in th Madrid Hydrographic Society. This states: "We knev nothing at all about them until discovered in 1762 b the Aurora which gave them its own name. But in 1790 they were seen again by the ship *Princess,* of the roya shipping company of the Philippines. It was com manded by Captain Manuel de Oyarvido who showed us the ship's log at Lima and furnished us with infor mation about the position of that land. In 1794 the corvette *Atrevida,* going there expressly to take exact details carried out all measurements required and found the longitudinal difference between these islands and

ιe port of Soledad in the Malvine (Falklands). There
ιre three islands, very close to the same meridian; the
ιentral one is somewhat lower but the other two can be
ιeen at a distance of nine leagues. The co-ordinates are
ιs follows:

South Island; 53 deg. 15 min. 22 sec. S.; 47 deg. 57
    min. 15 sec.
W. Central Island; 53 deg. 2 min. 40 sec. S.; 47 deg.
    55 min. 15 sec. W.
North Island; 52 deg. 37 min. 24 sec. S;. 47 deg. 43
    min. 15 sec. W.

One can read about other islands in those parts in the
ιeport drawn up by the same expedition and probably
·y the captain, J. de Bustamente; but no traces of these
ιr of the Auroras were ever seen again. It is absurd to
·elieve, as some do, that it was due to a mirage; the
reports we have are too conscientious and detailed and
the ones we have referred to are, not the only islands
ιeen and approached by travellers. Actually the Auroras were sighted again in 1856 by the crew of the
Helen Baird and for the last time in 1892 by the
Gladys. The ship's log tells us the following: 26th June;
we have seen a land which seems to be a long island
. . . with two hills giving the impression that there are
actually three islands. The hills had no trace of snow on
them (here, if not before, we must abandon the idea
that it might be icebergs quite apart from the fact that
icebergs keep moving). At 8 we saw another island; the
part I saw showed a steep incline of moderate height
towards the south; greyish but free of snow . . . There
seemed to be a way across this island in the direction
of the first."

In 1670 a Dutch sailor called Lindeman found an
island in the southern Atlantic which he called Saxemberg, about 600 miles north-west of Tristan da Cunha
almost half-way between the extreme south of Brazil
and South Africa. Afterwards two other ships tried in
vain to find the island. So it proved in the end for the
American sailing craft *Fanny* in 1804 and the *Colum-*

bus in 1809 after which Saxemberg was never seen again.

If we leave from the mouths of the River Niger and go direct south we meet the island called Bouvet at precisely the same latitude as the Tierra del Fuego, discovered and re-discovered several times and called a pure figment of the imagination till its existence was proved and gave rise to a dispute for ownership of the world's loneliest island; a dispute finally settled in Norway's favour.

The British captain G. Norris of the *Sprightly* set foot on Bouvet in 1825. A few days before he had discovered other pieces of land to the north-east and had called the chief one Thompson and the three smaller ones (hardly more than reefs) Chimneys because of their odd shape—they were treated extremely harshly by the sea. But these also, being low-lying, were soon swallowed by the sea again.

Half-way between the Auroras and Buenos Aires, about 1500 kilometres south-east of the city a "remarkably large and pleasant island, with a good port to the east" was found in 1675 by Antonio de la Roché which he called Isla Grande yet only a century afterwards there was no trace of it. But strange rumours were heard about it: the chronicles of Spain talked about a disembarkment on the Argentine coast between 1770 and 1780 of "white men, blacks and Indians" who were supposed to have been the survivors of an Atlantis colony (a theory still heard between the two world wars) which kept itself going on the Isla Grande for millennia until the island was destroyed. Other people say it was a shipwreck that Antonio discovered— the island had never existed. Unfortunately we have insufficient evidence either to confirm or deny this story.

Even Mu was supposed to have had its colony—the Dougherty island found by the whale-hunter from America called Swain who was modest enough to give it his own name. A few years later the land was seen by Captains Gardiner and Macy who said it was rich in seal-life and algae-covered rocks. In 1830 commercial easons brought the idea that it might be looked at more arefully. The American brothers N. B. Palmer and A. S. Palmer tried to do so but their accounts were so onfused that what was actually seen was never clear. But in 1842 Dougherty, a British captain, found the "kingdom of seals" and gave Swain tit for tat by renaming it after himself—since when it has always been Dougherty Island. Much later very many sailors between the latitudes and longitudes indicated by him 59. 20 S.—120. 20 W.) said they had seen the vanished land. Others continued to deny its existence while till others claimed it had never vanished. If this were o then it would be the island farthest away from civilization at about 3,500 kilometres to the west of Cape Horn. If Dougherty is really there it must have been denied to men for a long time. But who knows if its ancient inhabitants were not the "monsters" whose anding is recorded by the legends of several Polynesian peoples? These creatures would have been "covered in skins like animals"; we tend to think that the possible "evacuees" would hardly have hesitated to get rid of their furs as soon as they arrived in a warmer climate—but the legend could simply refer to men who were more hairy than the normal Polynesian peoples.

But let us return to Atlantis, which according to certain authors could have had something to do with the shout of "Land!" uttered by a member of the crew captained by Christopher Columbus in the early hours of October 12th 1492 (or October 21st according to the Gregorian calendar). The first island seen by the navigator—Guanahani to the natives but Saint Salvador to Columbus—was identified by most with the modern Watling; but although it may be certain that the same island is in the Bahamas it is by no means sure that this was the one meant, since it seems, rather, that Watling has nothing to do with it and it was simply left to further heated discussions. The log-books belonging to Columbus were lost (only the bishop Las Casa left extracts which still survive) and the sole map available is that written eight years afterwards by Juan de la Cosa, a companion of Columbus and owner of the

Santa Maria. And such a map superimposed on curren
ones shows islands which do not exist.

Once again we come back to submerged lands, an
in our case they would be countries about which ther
were still living traditions regarding beings of a su
perior civilization. Let us remember that the loca
myths (later destroyed wantonly) tried to explain to
the Columbus messengers—as the great Genoese wrote
—that "they knew how the white men had arrive
from the home of the gods and how about fifty of thei
fellows had begged the white men to take them bac
with them into the sky of the immortal gods." There
must once have been many islands between the Bahamas and Bermuda and then sunk at different times
one of which is the legendary Mayda, of which it was
said from 1600 on that there were people on the island
who practised all sorts of magic—including the ability
to hover in mid-air.

CHAPTER SIXTEEN

UTURE HOSTS

'With a bound he reached the top of the precipice: his
armour shone like rainbows and the sun formed a halo
ound his forehead. He seemed to Dona to be much
aller than warriors of his own tribe, who walked bent
down. With all her heart Dona would have liked to stop
him, pulling at an edge of his cloak or the wake of the
ight which emanated from him. But he went on towards the edge of the cliff and from the stick which he
held in his hand there flashed a sheet of lightning, one
only. And the striped worm vanished in a blaze of
horror and the winged salamander melted and the
beach before the Being stayed clear, stained with black
and foaming blood. The other monsters fled, vanishing
in a cloud. The tribe which had run for shelter in the
rocks burst into a shout of triumph. Dona also shouted,
but with horror. A second salamander came down vertically on to the platform with its jointed legs stretched
out and Bruce Morgan staggered under its weight. They
struggled with their bodies close together because Morgan had dropped his disintegrator which would have

been useless at such a short distance. The monster
joints penetrated his armour, its tentacles and sucker
trying to find an opening.

"Dona, all muscles tensed, looked on, wonderin
what to do. Perhaps the harpoon, but she hesitate
again when she saw a joint of the armour split and th
blood spurting out. Morgan supported himself agains
the rock. The creature's inhuman green eyes penetrate
his own and he felt as if he were being paralysed. Bu
Dona urged on the wolf, and two elastic shadows leap
forward together, the steel jaw of the beast tearing a
the Medusa's fat tentacles while the girl's hands lifte
the spear.

"Erg had hurried to help Dona: his lance stuck int
the monster's neck and a stream of black blood gushe
out. Getting free, Morgan averted his gaze from th
creature's dimming eyes, already veiled in death. The
the Medusa rolled on the rocks and the young hunte
gave it the *coup de grâce* . . .

"Dona led him back into the cave where h
stretched himself out, the disintegrator at his elbow. H
was exhausted but his mind was clear: 'this planet i
in the Jurassic, if one considers the saurians' h
thought . . ."

This episode is taken from a novel by Charles Henneberg—*La Naissance des dieux*—and relates the adventures of some astronauts who land on a young and
savage planet, thus reliving the great myths of antiquity.
As in Henneberg's book the Earth no doubt also had its
Bruce Morgans who attacked dinosaurs and other terrifying monsters of prehistoric eras. And if it makes us
smile to think that Lucifer might have been a power-
hungry scientist (or deformed poet full of inferiority
complexes) certain symbols and myths common to all
widely-scattered populations do suggest some highly
controversial questions.

Do we all come from space?

"If we allow for the corruption of the most ancient religious concepts and of their symbols," wrote Max

Müller, "we shall find ourselves dealing with some surprising facts." For instance, God has the same name whether we look at Indian, Greek, Italic or Germanic mythology. In Sanskrit it was Dyaus and Zeus in Greek; Jupiter in Latin and Tiu (Wotan?) in Germanic. Thousands of years before the time of the Vedas or of Homer the forefathers of the whole Aryan race worshipped an invisible being under the same name, the name of the light and of the sky . . . The word Dyaus did not simply mean the blue sky, nor the sky in personified form: in the Vedic scripts we find Dyaus Pater and in Greek Zeu Pater; in Latin Jupitar then Jupiter. All these expressions derived from the one in use before the three languages—as Churchward notes—were split up, when such terms meant Celestial Father. "The sun," said Churchward later, "was never regarded by our forefathers as a divinity itself but as a symbol of the Divine . . . a monotheistic symbol, rather, existing thousands of years before Egypt, Babylonia, Peru and Mexico were civilized . . ."

The oldest myths are full of gods and semi-gods who "came from the sky" and it is interesting to see that such beings were not considered as creators themselves but as ambassadors—direct or indirect—of the Supreme Being. If we accept these traditions should we not picture the cosmic explorers in a light similar to that in Henneberg's story, as "guests" of the future, coming from a more advanced planet than ours to bring real civilization to Earth if not life itself? In this respect we should stop to consider what the Soviet scholar Viaceslav Saitsev says in his book *On Earth and Sea:*

"What was the origin of man like? This is one of the biggest mysteries on Earth, to which we can reply only with three theories:

(*a*) Man is a product of Earth's evolution.
(*b*) Man is a creation of the Lord.
(*c*) Man is one link in a long evolutionary chain begun on some other planet and continued on ours.

"The first is a logical idea supported by science, but with an important factor not yet explained: it is in fact not as yet explained how man came from the ape-state; and the creature which would have had to be the first human being on Earth has never been discovered. The second theory raises certain doubts, as it is impossible to imagine how a sudden act of creation could have produced him. The third hypothesis is certainly worthy of study. Some myths say that human evolution took place on some planet in the Universe, and after a first formative period man would have reached Earth and continued to develop here. Some scientists believe our world is not yet old enough for intelligent beings to have grown here spontaneously from protozoa to their present-day level.

"According to a Slavonic tale 'man was created far from the Earth and very long ago. When God had finished creating He commanded the angels to take some human couples to Earth so that they should multiply there. The angels spread the couples over the world and wherever they set up home they multiplied. Perhaps when Earth is nearing its end, God will again take men somewhere else so that they may reproduce'. The mind which worked out such a tale must have been an elaborate one, fully developed. Though there may be fantasy here it is not without sense. It is necessary to return to the ways our ancestors thought and to consider how they would amplify their views when dissatisfied with what the priests told them. However it is, the fable expresses the idea that humanity as we know it today would not have been the first race of intelligent beings on Earth, and that it followed other races which became extinct as a result of remote cataclysms. According to central and southern beliefs, 'human' beings made of wood and clay populated Earth before we ourselves came here. One variant of this is mentioned in a Slavonic text in the Leningrad Library of the Academy of Sciences of USSR. It says that a man 'made with a wooden heart' was created before Adam. Several details of such legends cannot be taken seriously but the idea expressed here of evolution being the result of error and experiment, with nothing permanent in the world is very surprising." In connection with Einstein's theories Saitsev surveys the problem of communication between Earth and other worlds:

"In ancient times and during the middle ages many scholars thought that time went by more slowly in the sky than on Earth. A popular maxim says: 'a minute to God is longer than a whole human life,' and Psalm 39 (verse 5) states: 'Behold, thou hast made my days as an handbreadth and my age is as nothing before thee . . .' A Japanese legend from the *Nippon Mukasi Banasi* tells us how a man might become young again from a journey in the sky and would no longer find any of his family descendants. Similar events occur in a Russian tale included in the collection by A. N. Afanasiev and in a Ukrainian myth in Levcenko's anthology, in which it is said that three of our years are equal to thirty of God's. Strangest of all is the apocryphal Enoch story in which, according to religious texts, he was carried alive into Heaven before the Deluge and still lives there. The same theme is dealt with in the apocryphal account of the so-called *Visions of Isaiah,* presumably written in the second or third century B.C. The prophet Isaiah had begun to doubt his own faith and the power of the Almighty, who seized him for this reason, took him into the heavens and made him change his mind. At last Isaiah, seeing that he was to be taken back to Earth, said: 'But why so soon? I have only been here two hours'. But the divine messenger said: 'Not two hours but thirty-two years'. He would hardly have heard that with any pleasure, seeing that he would on his return there have to suffer death or advanced old age. 'Why must I return to my old flesh and bones?' And the angel would have reassured him with the words 'Do not fear; you will not be old when you return to Earth'.

"At the beginning of the twentieth century Albert Einstein revealed the possible caprices of time in the case of journeys approaching the speed of light. Such things could be tested only in laboratories till now, by mesons, but the writers of science fiction have already conducted their hero through adventures like those of Isaiah. Presumably the ancient idea of possible immortality does not only reflect the longing for an external God but also the idea that time can, under certain conditions, change its speed."

The womb of life

Father Francisco Ximénez was twenty-four years old in 1688 when he landed in Guatemala as a priest. Travelling across the country he learnt the many idioms and languages with amazing ease and thus came in contact with their traditions. Cortéz had ordered the Indian soul to be destroyed but Ximénez was unwilling: his belief was love and his weapon was understanding, both of which were to gain for him the confidence of the natives to the extent that an old chief told him the secrets jealously guarded from the Spanish conquerors; the secrets of the *Popol Vuh*, the *Maya Bible*.

"It is not easy to imagine his amazement when faced with the ancient quiché text," wrote Wolfgang Cordan, "an amazement soon changed into enthusiasm. It was a creation of the world in which the gods had cried 'Earth!' and so Earth came into being. There was the Deluge; and the raven which indicated a new expanse of land flowering from the waters, like the sea-passage confronting the tribe of Israel; and there was a shining star in which Ximénez identified the star of Jacob since it could not be that of Bethlehem."

The likeness to the Scriptures is anything but rare, and not only in the *Popol Vuh*. One of the tablets found by Niven, for instance, pictures the creation of woman according to an idea which is not only biblical but is referred to by many ancient peoples. And it seems to us here peculiarly significant that the Polynesians should say (as noted by Churchward): "from the bone of a man He fashioned woman and called her Eve." As for other sections of the Old Testament have not the Maori a text very like the story of Abel and

Cain? And do not the inhabitants of Fiji record a building just like the Tower of Babel? Or the Polynesians'
story of an ark in no way different from that of Noah
—except that they say it was built on one of their
islands? Several of the *Popol Vuh* exploits e.g. the return from the kingdom of the dead have their equiva-
lent in the most numerous traditions. The same thing
can be said about the fertile virgin theme which would
have a direct reference to the "cosmic egg", says
Churchward, the first fruit of the Creation. He also
adds, from another remote myth, that "life would arise
from this egg, each such egg being called 'a virgin of
life' or 'Hol Hu Kal' which tradition says means 'to
open the womb of life'. It is just for this reason that the
ancients speak of the sea as being the mother, since life
appeared in fact in the sea first, or at least in water,
thus opening the virgin womb."

But what seems more extraordinary to us is the appearance of the cross, with all the variants known today, in so many peoples of antiquity. According to
Churchward this means "the four powers of creation",
the "four cardinal points, terrestrial and cosmic", meaning the Creation itself. The "sun disc" would bear the
same significance, afterwards associated with the
swastika, the St. Andrea cross, the lotus-flower and so
on. The cross cut on Niven's tablet 1231 would represent the same notions in the primitive galaxy—like
various Maya designs, for whom the cross would have
been the symbol of divinity, as it is for us. The god of
the Maya cross is Ah Can Tzicnâl, an expression meaning the Lord of the four corners of the world—but
also the Universe personified! Regarding this there is a
curious remark by the Guatemala monk Antonio Batres
Jaurequi: as is well-known, the last words of Jesus
were: "Eli, lama sabac thani", said in Aramaic; and it
is to this that Jaurequi refers in his work *The History of
Central America*: "Such words come from the Maya
language, the oldest known, and which really read:
'Hele, Hele, lamah sabac ta ni'. This means 'Now I feel
weak and my face is hid in darkness'."

The Conspiracy of Silence

It is important to note that "official" science has persistently denied any validity to the discoveries we have mentioned; so we will now refer to Niven's tablets, first dismissed as non-existent, then thought to be the fruit of a colossal hoax until finally regarded as authentic statements—though even then an attempt was made to shroud it all in silence.

"Scholars of our day," says archaeologist J. Warren, "accuse the Church of having hindered progress; they attribute to the ecclesiastics what in effect has been the consequence of the times in which they lived. And now they are the first to follow the line of conduct attributed to the Church itself and refuse to consider any factors which could prejudice their dogmas." And Herbert Kühn in his work *Ice Age Art and Discoveries* says: "For those people logical arguments have no value . . . But if they examine the situation carefully they would find they are totally wrong to blame the priests entirely for this attitude. In fact there is not a single word in any Church texts about opposition to excavations or the uncovering of the skeletons of primitive men or the artefacts of the ice ages. Not even a hostile statement about the Altamira paintings. On the contrary many ecclesiastics are themselves archaeologists. The truth is that there is good reason to refuse to recognize the claims of progress and science—which is the fear of launching an attack on the theory of evolution. It was of course only by dint of great labour that people managed to spread the idea of an evolution having produced the men, animals and plants we have today—an idea which replaced the static concept of tradition, the notion of creation in one phase.

"The whole evolutionary system regards the earlier as the simpler form and thus the later one as the perfected. If the history of ancient art had included only primitive works, then of course they might have been placed according to the classical concepts of evolution.

But it is quite a different matter when we consider the Altamira cave drawings which have such perfect artistic expression they could be ranked with a Monet or a Manet. Now how would a cave-man have been able to achieve such flowing lines and contrasts of his chiaroscuri, that is, everything which the art of the nineteenth century had won after great subjective struggles against the old academic points of view? This was a great blow to the successes gained by natural science . . . Darwin's dogmas had already, by 1880, left the state of being mere teachings, so that everything which could not be put into the evolutionary picture was destroyed, and the new spiritual attitude soon dominated the whole of Europe, becoming so rigid it could no longer understand or agree with reality."

And in connection with the Altamira caves let us again quote Herbert Kühn: "Prehistoric art of such importance to the world has come to light like a misunderstood, unexpected miracle: there were no traditions, fables or myths connected with it. This was a vanished world, a realm of the distant past, buried for tens of thousands of years . . . But then it emerged from the bowels of the earth and spoke in a clear voice to men who would not listen; men who would not believe clear, independent evidence—they were afraid, not merely doubtful. Then still more evidence appeared, new fragments of a strange world, self-sufficient; but this artform was too elaborate and could not be set into the traditional picture of evolution . . . antiquity is the period from 400 B.C. to A.D. 400—almost a millennium. Would there have been any period with a naturalistic art before this time? What an absurd thought! The more one goes back into time the more abstract and primitive must art become. It is quite impossible and contrary to the concept of progress that in the glacial ages between 100,000 and 10,000 years B.C. such a form of art could ever have existed: since wherever art occurs, there must be thought and knowledge of the world to cause it. Ice-age man, this mere troglodyte, cannot have created a true art. His must have been only a stuttering . . . it is impossible that he was capable of a level only reached much later in the Renaissance.

"Nonetheless it is so, even if such things cause scandal, irritation and unpleasantness. That is the reality. It is not the duty of the mind to create facts: the facts exist—and mind must learn to place them correctly into the whole historical picture."

CHAPTER SEVENTEEN

EXTRATERRESTRIAL TEMPLES

Marcahuasi is only a desert plateau, burnt by the sun and split by dryness, wind-battered. A lunar-type gash 3,800 metres high, to the west of the Cordillera of the Andes. Three square kilometres of burnt-out horror, accessible only by mule. What could be found there, apart from fever and delirium? And yet Daniel Ruzo, a well-known Peruvian explorer, went there on the basis of vague traces of ruins and old texts and myths, or mere fragments of them. And it was there that he found, surrounded by figures of prehistoric animals dating back at least to the Secondary (from 185 to 130 million years ago), strange sculptures which seemed to say nothing, but at the summer solstice became visible and showed human faces.

This was not the end of the marvels, since he also saw a hill representing the calm face of an old man. When he photographed it and examined the negative he found that the features had changed into those of a young man in his prime! What mystery did the enigmatic face of Marcahuasi hide? Nothing we know was able to produce this change, apart from a roll of film and it would certainly not have been easy to carve such a thing even for an artist with all the resources of modern times at his disposal.

"On the banks of the canals which once must have given Marcahuasi the appearance of a garden of tropical splendour, as on the shores of Titicaca lake," the American McDonald tells us in references to the discoveries of Ruzo's as well as to the writings of the Spanish chronicler Diego d'Alcobaca, "there arose statues to which the light-effects and the reflections from the water gave an impressive show of life." On this side of the Atlantic we find such effects only at certain hours of the day—for instance in the imposing megalithic complex near the coasts in Southern England—at Stonehenge and Avebury, which had been studied for forty years by Péquart and Le Rouzic. And in Carelia there is a spectacle which is still more surprising and called by Konstantin Lauskin 'prehistoric cinema'.

"The Russian archaeologists working in Karelia," said Lauskin in the review *Snanje-Sila*, "have brought to light hundreds of villages dating between 3000 and 2000 years B.C. (it seems fairly certain that men were settled here around 6000–4000 B.C.) as well as rock-drawings which can be regarded as masterpieces of primitive art. On the eastern bank of the Onega they found about 600 sketches, a real gallery over the centuries. With knives only made of rough stone the artists cut figures of men, animals, birds, fish, reptiles, lunar and solar symbols—all on hard granite. These men must have had a clear idea of what they wanted to show, also acute vision and steady hands, since a wrong cut in the sharp silica could have ruined the picture for good: granite is a canvas which will not allow corrections. The choice of site is also interesting, since they picked on rocks rising vertically from the lake waters. It would have been much easier to operate nearby, so why did the artists ignore these spots?

"The designs on the cliffs become clearer in the sun's rays at sunset, and it is clear that the artists chose them precisely because of the light-effects, not because of wishing to run risks. I have had the luck to see some of these drawings on the promontory at Perinos (where there is a noteworthy collection of them) during the summer solstice and one of them might well have been called Crime and Punishment of the Frog. Before the sun went down the designs seemed confused, so that they could hardly be distinguished from below. But when the sun neared the horizon the granite shone dark-red and the variously coloured lines of the patterns were very clear. This is a magnificent spectacle which can be scientifically explained. Granite has a granular structure which is easily polished. The Onega granite has been polished for thousands and thousands of years by the water while the lines of the carvings on the smooth surfaces of the rocks maintain the above-mentioned granular structure. The designs are full of countless little crystal prisms reflecting much more light than the smooth surrounding areas. Thus the incisions become alive, though such luminous effects are not the only ones they have. They become alive almost before the sunrays touch the rocks and the frog seems to turn to an elk, while the hunter makes a movement with the hand (here the imagination can complete the story: the hunter has just thrown the axe with his right hand and puts out his left arm to keep his balance) as the camp-fire flickers. This spectacle on the granite lasts a quarter of an hour till the setting sun makes the designs grow weaker.

"Another marvel! But here too there is a scientific explanation. Think of some luminous signs: if the light goes on and off regularly the signs will seem to be moving. The same effect can be seen here—groups of tiny prisms on the unequal surfaces of the designs act like lamps, so that at certain moments some will become more luminous than others. The intensity of the light reflected will thus be different, as certain parts shine more than others. The rocks absorb two currents of light: one comes directly from the setting sun while the other is reflected from the lake. Both light sources are moving and whilst the sun is setting the angle of incidence of its rays is constantly changing likewise; whereas the water plays the part of a reflector. The incidence of the rays makes the various groups of prisms shine which gives the onlooker the impression that the whole design is moving . . ."

The Mystery of the "cat-man"

Such bizarre works must have been created on principles common to both sides of the ocean. But because they were carried out in times much closer to ours—however amazing they can seem to us from the point of view of "official" science—are they not really just rough copies of the ancient and ageless masterpieces to which we have referred? This question admits of only one answer—the one concerning the theories about a vanished continent—of which there is now nothing but the pale reflections of records wiped out by apocalyptic cataclysms.

The common denominators amongst the populations of Asia, America and the southern regions of the Mediterranean are innumerable. Let us look, with Serge Hutin, at one of the most enigmatic monuments of the past. "Scholars," he says, "have often pointed out similarities in religious architecture. For instance, there are pyramids in the Mediterranean area but also in the Gulf of Mexico. And against an often quoted objection we must also consider that even the 'teocalli' of the Aztecs and the Maya are really pyramids whose geometrical completeness is striking; and despite certain undeniable differences show the same structure of religious concept as those of the Nile valley.

"As for the materials used, Mitchell Hedges, an American Egyptologist, believes he can prove that the blocks in the Giza pyramid are not Egyptian syenite but come from South America. All the analogies between the Old and the New worlds have the problem of Atlantis. In the last analysis either one has to admit the existence of direct contact between the Maya and the Egyptians or one has to agree that there was a communal source between them. One must bear in

mind certain remarkable differences but these are quite
easily explained on the basis of the theory that there
was one origin but two independent lines of evolution."
But let us look at three amazing figures exhibited in the
National Anthropological Museum in Mexico City; the
so-called "old" god of an assumed "Olmeca" origin,
found in the State of Veracruz (Cerro de las Mesas)
one of the famous bearded white men spoken about in
innumerable chronicles of central and southern America. He is here represented wearing a very strange headgear with crosses on it; the second one in terracotta and
with typically oriental features of Tlatilco comes from
the preclassical period, while the third is another terracotta of the same time and place—an undoubtedly
negroid type of individual. Such statues could almost
give us additional proof of intercontinental contact in
the remotest times but they do not bring us with abso-
lute certainty to the origins mentioned by Hutin.

Where can we look for them then? In the Amazon
ruins found by Marcel Homet in the Serra do Machado,
countless ages old? Or among those dolicocephalous
(long-headed) creatures with the strange features, to be
seen in the Mexican anthropological museum, one of
which comes from the State of Nayarit and the other
(whose dress suggests a space-suit) from Jalisco State?
Or should we look among the "flat-headed beings" of
the Cauca Valley in Columbia, which have been reproduced in precious metals, stone sculptures and ti-
tanic rock carvings? And what about the cat-faced men
found everywhere in central and southern America?

Traditional science thinks of these as inspired by the
jaguar-cult, but against this theory is the fact that these
statues are also found where the jaguar-cult never
existed and where traditions allude to the unknown
people as "foreign warriors" or "warriors of the night"
or even as "gods descended from the moon". In the
imposing collection in Mexico City there is a mask of
Tlatilco with his vacant oblique expression and mouth
wide open in its unforgettable sneer. It is like some
creature totally alien to anything on Earth: a monstrous
relation of the Olmeca jade figure from Cerro de las

Mesas with its rounded pupils, triangular nostrils and
long dilated lips which came to light in Pueblo State
(Cozcatlán). And a relation, too, of the "cat-men" or
rather of their heads carved in huge stone blocks with
an amazing realism which swarm in the Mexican forests. It was the Olmecs who created them, but how these
people—who it is said did not even use roads—managed to carry out such masterpieces and transport them
through the forests for hundreds and hundreds of
kilometres, is still an insoluble mystery.

Their helmets are the most striking things about
them, but they have the same costumes as those carved
on the slabs of rock at Monte Albán in southern Mexico—costumes or suits which at once suggest spacemen's
clothing! The extraordinary myth goes with us across a
large part of what we now call Latin America, down to
Chavín de Huántar, in western Peru where the unknown culture once flourished discovered by the Indian
archaeologist Julio Tello; and where the world's most
enigmatic temple to the "cat-god" also rose: a temple
full of feline features, from the eyes to the nostrils and
from the teeth to the claws. But is it only a temple? Is
it not perhaps a monument to the astronauts of the
Chavín civilization or to something intended to simu-
late a cosmic engine, as people say who see similar
ones in the figures adorning the Gate of the Sun at
Tiahuanaco; a representation at the same time of an
interplanetary cruiser and the physiognomy of its occupants? These are not just fantasies; we are only saying that the characteristics here are so different from
anything else we know that some such hypothesis as this
is definitely favoured.

"Of the Chavín culture," says the Frenchman Olivier
Pecquet, "we know next to nothing. It seems that these
people may have appeared suddenly and built a network of fortresses in almost all the valleys of the northern slope; they then disappeared, leaving behind those
stone sculptures which remind us of their brilliant technique and the tradition of the terrible jaguar-cult . . .
The Castillo, the temple of Chavín de Huantar, is a

marvellous piece of architecture; the building has three floors, linked by means of stairs with balustrades. *Each floor has its own ventilation system, yet it has neither doors nor windows apart from the entrance!* The external walls are made of enormous blocks of stone, among which there are sculptured stone projections like gargoyles. The obelisks have very complex shapes with columns and carvings of condors, cats and devils, the latter lying about here and there, ruined by the years . . ."

It is not difficult to understand how some modern students have seen details in pre-columbian works which give rise to sensational theories: The Mexico City Museum of Anthropology show in addition to the works already quoted here some zapatoca funerary urns with "crowned" heads such as allow one to imagine with a modicum of restrained fantasy (as one Soviet worker happily puts it) some kind of "spatial" headgear, complete with radar antennae one might well think.

The mask of El Dorado

Images of space-ships, stars, feline symbols: here is that splendid and bewildering phantasmagoria even sparkling in the impenetrable jungles of the Amazon. El Dorado is a legend which has fascinated restless souls for centuries and in the course of the last three centuries has attracted according to the official archives of Seville, Barcelona and Buenos Aires (though it is thought the number may be at least five times as large) 72 expeditions to face the endless dangers and, in many cases, death.

The first note about it comes from Pizarro's deputy in 1509, Pedro de Orellana. People say that instead of completing an official mission he preferred to go off on his own looking for easy booty; afterwards he avoided trouble from his employers by inventing hair-raising stories about having met warriors "without heads", Amazons and people from a land called "Manoa" where everything was made of gold, from the pavements to the roofs of the houses, and governed by "El hombre dorado"—later called El Dorado.

Pure fiction? It certainly is, largely. But not just De Orellana's invention; it is the result of traditions he met everywhere on his travels. Belalcazar, another of Pizarro's lieutenants, confirms it by simply repeating accounts heard from the Indians settled east of Quito. He was told, as were many other Europeans, the history of a king of divine origin who lived in a gold palace which shut out all the light. This king was supposed to have been "the son of the sun and the sun itself": a kind of golden mask covered the lower part of his face and not even his servants were allowed to see him, since when they approached they had to do so backwards. Only once a year he showed himself to his subjects, covered in gold-dust, when he went to a lake and threw necklaces and jewels into it for the "demon of the deeps".

A daily Milan newspaper, *Il Giorno,* said in this connection: "Nobody could ever claim having seen El Dorado, and yet in 1700 a Spanish commentator on Belalcazar's diary was able to describe the palace of 'the son of the sun' as if he were looking at a photo of it: 'The palace of the Emperor Moxo rises from the centre of the lake, and the gates of the palace are guarded with pumas tied up with golden chains. Even the tables and the crockery are of gold. The island is full of gardens and artificial fountains where the waters rise from great effigies of gold and falls into silver basins. An artificial moon rises above a column of silver ten metres high which is so clear and brilliant it sends the purest rays across the lake when the sun strikes it'."

There is plenty here to strike the devotees of the "space hypothesis" as tied to the remote past of our planet; from the palace itself, hermetically sealed to represent an astronaut's ship to the "mask" of the enigmatic king—which could well be a space respirator; from the offerings to a ruler so deep no meaning could be attached to it, to the griffins reminding us of the "fire-bird" or "celestial dragons"; from the pumas meant to recall the physiognomy of the "cat-men" to the island's idyllic scenery with its temples and distant views; from the attributes of El Dorado himself to the lunar monument whose light effects remind us on the one hand of the statues mentioned here and on the other (with the reflection of those "most clear rays" from the lake) they suggest something of what the imagination of a man living in the first half of the sixteenth century would have been able to add.

Cosmic eggs

For many of its verses the description of El Dorado can be likened to that of Tiahuanaco the very ancient Peruvian city senselessly destroyed which was once situated on the banks of the lake of Titicaca, its ruins now being about 25 kilometres from that lake—because of continued drop in water level. Archaeology is still trying to penetrate its mysteries. Some people, like the German scholar Posnansky, who saved everything he could save there, thinks it was built around 16,000 years ago on the ruins of something built by the "fair-haired giants" 200–250,000 years ago, as mentioned by native legend. Perhaps something can be said of the city sunk in the middle of the lake and recently discovered by three Argentinian workers. The theory is becoming more and more acceptable that Tiahuanaco first arose from the sea and then later thrown up to its present-day height like the Cordillera of the Andes by cosmic catastrophes that changed the whole face of the globe. Where in fact do the gigantic monoliths come from? How would its inhabitants have been able to live on that desolate plateau today lashed by all the winds and hostile to any form of farming?

We cannot say for certain that McDonald is wrong when he states that Peru probably holds the most vital secrets in the world "of which we have neither name nor date" woven between Titicaca and Chan-Chan, the city of the snake-god whose ruins seem to include the architectural qualities of all the ancient civilizations; between the extremely long wall which, found around 40 years ago by the Johnson expedition, snakes its way from high peak to deep valley, and the Maras amphitheatres so astonishingly like the Mediterranean ones; and the mysterious constructions built along the flanks of impenetrable mountains with the Nazca pictures which can only be seen from above and have been clearly seen by areial reconnaissance.

Professor John A. Mason, a more traditional-type archaeologist, and member of Pennsylvania University, rejects the wilder notions of his colleagues but still cites the oldest Peruvian traditions and refers to the "habitable qualities of the stars" as mentioned by the texts centred on the "descent of gods from the constellation of the Pleiad".

"One legend reported in the well-known book *The Earth* by Jean Elisee Reclus," says the Soviet scholar Saitsev, "tells how the first Peruvians were born from a bronze, gold and silver egg which fell from the sky. A variant of this is represented by the famous Tassili drawings, found by Lieutenant Brenard in the heart of the Sahara. Shortly afterwards the site was examined by the French expedition led by Henri Lote . . . Besides animal drawings and hunting scenes the sketches themselves show us strange figures wearing garments which seem to be space suits and round helmets. The latter are clearly joined to the former and evoke neither ritualistic headgear nor dress appropriate to hunters, who—as certain scholars think—used helmets made of oyster shell. Lote called these mysterious figures Martians and said how one of them looked like 'a man emerging from an egg-shaped object covered in concentric circles . . .'

"But the parallels do not stop with the Tassili drawings or the Peruvian legends. Later on in another part of the world the same subject was dealt with again by ancient sculptors, some of whom created Castor and Pollux, Helen and Nemesis with bits of egg-shell on their heads, since such people were born from celestial eggs according to Greek mythology. How could this idea spread—the birth of a man from an egg? Perhaps as a recollection of the world of birds and fish? But why would such an egg have fallen from the sky? One central-American legend tells us about direct descent from space on the 'teeth of the lion'!

"The absence of any established interpretation leaves the door wide open to what might appear to be a fantastic supposition: to the theory, that is, that the 'celestial egg' can have originated like others in the transformation of real events. Our remotest forefathers must have seen creatures emerging from space vehicles and naturally have thought they were beings born from an egg which fell out of the heavens."

CHAPTER EIGHTEEN

FORMED FROM A STAR

"In the remotest past
Millions and millions of moons ago
The first of mortal men was cast down
On this world by the great Wo-Kon.
The first Dakota was formed from a star;
He hurled him and watched him as he fell
Through the darkness until he rested
On soft soil. He was not wounded
Wa-kin-yan, the first Sioux.

From afar we see the days of summer
Setting in a golden splendour
Towards the mystic region of the legend
That remote land in the West,
The land of the house and the story of the Red Man,
Country of myths and strange customs,
Valley of dark unwritten history.

This is an extract from the American Indian epic
called *Chon-oopa-sa* and is attributed to an unknown

poet Pa-la-ne-a-pa-pe. James Churchward mentions him in connection with his theory that man originated from Mu—which is just what is meant by "That remote land in the West, The land of the house and the story of the Red Man". We could easily replace Mu by the area normally given by science to the origin of the Redskin. But more interesting by far are the allusions to the "first Dakota formed from a star" and his journey to Earth "through the darkness"; which could be a synonym for cosmic space as in many American traditions and could lend support to the notion of a landing on Earth of beings from another world an unimaginably long time ago.

It seems important to note that Churchward did not actually allude to such theories himself (in his time astronautical matters were not even a vague dream) though the idea recurs with curious frequency in Indian lore.

"The inhabitants of Earth," wrote the *Ottawa Journal,* in an article on these myths, "were first on other planets: all human beings descend from people of distant worlds." And another Canadian journal, *Topside,* says: "The writer has recently met Chief Mezzaluna of the Piute tribe. In an answer to the question Where did the North American Indians come from? the following was stated: 'According to our ancient traditions the Indians were created in the sky by Gitchie Manitou, the Great Spirit, who sent down here a big thunder-bird to find a place for his children to live. He discovered this land . . . and brought Indians to settle on it. They were taught to use the land wisely and never abuse its natural resources'." "The Hiden Indians," says Churchward, when discussing Indian legends, "of Queen Charlotte Island possess one of the most interesting and beautiful totem poles I have ever seen. On top there is a great bird like an eagle, called 'Thunder-bird' and all along the pole itself stretches the carving of a fish known as 'the whale that kills'; while half-way between its head and tail there is the carving of a man—'the man with the iron head'— about to stab a spear in its back. This was interpreted to me by a local sage as follows: 'The thunder-bird represents the Creator. Its glance is like a spark and the clapping of its wings is thunder. In the days of the Deluge the man with the spear was very much loved by the thunder-bird, by the thunder-god and by all the other gods. When the Flood cleared the face of the world, the gods feared for the life of the iron-headed man, so they changed him by miracle into a salmon with an iron head. During the flood the leader of humanity, transformed in this way, lived in the waters of the river Minish. He collected timbers for his house but found many things wanting for its construction. Then the thunder-bird appeared and showed the man, after lifting his mask, a human face: 'I am a man like you and shall collect timber for you. I shall stay with you to establish your tribe and to protect you always'. Then the Thunder-bird made a group of warriors appear, completely armed. This was the origin of the people of Haiden'."

Churchward adapted this symbolic legend for his Mu theory—"mother of all races"—and tends to think the survivors reached other lands by means of boats, since some of the oriental drawings indicating their means of survival are in fish form. It is quite clear that before the space age certain legends must have seemed completely senseless, sheer fantasy or religious concepts unconnected with reality. But things are different today and in the light of present-day knowledge we could perhaps follow the story as told by the Indian sage a little further: "With thunderous noises and flashes of light a missile descended on Earth and left a group of observers there of whom perhaps only one survived. Faced with a terrifying flood the visitor looked for shelter in a world invaded by water, but his colleagues on board the space ship, thinking he was in difficulty as he did not return sent an expedition which when it arrived on Earth also helped the survivors from the Deluge by setting them off towards some place where existence was tolerable." The "sole survivor" would be the iron-headed man, if we remember that this head became a mask much later which hid human features—an astronaut's helmet? And the "salmon of iron" an unsinkable, hermetically sealed glass case—quite likely, since we also would give our spacemen such equipment if they were going to land on other worlds mostly covered in water.

The torn canvas

Something still more amazing must have happened in North America: an event or series of events likened by some students to gigantic thermo-nuclear explosions. Among such scholars we can count Mihail Agrest, a Russian mathematician and physicist, who sees this type of ending for Sodom and Gomorrah. Faced with the sinister spectacle of the Valley of Death in California and Nevada Desert, Agrest starts again with the study of the most ancient ruins, with the fused rocks and vitrified sand which cannot be due at all to volcanic eruptions but which have eternally changed a once verdant land into a nightmarish desert. What events took place here thousands of years ago? We shall probably never know; among the traces of men who a million years ago began their arduous ascent to the Santa Maria culture, fantastic ruins arise from Death Valley; and the inexplicable traditions of the Apache Indians (who even today bow to the Mediterranean god Ammon-Ra and can describe Tiahuanaco without ever having seen it) stretch into fathomless chasms from which other mysteries crop up with mythological connections.

There are above all the mounds, the artificial hills mentioned in the first part of this book (page 90 et seq.), but we can ignore the suggestive theories according to which they were made in a limited number of shapes the world over; even if there is, near Stonehenge, a snake formation said to be the exact duplicate of one not far from Peebles, Ohio. Let us rather consider the mound-builders calendar as it is called, found carved into a rock in the river Ouachita (Hot Springs, Arkansas) with its year divided into 13 months and represented by the following symbols:

1. An unclear carving: could be a bird with unfurled wings—probably the Thunder-bird.
2. A sign like the Maya month of Zac, the month of the snows.
3. An unidentifiable sign.
4. A fish going upstream—could be a reference to the iron-salmon.
5. A sign which Churchward thinks can be identified with a letter of the Mu alphabet.
6. A lotus-flower, a development of the cross.
7. Unidentifiable: but nearby is the head of a snake suggesting emblems of the plumed serpent.
8. A symbol which, according to Churchward, would have religious significance in various Asiatic lands.
9. Unidentifiable drawing: some think it indicates August-September.
10. A drawing apparently indicating falling leaves.
11. A spider.
12. Profile of an animal, probably a deer.
13. Profile of another animal, probably a bison.

One special thing about all these is the spider of the 11th month which is cut—heavily inscribed in circumferences and producing another circle with a cross or the solar disc—into a number of the mound-builders works in Missouri, Arkansas and Tennessee. The spider emblem can be found, says Churchward, on several of the discoveries made by Schliemann, the discoverer of Troy, as well as in Crete, Cyprus and Polynesia. With regard to the latter Churchward mentions obscure legends according to which the spider would have been able to leap into the sky if not held back by the cold. If we want to see the animal portrayed in its usual perfect form we must go to Nazca, to that stellar Atlantis in which one can see a series of drawings intended for attracting the attention of astronauts who had landed on Earth ages ago.

And if we feel inclined to accept the theory of contact between all the ancient cultures we find an expression of this in a Polynesian legend which mentions a network of impossible complexity interfering with later travels by spacemen who landed on Earth.

Message in dust

Which and how many pages of the unknown history of Earth lie buried under the prairies and forests and cities of North America? We owe the following notes to Alessandro Riario Sforza, an Italian student of these matters: "Alexander Bradford in his New York 1834 edition of *American Antiquities* tells us about one of the larger American caves under the San Antonio waterfall with its walls covered in hieroglyphics, but so adorned with moss and eroded with age that there was nothing intelligible left in it. Bradford also said that in Illinois there was a huge cave with a mineshaft (the cave was about 122 metres round) where excavators brought to light some pottery like that of the mounds—and found here at a great depth but it is a pity Bradford, usually so meticulous, did not specify the depth. The queen of caves in North America is still the Mammoth Cave, the Kentucky mastodon cave or grotto which branches off to form many others. The entrance is over 10 metres wide and six high with a corridor about 15 metres long. This gives way to a very narrow passage which shoots off into darkness. When you cross the threshold you go into a "room" 183 metres in length and 27 wide, with its walls consisting of massive boulders. From here start various twisting tunnels—thought by scholars to be due to the erosion caused by large subterranean rivers which have now vanished. Through a series of corridors one comes to the so-called Haunted Chamber; and the first people to go there, in 1800 discovered some mummies, or so it is said. Others were found in 1810 when there was excavation going on for saltpetre, and in his book *Excursion to the Mammoth Cave* Davidson describes how the bodies were interred again so as not to disturb the peace of the spirits. The mummies were wrapped and had funerary equipment beside them, together with jewels. Another explorer, Stephen, described them in his book published in New York in 1841 and he reproduced the drawings. There were hieroglyphics, palaces, colossal statues and pyramids—like the ones in Egypt."

But unfortunately we have no further evidence. Some archaeologists (Wilson, Rush) remind us of the ancient cultures of central and southern America rather than the Egyptian one. Alessandro Riario Sforza could also support this when he refers to Stephen's recordings: "If, in general, the Egyptian hierologlyphics remind of reality those of the Mammoth Cave give us notions of imaginary beings."

Sforza also says that in 1868 during coalmining in Ohio an enormous mass of the mineral got loose and revealed a wall literally covered in hieroglyphics and arranged in horizontal rows at a distance of about 7.60 metres from each other. They were never deciphered and the wall crumbled away and so the enigmatic message from the unimaginably distant past failed. Then there is the case of Tom Kenny, a farmer in the Plateau Valley, who found at a depth of three metres under the ground a piece of pavement consisting of hand-made, smooth, symmetrical tiles. The analysis of its mortar proved that it was of different material from anything else in the valley and experts had to admit it dated back to anything from 20 to 80 thousand years ago. But Frank Edwards, in Strangest of All (New York 1956) tells us that tiles and pavements have been found elsewhere in the strata where the three-toed horse occurs—in the American Miocene—and this dates from 6 to 30 million years ago!

We cannot share the view of Edwards on the basis of a single piece of evidence, but it is on the other hand just as clear that the history of the world does not follow the road which the pontiffs of science insist on giving to it.

CHAPTER NINETEEN

A CHALLENGE TO SCIENCE

Mr. Kishi woke up in the dead-of night, rushed towards the door and stumbled against a stool. His wife and son then woke up with a jump. "What's the matter, Father?" said the boy, "aren't you feeling well?" "Oh no," said the old peasant, shaking his head, "it is something which happened outside. Very odd. There was a rumble of thunder—didn't you hear it? And that green light, everything green . . ."

Mother and son looked at each other alarmed, as they had heard no noise at all and seen no green light. But Kishi looked like a sleepwalker yet was aware of everything around him. He opened the door and slipped out while his wife and son went to the window where they saw him creeping along until he suddenly straightened up and moved his hands as though trying to calm someone in front of him. He stayed there about five minutes, waving his arms up and down as though talking to someone and then went back indoors. "I can't understand it," he said, "I just can't understand it."

"But what happened?" his son asked him.

"Did you see it too?" Kishi asked. "It was a great dragon of fire which we thought was a meteorite. Why it pitched on our field I don't know but I saw two little men get out of its belly and they started talking to me in a language I didn't understand. I tried talking to them but it was no use. They went back into the monster's belly and . . ." The old peasant suddenly stopped and fainted. His wife and son got him back to bed very apprehensively but immediately afterwards he seemed to be sleeping peacefully. The following morning when they mentioned it Kishi looked at them astonished, and said: "You must be mad—I slept like a log all night!"

Tales like this one, by the Amercan journalist W. Jones, are quite frequent in Japan. This case is hardly likely to be pure somnambulism and scholars less tied to traditional views think it might be a case of atavistic phenomena not yet explained by science. We could support this with similar cases if necessary though this is not really our purpose.

The bridge amongst the stars

Of winged monsters and stars settling on Earth or of beings emerging from the bellies of dragons the ancient texts and legends of Japan are full. They also tell us of odd events which if seen in a modern light tend to support even odder hypotheses. The *Kojiki* or *Chronicle of Ancient Things* is one of the earliest texts written in 712 by the chamberlain Hiyeda-No-Are but containing much older tales handed down by wandering singers; and it was translated into Chinese in 720 by Toneri, who called it *Nihongi* and dedicated it to the Empress "as proof of her descent from Amaterasu, goddess of the sun". But the *Nihongi* gives us accounts about the appearances of unknown celestial objects which are quite odd enough in themselves. "A big star went from east to west," we read among the events of 637, "and there was a noise like thunder." The people talked about a falling star but the Buddhist monk Bin said: "It is not a shooting star but the Heavenly Dog whose bark is like thunder."

"The Heavenly Dog," says Drake in *Spacemen in the Middle East*, "is the star called Sirius. But the monk is referring rather to an ancient Chinese text, *The Book of the Mountains and the Seas*, in which it states: 'On the mountains of the Celestial Gate there is a dog called the Celestial Dog whose shine ploughs across the sky like a star several poles long. He travels like the wind and his voice is that of thunder!' The reference to length could mean a space vehicle while the name itself tends to make one believe it came from Sirius."

Other extracts from the second volume of the work possibly concerning interplanetary travel are:

640: 7th day of 2nd month of spring a star entered the Moon area. 642: In the autumn, 9th day, 7th month, a guest star entered the Moon in the reign of the Empress Ame-Toyo-Tokora-Ikashi-hi-Tarashi-Hime. 681: 9th month, 16th day. A comet appeared, and on 17th day Mars entered the Moon. (This clearly does not mean Mars but some other body with its reddish colour. It is interesting that the *Nihong* spoke about comets and meteorites, while the term "star" does not refer to them but to something else.)

682: 8th month, 3rd day, a great star passed from east to west. 692: Autumn, 28th month, reign of the Empress Tokama-No-Ara-Hiro-No-Hime. The imperial chariot was returning to the palace at night when Mars and Jove (This does not refer to the Mars and Jove as we know them) appeared with a great light which came on and off four times.

Drake says in this connection: "Doctor Yoshiyuki Tange tells us of a Hokkaido legend recording the descent of Okikurumi-kammi (the ancient god Ainu) at Maiopira on board a shining 'shinta', a vehicle used by those people. The god would have taught to the Ainu 'the just and rightful way to live' and exterminated a devil. The *Nihongi* then tells how in 667 B.C. the Emperor Kami-Yamato-Iharo-Biko spoke with his celestial forefathers who had then gone home on board an 'oscillating celestial vessel'[1] and going back in time for over one million seven hundred and ninety-two thousand four hundred and seventy years—certainly something which will never fail to amuse our scientists . . . Before the nephew of Amaterasu, Ninigi-No-Mikoto descended from the sky on his 'floating bridge' (a cosmic vehicle?) he told how at the sky crossroads there was a strange god whose nose was seven hands long and from whose mouth and back came a vivid light . . . The goddess Uzumehime approached the stranger who presented himself as Sarute-hiko, saying he also meant to take an abode in Japan and offered a 'flying bridge' or a 'celestial bird'. The nine suns over Japan in 9 B.C. give us some analogy perhaps with the ten suns which appeared over China in 2346 B.C., nine of which fell to the arrows of the 'divine archer'. On both occasions the people were at war and the sun-worshippers thought that the phenomenon of 9 B.C. was a sign of divine wrath with the Yamato dynasty, which had thrown its own people into slavery."

We might also look at Tibet concerning space travel, which before the Himalayas arose would have been a "flat fertile plain, peopled by Mu survivors" a tradition which reminds us of the notion that the sinking of Atlantis might have meant the raising up of the Andes —but a great deal of Tibetan myth is obscure: its first king Shipuye was followed by the "Seven divine thrones" and then the "two high beings"; events related to the "divine dynasties" of Vietnam, India, China, Japan, Egypt and Greece. Then came the "six reigning sages", the "eight monarchs of the world" and the "four powers" which suggest the semi-gods and heroes of mythology. The first Tibetan king of historical truth is, however, Nami Sontson, who in the seventh century engaged in victorious warfare and extended his sway from China to Persia.

"The vast literature concerning Tibet," says Drake,

[1]From this, perhaps, we get the notion in the term "shinta" of cradle or home of civilization—and the Ainu might have brought the solar disc.

"is little enough known in the west: yet the archives of the lamaseries as far as riches go could rival those of the Vatican. The 'Kanjur', for instance, has 1,083 works, one of which, the 'Tanjur', has 225 volumes. Only persons with proper scientific knowledge can explain the important parts of these works—while the Indian texts refer to the secrets of anti-gravity (weightlessness) of telekinesis and the exploitation of cosmic energy.

"It is odd how often the things which we might label as science-fiction today occur in Tibetan legends, one of which relates how a boy with a 'deformed' head married the daughter of a god living in the celestial regions. The god descended to earth 'in the form of a shining duck'." Is this another version of the Firebird?

"One colourful Tibetan tale," Drake goes on, "describes Sudarsoma, the city of thirty-three gods which rose in space and was encircled by seven walls of gold . . . a marvel of gold, silver, beryl and crystal, where the divinities would have had 'power of materialization', taking everything they needed from the trees (are we not approaching this state, too, with the synthesis of chlorophyll?). After having conquered the whole world the king Mandhotar would have been forced out of his lust to subjugate even Heaven, but his wild ambitions would have brought his death. Now while Mandhotar was in space the city of the 33 gods would have been attacked by the Asura who, after a terrible battle (with amazing arms like invisible rays and flying horses etc.) would have been defeated and hounded back into space."

Many fantastic stories derive from Tibet and it is certain that if its inhabitants had the powers attributed to them then, their history—especially after the second world war would have developed in a very different way from the one we know. But it is still amazing considering the faculties of the Tibetan monks—though perhaps even these would be of little importance if we could know about their unimaginable past.

Electric discs

Fantasy has definitely played its part in whatever has been handed down to us in mythology but it would be wrong to think everything was due to this; if we follow Saitsev, for instance the facts are true enough. "The report of a Chinese archaeologist," he said, "amazed the world when it was published in 1965, because he had put together from ancient fragments an astonishing theory about space-ships having visited Earth 12 thousand years ago. According to the German review *Das Vegetarische Universum* the last quarter of the century saw archaeologists exploring caves in the Bayan-Kara-Ula mountains on the China-Tibet borders. They found 716 stone discs with drawings and indecipherable hieroglyphics which were thousands of years old. They had a hole in the centre like a gramophone record from which a double groove traces out a spiral to the circumference. They were not sound tracks but a kind of writing—the strangest in the world. The experts racked their brains in vain till some Chinese archaeologists solved the puzzle—which so astounded them that the Peking Academy of Prehistory stopped publication of what was revealed. But permission was finally given and the work came out under the title—rather clumsily —of *The grooved script concerning space-ships which, as recorded on the discs, landed on Earth 12 thousand years ago*. The Bayan-Kara-Ula caves have been peopled by the Ham and Dropa tribes—a weak race, diseased with rickets. Average height only 1 metre 27 centimetres and as yet without any proper ethnographical classification. "The Dropa," we read there, "descended from the clouds on their machines while our own forefathers hid ten times in the night in caves. But when they understood the sign language of the Dropas they realized that the newcomers meant them no harm." Other Ham writings describe the grief following the loss of the tribe's space-ships during a dangerous landing in high mountains and the failure of the attempt to build a new one . . .

"When finally freed of all incrustations the discs were sent to Moscow where it was found that they contained large amounts of cobalt and that they were rhythmically pulsating as though they had electric charges in them. Those discs were, and still are, a challenge to science!"

Other Chinese fables tell how little yellow creatures descended from the clouds and found repulsion on the part of Earth's inhabitants because their yellow faces, big heads and small bodies were so ugly. Some were attacked.

Such legends appear to be confirmed by science, since in some of the same caves, tombs and skeletons were found 12,000 years old. The remains belonged to a humanoid race with big heads and small bodies we would call rachitic—a new type of extinct monkey, said some archaeologists in China. But no monkeys we know of bury themselves carefully after death as these were and neither can they write or draw. A further amazing fact from the caverns is the wall drawings of the sun, moon and stars interspaced with crowds of small circles the size of peas which seem to be approaching Earth, in a mountainous zone.

CHAPTER TWENTY

THE ROCKS OF SIRIUS

"About 15,000 years ago," said the French scholar F. Lagarde, "the Babylon priest Kidinnu (also an astronomer) knew the facts relating to the yearly movement of the sun and moon with a precision excelled only in 1857, when Hansen managed to obtain figures with an error of only 3 seconds. Even more amazing is the precision shown by the ancient sages when predicting lunar eclipses. The Oppolzer method has an error of seven-tenths of a second of an arc while Kidinnu's were nearer two-tenths. The fact that such results had been reached without telescopes, watches and all the other equipment we depend on seems quite incredible—this at a time when Aurignac man was still cutting his stones."

And the surprises have hardly begun: let us remember that the Assyrian god Nisroch (he corresponded to Saturn) was always represented by a ring and that a cylindrical Assyrian seal was the emblem of the planet dedicated to the goddess with a ring; which means they were aware, surely, of the circular nature of the celestial bodies and the orbits around them.

But there is something else amazing: "The Shilluk of southern Africa," says Professor Jean Servier, ethnographer at Montpellier, "call Uranus *three* stars; which seemed mad to the author who pointed it out but it was forgotten that when Herschel discovered Uranus on March 13th 1781 he observed later, in 1787, its two chief satellites; so only in that year could he explain the 'Uranus Three Star' term which the Shilluk had used since time immemorial—let us pardon them for having said three instead of five. Thus even without telescopes they had anticipated Herschel, thanks to generations of their own people who sat there in the Savanna with their eyes riveted to the skies."

Professor Servier also points out that the Dogon of Bandiagara, in Mali, similarly described the Sirius system as three stars, one of which was held to be the farthest away of all and of a metal brighter than iron, of which a tiny grain would weight more than "480 donkey-loads". "Our ideas," he says, "are not any more precise than these. A Sirius satellite called Companion was discovered by Clark in 1862, but even when in its most favourable phase (from our point of view) it could only be seen with the aid of a powerful telescope. Its density was calculated some years ago—and was found to be fifty times greater than water so that a small box full of it would weigh a ton. Astronomers admit today that besides Sirius (Sirius A) and Companion (Sirius B) there must be another star in the system, Sirius C; and they are still far from the day when they will be able to describe its orbit even roughly, as the Dogon do. The satellites of Mars were known before their 'discovery' in 1887 and it seems they were known even to the Sumerians. How it was all known is inexplicable unless we return to the theory of spacemen having come to Earth to instruct humanity in its own wisdom." F. Lagarde (whose views, we must honestly admit, we do not entirely share) has this to say about the matter: "According to Professor Agrest some prehistoric astronauts would have given the

calendar to the Maya. They were the 'gentlemen Dedz-
yan' of Indian tradition who had brought fire to Earth,
likewise the bow and the hammer; and they too were
the ones who supplied the Dogon with their knowledge
about the obscure Companion satellite; and given to the
peoples of the Mediterranean the information about
the tenth star of the Pleiades."

The Merowe missile

But many discoveries tend to make us ask if the ancient
peoples really were without optical instruments; and
whether we accept or reject the space theory we shall
find ourselves facing awkward questions. Leaving aside
the Hellenic references to the "preselenites" who lived
in glass houses we must still agree that the history of
glass goes back into the remotest antiquity. For long
held to be a Phoenician invention, found, says Pliny,
by using blocks of saltpetre to balance the cooking
pots on the fire which would make the blocks fuse with
the sand—it is now realized that such an idea is
absurd since no ordinary fire could produce enough
heat for a process of this nature. It is much the same
with the idea put forward by Giuseppe Flavio that the
Hebrews would have discovered it by setting light to a
forest.

Actually it appears in different epochs among peoples; the Indians knew it from the remotest eras (the
Germanic "glas" derives from the Sanskrit "kelasa")
and so did the Egyptians and Chinese—the former undoubtedly knowing about it before 2500 B.C. This is
proved by the rock-drawings of Beni Hassan, in which
there are designs showing men making glass; and then
there are the artificial pearls found at Thebes and covered in hieroglyphics. But the first instructions regarding its making come from King Assur-bani-pal of As-
syria: "60 parts of sand, 180 parts of ground seaweed,
5 parts of saltpetre and 3 parts of chalk"; all the
necessary ingredients if somewhat in the wrong proportions, but it would give a hard paste suitable for
the manufacture of small flasks, pearls, etc.

It is said that among the Greeks the art became lost but flourished again at the time of Alexander the Great. The Romans certainly appreciated it after the conquest of Egypt and Augustus claimed from the tribes conquered everywhere a proportion of his taxes in glass. Production of amphorae, vases, goblets of glass etc. all began in Italy about this time, as also the famous "chalices of gold"—formed by a thin sheet of the precious metal covered in glass.

Aristophanes says that spheres of glass were sold in Athens and Pliny informs us that Emilio Scauro, one of Sulla's generals, had a three-floored theatre built at Rome for 80,000 spectators: the first floor was of marble, the second of glass and the third of gilded wood. Pliny also said that Tiberius had a man killed who made pliable, unbreakable glass so that the secret should never be divulged. Shatter-proof glass about 1,970 years ago should not astonish us if we bear in mind that objects of this material were brought by the Romans to the finest level of perfection—of those times —but perhaps equalled only by the Egyptians. At Pompei the excavators dug up several sheets of glass of the sort we make today. This of course does not prove the existence of optical lenses yet we notice that Cicero speaks about a version of the *Iliad* "written on parchment so small it could all go into a nutshell". And similarly Pliny notes that "Mimecide had carved in ivory a chariot which could be covered by a fly's wings". The French astronomer Théodore Moreux mentioned a seal in the "Cabinet des Médailles" containing 15 figures in an area of seven millimetres radius; a miniature masterpiece called the "seal of Michelangelo" though undoubtedly of a much more remote age. It seems obvious that such objects could only have been achieved by means of the optical lens. "In 1903," Moreux says, "I was asked by the government to make a study of the total eclipse of the moon visible at Sfax. After we had finished our work we thought it would be nice to see Tunisia—we could hardly leave without having made a trip to Carthage ... Of the ancient city nothing is left except a village where the port for those terrible Carthaginian ships used to be. Father Bianchi has built a seminary there and a cathedral whose walls stand out sharply against the deep blue of the sky. Ancient Carthage no longer exists but reverent hands have uncovered the ruins of that distant life. Father Delattre took us round his museum where we admired the cameo of a horse scratching its ear. I said 'The people of those days didn't have eyes any better than ours, so how could they make such things in so small a space? Give me a magnifying glass so that I can admire its mane . . .' A minute later Father Delattre showed us a true, slightly convex lens the size of a button which was unfortunately opaque though no doubt originally transparent. We would still have had our doubts if Father Delattre had not shown us another lens, in rock-crystal this time and perfectly cut—it enabled us to examine the cameo. I thought I was holding in my hands the proof that the ancients had a knowledge of glass; being delighted I told some scientists about it and was astonished to hear that the great English physicist Sir David Brewster had exhibited at a meeting in Bedford a piece of rock-crystal shaped like a lens and found—in excavations at Ninevah!"

The road from these lenses to large modern ones is of course very long, but Moreux thinks our forefathers even reached this state themselves; otherwise Democritus would not have been able to say that the Milky Way (thought by the ancients to be drops of milk from the breast of Juno!) was formed of a multitude of stars and that "the confused mixture of their light is the cause of their phosphorescent whiteness".

Two centuries later came news about the mysterious instrument which Ptolemy the Third (Euergetes) had fixed on the top of the lighthouse at Alexandria, a device which could "detect distant ships"; and it is equally odd that some of the ancients talked about seeing stars "through tubes", which Moreux questions in the sense that he does not known if it is a simple tube which would concentrate the view—or perhaps a real telescope? To support the latter view he refers to Merowe, the old Nile city, capital of Nubia from the fourth century B.C. to the third century A.D. and revealed during the Garstang-Sayce excavations of 1909-10. During these Professor John Garstang of Liverpool found a building which after careful examination proved to be an astronomical observatory. Not only this but on one of the blocks there was a drawing which could have been an antenna or even a missile!

Iron from Ethalie

Even if only in rough outline we should consider the story of the Queen of Merowe and her bejewelled figures of winged and cat-like creatures. "We do know," says Walther Wolf in his book *Discoveries in Egypt,* "that in the last decades of the eighth century B.C. Egypt fell under the rule of the 'Ethopians'—which was brought about by a ruling family in Nàpata, a city at the Fourth Cataract which from the time of Thutmoses was the centre of the southern Egyptian empire. In 655 B.C. the last 'Ethopians' had to withdraw from Egypt and their plans for world power came to an end, although the Empire of Kush might still maintain itself for a further thousand years. But it was clear that Egyptian political and religious influence was dominant even if local power and much later the Greek and Roman forces were at work. Though the capital was Nàpata a branch of the royal family stayed at Merowe, by the Sixth Cataract in the district known today as Shendi. Here in the sixth century B.C. the residence was established, largely as a result of the Merowe's growing commercial power—based on iron ore deposits. About 200 B.C. the people of Merowe had developed a type of cursive alphabet like Demotic as well as one based on the Egyptian model which they used for their monuments. Both the alphabets were deciphered in 1911 by F. L. Griffith but in spite of this the Kush language is still not understood."

Their scientific knowledge and practical ability in metallurgy, especially gold, must have been highly advanced according to the German goldsmith Treskow who found that they knew the granular method for their necklaces etc. In 1850, during excavations under the El-Ghiza Sphinx the famous Egyptian expert Mariette had revealed at a depth of some seventy metres a number of gigantic structures, containing artistic marvels. "The date of the building of the Sphinx," says Charroux in this connection, "is lost in the mists of time; so the ruins found by Mariette, heaped up with the soil from thousands of years, must be much older still. Among the objects discovered, according to the 1850 text published, were 'tiny things of gold so light in weight one would think they were made by the process (ultra-modern) known as galvanoplasty'."

The American Richard Morris talks about large, peculiar boats lying in Tyrrhenian depths which suggest by their shape those of Egypt and with cargoes of gold, iron and other metals still visible. This of course is just Morris's tale (he being a frogman, not a scholar) but we must not forget, however, that the ancients' journeys were longer and their cargoes often bigger than the history books usually suggest; similarly with the iron-ore workings on Elba which are about ten times older than we thought.

"The Greeks in Homer's time," Charroux goes on, "already knew the island, which they called 'Ethalie' because of the smoke and soot arising from it so we may conclude the mining has been going on there for at least 3,000 years."

Voice of the Dawn

"We do not know Egypt: we only deceive ourselves into thinking we do." This statement, attributed to Professor Howard Carter, head of the famous expedition which found the tomb of Tut-ankh-Amon, reminds us of what Walther Wolf wrote: "We know today that there was a most remote Stone Age in Egypt. The celebrated African explorer Georg Schweinfurth (1836–1925), who founded the Cairo Geographical Society, during his wanderings through all the Nile valleys of the higher regions near present-day Luxor found flint artefacts even older than the stone implements. They were also discovered later in many other parts of Egypt, and western Europe too. It was thought no link could be established between old and new Egyptian stone ages till discoveries came to light dealing with recent stone and copper artefacts (eneolithic): "It was a clear red pottery alternating with yellowish or pink and on it we find painted various ships of a reddish-brown, dancing women, flamingoes and antelopes. At the same time they produced stone vases of a yellow alabaster and coloured breccia; also in green slate and red granite, all with great richness of form. Copper takes the place of silicon more and more, while the ditches for the burial of the dead were lined with rectangular bricks. These were also found in the Aegean Islands, Palestine, Syria and Mesopotamia."

"But how can one explain this course civilization took?" Wolf asks, "Are they simple evolutionary steps or are there other social strata involved—such as nomads and farmers perhaps—or totally new ethnic groups?"

Maybe the latter idea is correct but Wolf is right to question it since probably nobody will ever know, where the Nile dwellers obtained their astounding knowledge. We can often follow a people from its infancy; but of the Egyptians we discern their maturity and perhaps their decline—but their beginnings are so muddled and vague even the boldest theories might pass—such as the idea that their culture came from somewhere else, of which there are hardly any traces left.

Did the radiography carried out on a mummy kept in the Darlington museum, England, in 1964, reveal the presence of an artificial hand? "It is the first example in ancient times of artificial limb practice," said Professor Thacker of the Institute of Oriental Studies at Durham University. But there are others who think this is just a rough imitation of much better ones dating from a previous epoch which has vanished from memory; and that earlier Egyptian arts reached a peak of which we can get only a vague idea by admiring the pyramids and other gigantic monuments which have victoriously withstood the ravages of time.

The Greeks spoke about "singing houses"; unfortunately we are not sure what they meant but some believe it to be devices for the automatic opening and closing of temple doors: a kind of concealed "carillons" activated by weights or by the footsteps of the passers-by. The expression reminds one of the famous statue of Mennon[1] which was built around 1500 B.C. together with its gigantic "twin" and gave out a thin, high-pitched sound like a chord on a harp. It was a phenomenon heard for about 200 years; Strabo mentioned it in 90 B.C., Germanicus in A.D. 19, Juvenal in A.D. 90, Pausanius and the Emperor Hadrian in A.D. 196. The huge statue seemed capable of greeting the rising star. The sound at first was said to be sweetly melodious but we must not forget that the monument was disfigured in 524 B.C. by Cambyses and damaged by earthquake in A.D. 27.

During the reign of Septimius Severus the Memnon statue fell silent. Many believe the sound was caused through a fissure, closed when restoration work was done to the statue on the orders, perhaps, of the Roman Emperor. But why in that case was the sound heard again during the last century, according to the Paris *Revue Encyclopédique* of 1821? Another accident perhaps due to imperfect closing of the famous fissure in the structure. But what made the noise? There are many theories, among which the Frenchmen Langlès and Salvert discuss a complex mechanism hidden in the depths of the statue, activated by the sun working on a lens hidden in the figure's lips; a notion which is acceptable to many. Others think it is quite a natural feature, but their theory seems untenable if we remember that similar sounds were heard at sunrise in the granite cave at Syene; also in a Karnak temple by three students accompanying Napoleon during his

[1]It was the Greeks who called it by this name because of the sound emitted at dawn—and thus the association with the mythical Son of Dawn. But actually it was a statue of Amenhotep the Third.

Egyptian expedition—Professors Jomard, Jollois and Devilliers.

In this connection mention should also be made of the famous Labyrinth referred to by Strabo, Herodotus, Pliny, Diodorus and other celebrated classical writers. "I have seen the Labyrinth," says Herodotus after having visited Egypt in the fifth century B.C., "and it is beyond all description. Of course, the pyramids are huge and any of them is equal to the biggest Greek works. But the Labyrinth excels even the pyramids; it has twelve covered courtyards, arranged in pairs facing each other . . . there are two sorts of rooms, one type being underground and the other at ground level; and a total of 3,000 rooms between the courtyards with innumerable paintings of all sorts . . ." Strabo, who took his time over it in 25 B.C., thinks of it as a temple "with as many rooms as there are provinces in Egypt", consisting of a maze of rooms, passages and covered or uncovered corridors in which "no stranger could find his way without the aid of expert guides".

CHAPTER TWENTY-ONE

TOMBS FOR ETERNITY

"King Saurid, son of Salahoc, reigned in Egypt three hundred years before the Flood and dreamt one night that the Earth was convulsed: all the houses fell down upon men and the stars collided in the heavens such that their pieces covered the sun. The king awoke in terror, rushed into the Sun-Temple and consulted the priests and diviners. Akliman, the wisest of them, said he too had had a similar dream . . . It was then that the king had the pyramids built in that angular way suitable for withstanding even the blows from stars, with enormous stone blocks held together with iron hooks and cut with a precision such that neither the fire of Heaven nor the Flood could harm them. There the king and all the leaders would find refuge, together with their books, talismans and everything needed to ensure the continuity of the human race."

Thus writes Serge Hutin referring to *Travels in the Orient,* by Gérard de Nerval when trying to show that it is not absurd to think of the pyramids as existing before the time of Cheops, Chefren and Mencheres who would only have been able to make use of them for their own profit—even if posthumous. The pyramids would be thus huge archives, the contents of which disappeared during the Arab conquests.

"Guarding the Oriental Pyramid there was an idol of black and white flakes. He was seated on a throne of gold and held a lance which could not be looked at without the onlooker being killed," Serge Hutin tells us in a reference to another old legend. "The spirit associated with this was a beautiful, smiling girl who still appears today and makes people lose their reason when they see her. Guarding the Western Pyramid there was a redstone idol also armed with a lance, but wearing a twisted snake on his head; a spirit was nearby to serve him and he looked like an old man of Nubia, with a basket on his head and a censer in his hand. As for the third pyramid, this was guarded by a small idol of basalt on a pedestal also made of basalt."

In an Arabic manuscript called *Le Murtadi,* translated into French by Pierre Vatter (Paris, 1666) there is a description of some discoveries made by Mussulmans (Moslems) in the room "of the king" of the Cheops Pyramid. The raiders saw a statue in black stone which was that of a man; there was also one of a woman—in white stone—of a physical type quite different from that of the ancient Egyptians. Such statues were erect, with a bow in one hand and a lance in the other—also a vase "apparently of red crystal which when it was filled with water weighed the same as when it was empty . . ."

The pyramids and the cathedrals

It is odd how the belief spread in olden times that the builders of the pyramids had concealed, somewhere inside, the fabulous philosopher's stone or something which could give enormous powers to its owners. Caliph Al-Mamun was obsessed with the idea and looked everywhere but in vain. Then Melik al-Aziz in 1196 employed thousands of workers to pull down the three pyramids stone by stone until successful. The workers went at the smallest of the three pyramids for eight exhausting months, after which he gave the order to suspend all work when he saw that the edifice had scarcely been touched.

Some people have fanciful beliefs concerning mysterious links between the cathedrals and the pyramids, saying that the latter had been built for the sole purpose of hiding from the cosmic rays a terrible power capable of making countries fertile; we call this power, of whose waves we know nothing, the "philosopher's stone". One such writer claims to know where the philosopher's stone is: "In the Cheops Pyramid, beyond the first low corridor and the entrance to the 'Royal Chamber' there are granite facings to the walls of the antechamber and there are some vertical carvings in them. On the eastern wall here, a slab of granite reveals a projection, horseshoe shaped, about 63 centimetres in circumference and 20.5 thick. The lower part of the granite slab is exactly the same height as the roof of the lower passage: would the philosopher's stone not lie in such a container, this power which has destroyed a world?"

There are not a few students of the occult, especially in France, who maintain there are precise correlations between the pyramids and the gothic cathedrals, especially between the Cheops Pyramid and Strasbourg Cathedral; a view which suggests to us a number of generations transmitting ancient secrets and it is curious that Roger Peyrefitte says in his book *Les Fils de la Lumiére:* "The technique of the Companions was something different from a technique. When the Orly bridge was being built a defect occurred which they could not remedy without starting all over again; but the problem was handed over to a Companion—a man who had never read any textbook in his life—and he solved their difficulties. But some Companions overstate their powers: one of them said he knew the exact spot in Strasbourg Cathedral where you only had to put your finger to make the whole edifice crash." Another such person said the pre-columbians had "calculated the

xact time in which the fourth dimension met the three
nown ones."

Such things of course contain a good deal of fantasy,
ut it is not all pure imagination. So we must therefore
agree with Moreux that "by saying the pyramids are
only sepulchral monuments the modern archaeologist
alls into the error which would be as bad as that of
any future scholar who, if he had brought to light
after many centuries the ruins of our churches and
ad found the tombs of bishops and kings, had then
stated that such wonderful buildings were definitely
constructed for the purpose of doing honour to their
mortal remains. Just because the pyramids were used
as burial chambers it does not necessarily follow that
no other idea lay behind their construction."

But Moreux himself makes a big mistake in blindly
following the Scottish astronomer Piazzi-Smyth who
claimed to have discovered a universal unit of measure-
ment (the so-called "pyramid-inch") and was then
found one day by a student of his to be frantically
polishing a stone to reduce it to the size needed for
the establishment of his theory. We can, however, still
follow him in some respects.

"The pyramid stones," he writes, "are put together
with such accuracy that you could pass a pen-knife
blade along them without finding where they join; and
one of today's biggest United States contractors has
stated that we do not possess any machine capable of
making equally smooth surfaces as those connecting the
stones of the pyramids. There are six million tons of
rock in the Great Pyramid, which would thus require
600 locomotives able to pull a thousand tons each to
transport all this material. Egypt's entire financial resources today would not be enough for demolishing it,
so the architect, whoever he was, aimed at constructing
something eternal. People do not realize its size: this
mountain of rock exceeds the Cathédrale des Invalides
by a height of 40 metres, the Pantheon by 66 and the
towers of the Notre Dame by 77! As for the orientation, the façades of the pyramids should have been
aligned along the four cardinal points but this was not

exactly carried out except as regards the Cheops. The problem was very difficult. Of course, there is the compass today but everybody knows that the needle show Magnetic North and that every place must make adjustments.

"There is the astronomic method, the North as shown by the Pole Star. But even this is not exact although it is used in practice, since this star is not at the celestial pole, but describes a circle of radius one degree eight minutes around the ideal point of the celestial sphere which an imaginary extension of the Earth's axis would intersect.

"To put it simply, you could place two globes the size of the moon between the Pole Star and the celestial pole. The star we call Polaris would not have been so defined 4,000 years ago; since because of the Earth's oscillation the terrestrial axis points in somewhat different directions at different times. In 13,000 years' time our pole star will be Vega, the brightest star of Lyrae, but when the Great Pyramid was built the pole star was a star in the constellation Draconis. To establish the exact position of the celestial pole the ancients had to use other methods as they did not have certain precision instruments which we use today. The famous Tycho Brahe made an error of 18 degrees of an arc despite all his calculations when placing the Urianenborg Observatory; which happened a mere three and a half centuries ago in 1577. And the Paris Observatory—constructed in 1666—was not fixed any better, either because of carelessness or lack of skill. There came a great surprise for modern astronomers when they found that the orientation of the Great Pyramid was fixed with an error of 4 degrees 35 minutes. This could not possibly be due to chance—so we must admit that the pyramid builders had more ability than Tycho Brahe. For centuries our scientists have been looking for an ideal meridian and the choice fell on Paris first, then later on Greenwich. But now we know that the Great Pyramid meridian is ideal. Why? First because it passes through more land than any other meridian and secondly if we calculate the area of habitable land from the Behring Straits we find it divides exactly in two. Did the builders of the pyramids, then, tour the whole world and make geographical maps?"

Not only this but the height of the Great Pyramid is in direct relationship with the distance of our planet from the sun; and the distance of the Cheops Pyramid from the centre of the world is the same as its distance from the North Pole, therefore corresponding to the latter's distance from the middle of the Earth. How have they been able to do this if their cultural level was that which is allotted to them by traditional science?

The "absurd" chest

The Cheops Pyramid presents other mysteries, one of which is the manner of gaining entrance to the "chamber of the king" for the funeral procession—a subject people have been racking their brains about for years. When the Arabs attacked the pyramid inside they found a tough 'plug' of granite which could not have got there through the corridor as it was much larger than the latter. If it was purely a burial-chamber then the piece of granite must have been placed there from inside—from the royal chamber. Yet when the Arabs got into this room for the first time (ninth century A.D.) they found no sign of bodies or instruments but only a box of red granite empty from the time it was put there! Not only this but the box was larger than the upward passage leading to the chamber and larger than its entrance. Only one solution therefore makes sense: that it was placed in position during the building—but in that case it could not possibly contain the so-called "Ka" (the eternal vital spirit or soul) of the Pharaoh, who was still alive while its building was going on. It may be that the pyramid had not been built as a burial-chamber—only used as such later; just as it may equally be that later pyramids were used exclusively for burials. One thing is certain—that we are far from clearing up all the problems involved. This confusion gave rise to a host of silly theories—as

Walther Wolf has demonstrated when quoting some of them—like the one about the period of gestation amongst mammals being deducible from certain mathematical relationships within the Cheops Pyramid; but we will end with a quotation from the *Daily Telegraph*, October 19th 1966 concerning the Chephren Pyramid: "The monument is 143 metres in height and 213 wide, built over 4,500 years ago around a funeral chamber. Some archaeologists accept this and hope to discover, by means of 'operation X-ray', other rooms as yet unknown in the Chephren Pyramid."

But others do not share this opinion:

"Cheops ordered the building of the Great Pyramid around 2650 B.C. and it was done with amazing precision. Its four sides have been exactly built on the four cardinal points (was the compass known then?) while its height of 148.20 metres is in exact proportion to the 148,208,000 kilometres which lie between the Earth and the Sun—never calculated so precisely until A.D. 1860. Many archaeologists are convinced it was built not just as burial chamber but for astronomical and astrological purposes."

CHAPTER TWENTY-TWO

THE EYE AND THE SUN

I traverse the paths of the heavens . . .
I reside in the divine eye of Horus . . .
The eye of Horus gives me eternal life . . .
and when it shuts, protects me . . .
Surrounded by sparkling rays I proceed on my
path, and penetrate any place at my pleasure . . .
I traverse the cosmic solitudes . . .

Quoting from the famous *The Book of the Dead* Professor Solas Boncompagni emphasizes that the "eye" may be identifiable with the winged disc often recurring in Egyptian mythology and says: "Such discs compare with the emblems of Ahura-Mazda and the Assyrian winged circle, all showing a god in a flying and luminous body as if he lived there. He seemed to be the ruler of time and space to judge from *The Book of the Dead*—'the god of yesterday, today and tomorrow'. This may be compared with the Turin papyrus chapter 110 which reads:

> I land on Earth at the right moment
> when it is calm, according to all the texts
> from when the Earth existed

"The pronoun 'I' could mean Osiris, who was a semi-god rather than a true god whose mother belonged to the celestial beings (sky-goddess 'Nut') and whose father was Geb, the god of Earth. As he was brother and husband of Isis there is clearly a connection with Jove-Juno. But some consider him the god of light, like Apollo or Phoebe of the Greeks and thus different from Zeus, the Phoenicians' Adonis and the Persians' Ahura-Mazda. It seems as if a 'deus ex machina' is involved in 'I land on Earth' to help humanity at critical moments in its history. He is the leader in the Egyptian Pantheon of gods after losing his life in struggling with evil Seth and then regaining life and heavenly kingdom. Losing life on Earth meant an eternal one in Heaven, so this became common practice; but Osiris is also the father of Horus so even in this ancient pagan theogony the father and son have something in common and which unites them as one. This is the mystic trinity of life (Osiris, Isis, Horus) unchanging through the centuries; but Horus is 'he who flies up high' and 'he lives in his eye'."

Horus the falcon

So Horus (or Hor) does not seem to be mythological. When the archaeologist Jacques Jean Marie de Morgan (1857–1924) was director of Antiquities at Cairo he found near Naqâda a huge building 54 metres long and 27 wide. The building was thought by Morgan to be unique, without knowing that the same type, with variations here and there, was also in Lower Egypt and connected with a prehistoric kingdom with its capital at Buto. "Morgan was right," says Wolf, "in thinking it to be a prehistoric monument. He detailed it very exactly in his *Recherches* especially regarding its vases of stone and clay and implements of flint. There was also an ivory tablet with odd inscriptions and the name of a king; today we know that that king was Horus". Horus shown with a hawk on his head—but often with something like the American "firebird", in which many see the symbol of an astronaut. In 508 and 509 of the "formulae" translated by Kurt Sethe mention is made of Horus travelling into the sky "on metal" suggesting the falcon head of gold found in 1897 by James Edward Quibel in the "city of falcons", ancient capital of the third province of the Old Kingdom. Many of Quibel's finds were very like precolumbian ones.

Mexican Heliopolis

The Egyptian sun-temples were not places for gods to live in but meant for people to worship the sun and other stars; and in the big temple at Heliopolis, the Egyptian capital six thousand years ago, there was a huge obelisk which some Soviet scientists thought might represent a missile—with its base as a launching pad. Here, too, there were many architectural features like those of Teotihuacan. From this stage of complex building it is not far to the stepped pyramids of America and Egypt. "It is quite likely," Wolf says, "that the king intended the steps to lead into heaven after his death; the urge to reach the god of the sun and the stars often recurs."

So the basic idea does not change—and its realization is in the endless rooms and passages, in the enigmatic, dark and narrow corridors of all these buildings: but can we see in this urge for immortality and the sky a real imitation of astronauts and their ships? If we answer honestly then we cannot agree fully. But let us conclude with Herbert Kühn:

"Science is a creation whose grandeur consists in its endlessness: each scientist is required to bring light to the dark places, the obscure problems. But the changes and perfecting of things are usually small: deepened in one sector and then completed in another until a final picture emerges. The great transformations, on the other hand, are unexpected and exceptional. They are centres of struggle and only when a new item of knowledge can be sustained by many facts and in a manner such as leaves no room for doubt, can the new way forward be slowly accepted and so take its place in the great panorama of life. Thus it was with the discoveries of Galileo, with those of Copernicus and Kepler; and thus it was with the world of Darwin, though perhaps anticipated by Herder, Kant and Goethe."

PSYCHIC WORLD

Here are some of the leading books that delve in the world of the occult—that shed light on the po ers of prophecy, of reincarnation and of foretelli the future.